Contributions to Management Science

The series *Contributions to Management Science* contains research publications in all fields of business and management science. These publications are primarily monographs and multiple author works containing new research results, and also feature selected conference-based publications are also considered. The focus of the series lies in presenting the development of latest theoretical and empirical research across different viewpoints.

This book series is indexed in Scopus.

More information about this series at http://www.springer.com/series/1505

Ramo Palalić • Emil Knezović • Léo-Paul Dana
Editors

Women's Entrepreneurship in Former Yugoslavia

Historical Framework, Ecosystem, and Future Perspectives for the Region

Springer

Editors
Ramo Palalić
Faculty of Business and Administration
International University of Sarajevo
Ilidža, Bosnia and Herzegovina

Emil Knezović
Faculty of Business and Administration
International University of Sarajevo
Ilidža, Bosnia and Herzegovina

Léo-Paul Dana
Dalhousie University
Halifax, NS, Canada

ISSN 1431-1941 ISSN 2197-716X (electronic)
Contributions to Management Science
ISBN 978-3-030-45252-0 ISBN 978-3-030-45253-7 (eBook)
https://doi.org/10.1007/978-3-030-45253-7

This Springer imprint is published by the registered company Springer Nature Switzerland AG.
The registered company address is: Gewerbestrasse 11, 6330 Cham, Switzerland

To mothers, wives, sisters, daughters

—Ramo Palalić

To my family

—Emil Knezović

I dedicate this book to a champion, a woman entrepreneur who thinks out of the box: Michelle Brandstrup Jensen

—Léo-Paul Dana

To Michelle with great respect and thanks for teaching me so much!

—Léo-Paul Dana

Foreword

The modern world would not be the same without its persuasive female entrepreneurs. Throughout history, women have left an imprint on the world with inventive innovations, out-of-box business ventures, and unique accomplishments. Women have composite careers, indicated to as multidirectional patchwork, disputed that are dissimilar from men. Women's higher concern with others' welfare suggests that women are convinced of entrepreneurially beneficial upward influence approaches in comparison to men.

Examining the past empowers us to embed the fulfillment of women entrepreneurs in prospect, enabling us to understand what is unprecedented about their experiences and what threads tie them to women who live in a socialist country. The need to create positive entrepreneurial climate, to help women to change their destiny by deciding to be entrepreneurs, and to build up appropriate framework for facilitating entrepreneurship as well as to promote entrepreneurship education was also emphasized by the editors. The book topped archival background of female entrepreneurship across Bosnia and Herzegovina, Croatia, Kosovo, Macedonia, Montenegro, Serbia, and Slovenia. Consequently, entrepreneurs are facing a variety of challenges, notably over financialization, technological innovations, demographic changes, transcultural diversity, ethical interrogations, and political turbulences. Each country from the former Yugoslavia is unique and peculiar, but they share transition period common for most Central Eastern Countries. This book seeks to add contribution to the global women entrepreneurial challenges. The relevance of this book stems from at least three enrichment.

First, surprisingly, few empirical researches have examined the process of strengthening female entrepreneurship in transition countries. The authors investigate theoretical views and empirical evidence of female entrepreneurship and small businesses nowadays promoted in each former Yugoslavian republic. It tackles the essential issues of entrepreneurship challenges, entrepreneurship perspectives, entrepreneurial initiatives and innovation, policymakers for women entrepreneurship, small businesses, corporate entrepreneurship, institutional support to women entrepreneurship, etc.

Second, the importance of this book is sourced in the lack of concurrence with the literature about the attributes of women entrepreneurship for economy and growth in ex-Yugoslavian countries. Slovenia and Croatia joined the European Union, and other ex-Yugoslavian countries are, in the current situation, not close to that goal. In all ex-Yugoslavian countries, growth did not reach the expected level. It has been recognized that high economic growth, the opening up of opportunities, means that women will be more able to qualify for positions that were previously closed to them.

In the last 20 years, there has seen an increase in women entrepreneurs, but it is not permanently milk and honey. It is women, more often than not, who confront their career by fitting paid work into household responsibilities, as well as care. Therefore, there is much confirmation of the existence of the glass ceiling against women and the lack of women in CEO positions and as members of corporate boards. There has been little work that has involved a particular sector, which has endeavored to unpick the career paths of women to demonstrate their nonlinear structure and the effect of sectoral context on career choices. From that point emerges the third contribution: do women business owners in ex-Yugoslavian countries after transition experience unique gender-related barriers to run business? If, however, gender inequalities are unexplained by policy level, firm level, and owner level characteristics, the market interferences should be targeted at distinguishing market restraints such discrimination for female entrepreneurs.

In line with "*Women Entrepreneurship in the Former Yugoslavia*" themes, acknowledging democracy and the role of democratic processes in the higher wellbeing of all entrepreneurs, institutions, and society, there is a need to broaden society to put an additional focus on how may the gendered dynamic of entrepreneurship increase in-depth understanding in social firm relations.

Authors find those "strugglers" in different way as aspiring about their future entrepreneurial plans as good actresses, but their limited resources prove to be burden on their goals. An entrepreneur has to deal with several different types of obstacles and people and bring them together to integrated perspectives on goals and actions while continuing to draw upon their individual and diverse strengths and leveraging the complex interrelationships that go forward between them over time.

According to Nikola Tesla famous inventor and mind who was born in small village Smiljan, Lika, Croatia, who worked and invented in the USA, and has been recognized as a global visionary: *"Though free to think and act, we are held together, like the stars in the firmament, with ties inseparable. These ties cannot be seen, but we can feel them".*

Faculty of Economics and Business,
University of Zagreb, Croatia &
Nottingham Business School,
Nottingham Trent University,
Nottingham, UK

Marina Dabić

Contents

Editors and Contributors

About the Editors

Ramo Palalić is the Coordinator of Leadership and Entrepreneurship Centre at the IUS. Dr. Palalić's research interests are entrepreneurship, leadership, marketing, and small and family business management. As an Assistant Professor, Dr. Palalić teaches at all three study cycles in the above areas. Apart from this, he is actively involved in business projects in the areas of entrepreneurial leadership and marketing management, in private and public organizations. He has authored and coauthored many articles in reputable international journals, several books, and many book chapters. Additionally, he is serving a few journals as reviewer/editorial board member.

Emil Knezović is the Head of Department of Economics and Management at the International University of Sarajevo. His research and teaching expertise include human resource management, entrepreneurship, small business management, and marketing. So far, he published several articles in refereed international and national journals. He has been engaged as a researcher at several projects, among which is Horizon2020 Systemic Action for Gender Equality. Before joining academia, he worked in the real estate and transport industry where occasionally he still serves as a consultant.

Léo-Paul Dana is Professor at Dalhousie University in Canada. A graduate of McGill University and HEC-Montreal, he has served as Professor and President of the Scientific Council at Montpellier Business School and was formerly Marie Curie Fellow at Princeton University and Visiting Professor at INSEAD. He has published extensively in a variety of journals including *Entrepreneurship & Regional Development, Entrepreneurship: Theory & Practice, International Business Review, International Small Business Journal, Journal of Business Research, Journal of Small Business Management, Journal of World Business, Small Business Economics,* and *Technological Forecasting & Social Change.*

Contributors

Bostjan Antoncic School of Economics and Business, University of Ljubljana, Ljubljana, Slovenia

Jasna Auer Antoncic Faculty of Management, University of Primorska, Koper, Slovenia

Azra Bičo Faculty of Business and Administration, International University of Sarajevo, Ilidža, Bosnia and Herzegovina

Azra Branković Faculty of Business and Administration, International University of Sarajevo, Ilidža, Bosnia and Herzegovina

Léo-Paul Dana Dalhousie University, Halifax, NS, Canada

Vladimir Djurisic Faculty of Economics, University of Montenegro, Podgorica, Montenegro

Maja Has European Business School Zagreb, Zagreb, Croatia

Robert D. Hisrich Bridgestone Professor of International Marketing and the Director of the Global Management Center and International Programs, Kent State University, Kent, OH, USA

Maja Ivanović-Đukić Faculty of Economics, University of Niš, Niš, Serbia

Emil Knezović Faculty of Business and Administration, International University of Sarajevo, Ilidža, Bosnia and Herzegovina

Boban Melovic Faculty of Economics, University of Montenegro, Podgorica, Montenegro

Esra Memili University of North Carolina at Greensboro, Greensboro, NC, USA

Mihaela Mikic Faculty of Economics and Business, University of Zagreb, Zagreb, Croatia

Ramo Palalić Faculty of Business and Administration, International University of Sarajevo, Ilidža, Bosnia and Herzegovina

Saša Petković Faculty of Economics, University of Banja Luka, Banja Luka, Bosnia and Herzegovina

Veland Ramadani South-East European University, Tetovo, North Macedonia

Visar Ramadani International Balkan University, Skopje, North Macedonia

Nora Sadiku-Dushi University for Business and Technology, Prishtina, Kosovo

Dianne H. B. Welsh University of North Carolina at Greensboro, Greensboro, NC, USA

Women's Entrepreneurship in the Former Yugoslavia: An Introduction

Emil Knezović, Ramo Palalić, and Léo-Paul Dana

Abstract A vast of literature on entrepreneurship has been published in the recent period. However, the topic is relatively not new. Therefore, this introductory chapter explores the role and importance of entrepreneurship from a historical and contemporary perspective. Furthermore, we discuss the role of gender when it comes to entrepreneurship. Besides, we provide a discourse when it comes to the role of women in the former Yugoslavian society which was a key determinant of later women entrepreneurship movement. Finally, we emphasize the importance of this topic for former Yugoslavian states.

1 Introduction

The importance of small businesses to the economy has been an important topic in recent decades. Their contribution is observed through three major outcomes: economic development, employability, and innovation (Aceleanu et al. 2014; Berry 2002; Savlovschi and Robu 2011; Zaman and Vilceanu 1999; Knezović et al. 2020). This triangular contribution has been of immense importance to both state policymakers and practitioners who perform this activity every day throughout the world (Ramadani and Schneider 2013). A tremendous amount of studies emphasizes that this activity which is a combination of creativity and risk-taking is a world game changer (Fayolle 2007; Raposo and do Paco 2011).

Observing historically, one might say that entrepreneurship was present from the beginning of mankind. Originated from communication, trade was an activity that

E. Knezović (✉) · R. Palalić
Faculty of Business and Administration, International University of Sarajevo, Ilidža, Bosnia and Herzegovina
e-mail: eknezovic@ius.edu.ba; rpalalic@ius.edu.ba

L.-P. Dana
Dalhousie University, Halifax, NS, Canada
e-mail: lp.dana@Montpellier-BS.com

R. Palalić et al. (eds.), *Women's Entrepreneurship in Former Yugoslavia*,
Contributions to Management Science,
https://doi.org/10.1007/978-3-030-45253-7_1

was performed among the ancient people for necessity and/or opportunity. According to Gupta et al. (2018):

> profit-minded traders were dealing in goods and services in ancient Egypt, as well as in similar ancient civilizations .... business flourished as traders from different parts of the world encountered each other and exchanged various goods and services (p. 1).

The contours of entrepreneurship were visible in some of the most important historical projects, such as Egyptian pyramids, the Great Wall of China, or Venice shipping transports. In these times, the first sights of entrepreneurs can be found in the profiles of merchants and adventurers (Hebert and Link 2006). Later on, through the industrial revolution, and thereafter, the entrepreneurial opportunities were arousing (Robbins and Coulter 2012). The contemporary approach to entrepreneurship is dynamic. According to Ramadani and Schneider (2013), there is still a discourse when it comes to providing a universally accepted definition of entrepreneurship; however, the general framework is developed around several elements, such as:

> "innovation (new opportunities), risk-taking (moderate), combination of production factors, creation of a new enterprise, realization of profit, and ensuring business growth" where "entrepreneurship is the process of seeking innovative opportunities in uncertain and risky circumstances, combining effectively and efficiently the factors of production in order to achieve profitability and business growth" (p. 3)

Even though practical entrepreneurship is a historical phenomenon, the academic one is comparatively new. Regarding the development of entrepreneurship in terms of the research area, it is obvious that earlier studies were more leaning toward the personality concept of entrepreneurs while the newer studies were more oriented toward the complexities of entrepreneurial activities regarding contextual, structural, and individual determinants (Guo 2018). This interconnection led to something we label as an "entrepreneurial ecosystem." As Wright (2018) states "an entrepreneurial ecosystem approach recognizes the interdependencies between various actors and resources necessary to identify and exploit entrepreneurial opportunities" (p. 3). One of the pioneer studies that opened a field to a more systematic approach was the one performed by Schumpeter (1934). Very soon we had entrepreneurship in the educational system and curricula in Japan and the USA (Hannon 2005; Katz 2003). Today, we have hundreds of scientific studies regarding entrepreneurship that emphasize the importance of its commercial and non-commercial aspects (Wadhwani et al. 2017). Therefore, entrepreneurship is presented as a well-developed and organized discipline in academia that intersects several interrelated fields (Gupta et al. 2018).

Any kind of an argument regarding entrepreneurship and its contribution to different aspects of the economy and society cannot be made without referring to the role of entrepreneur. According to Hebert and Link (2006), this role has been discoursed as static vs. dynamic and the concurrent literature provides no less than 12 personalities of an entrepreneur. Furthermore, they present the entrepreneur's importance through the economic theory of production and distribution where entrepreneurs are a key factor of resource allocation in the system. In particular, an entrepreneur is described as innovative, risk-taking, and profit-oriented (Ramadani and Schneider 2013). Besides, Baumol (1990) offers the perspective that entrepreneurs are primarily focused on profit rather than on any other output which reflects in their improved social status due to the increased income.

The focus on the entrepreneur brought several perspectives over the years. The early studies were focused solely on the entrepreneur as a determinant of business success. One of the first extensions of this approach was made by Sandberg and Hofer (1987) who introduced factors such as strategy and industry as important determinants. However, there is still a large amount of research devoted to examining the characteristics of an entrepreneur to find the right profile. For example, Brockhaus (1980) highlighted several important predictors for entrepreneurial success, such as dissatisfaction with a previous job, job security in hands of others, internal locus of control, age, and marital status.

However, the focus on gender as one of the key entrepreneurial characteristics is relatively new (Birkner et al. 2018; Lansky 2000; Marlow et al. 2009) since this field was more or less presented as gender-neutral or male-dominant. One of the first studies addressing the phenomenon of women entrepreneurs was the one performed by Bowen and Hisrich (1986). The interest in women's entrepreneurship has been rising since then, but the relationship between the entrepreneur's gender and business success is still presented as a complex one (Chirwa 2008). This complexity has been supported by contradictory findings in the studies that compared female and male managers and entrepreneurs (Chell and Baines 1998; Kalleberg and Leicht 1991; Khalife and Chalouhi 2013; Radipere and Dhliwayo 2014; Watson 2002). Although the relationship between gender and business performance is rather unclear, there is obvious visibility when it comes to women entrepreneurs, and this has been emphasized by policymakers and governments through their efforts to make a supportive business environment (Knowlton et al. 2015). Such emphasis can be noticed on local, national, and international levels where:

> organizations, such as the National Women's Business Council among others, have highlighted the economic value of women-owned businesses to the overall economy, fueling growing research across academic disciplines to understand the antecedents, drivers, and outcomes associated with women's entrepreneurship ... the study of women's entrepreneurship has become an important academic discipline and policy area that can provide much-needed insights and new directions to highlight the challenges and opportunities facing women-owned businesses (Ozkazanc-Pan 2018, p. 103).

This is in alignment with the statement made by Birkner et al. (2018), where they highlight that women are one of the fastest-growing entrepreneurial populations and that they are important contributors to the economic and social development. However, the neoliberal argument that entrepreneurship is open and equal for everyone is shaky. According to Ahl and Marlow (2012), it is rather a gender-biased since women are positioned unfavorably compared to men. For example, Riverin (2005) stressed that factors such as basic psychological and demographic characteristics, access to finance, access to training, networking, and work–life balance are not favorable for female entrepreneurs. What is more interesting is that the women are mostly deciding for entrepreneurship because they have been rejected in a male-dominant business world. Such a reaction is labeled as a "push factor" (Reavley and Lituchy 2008). These imbalances are more obvious in developing countries where the differences are more explicit due to social structures and social roles that are embedded deeply in historical and cultural contexts (Metters 2017; Ramadani et al. 2013). However, Brush et al. (2009) point out that there is no need for a separate theory on women's entrepreneurship as long as the differences can be incorporated into a regular entrepreneurial framework.

Some of the studies suggest that the beginning of women's entrepreneurship in Europe, as well as the Balkan region, can be traced to the nineteenth century which has been characterized by the transition of economic systems to industrial that was supported by changes in social systems as well (Vuković 2015). In those times there was a slightly increased integration of females in society due to the importance of raising children (Gross and Szabo 1992). Such emphasis provided better opportunities for women to include themselves in other spheres of life such as businesses. However, the role of women in society, as well as the business in the Western Balkans, was nonexistent until the end of WWII. Thanks to their involvement and contribution during the war, women made serious progress in the sphere of emancipation in the period 1945–1990 (Simić 2011). Important progress was made in areas such as education opportunities, economic independence, and actual women empowerment. Some of the results were similarity in school enrollment (primary and secondary) between men and women and the higher presence of women in different social and economic spheres. According to Zaharijević (2017), the feminist movement appeared in Yugoslavia in late 1970 since there was more openness in terms of borders, literature availability, and travel opportunities. One of the important events in these times that supported such movement was the Bled seminar entitled "Woman and Development." It gathered 102 representatives from 40 countries with the main aim to tackle problems such as sociopolitical and economic differences among the countries.

Despite this, before the collapse of the system, the role of women was still marginalized. Jerončić (2015) points out that there was still a strong presence of masculine and nationalist culture in the region and that anti-nurturing environment for the idea of gender equality. The primary activity of women in the postwar (WWII) period was agriculture. However, it is hard to justify that they were considered as entrepreneurs since, as Zaharijević (2017) points, "their participation in self-management and the delegate structure of the socialized sector remained symbolic" (pp. 270, 271). It is evident that women were more part of enlargement than enrichment approach due to their multiple roles in the household and society (Milosavljević 1981). According to Mežnarić (1985), the ideology that Yugoslavia possessed was favorable for women although the main areas where women were engaged in the business were clerical and manufacturing work that showed clear gender segregation. To support this, Zaharijević refers to the data which show that 38% of the economically active population was women with a high degree of specialization in female stereotype jobs, such as nursery and school teachers. Furthermore, they were very unlikely to be in supervising positions. In particular, women entrepreneurship was almost nonexistent due to the nonexistence of entrepreneurship in general. However, the position of women was improving through the years resulting in higher women emancipation, social inclusion, and an active working population. This will result in a key determinant for the development of women entrepreneurship in the new economic system. As discussed by Dana (2010) and Palalić et al. (2017), it was almost impossible to promote women entrepreneurial values in this region. The actual equality transition started with the transition to the capitalist economic model that was focused on private ownership (Dana 2010). More women started to participate in business circles, increasing the probability of starting their own business. They shifted their stereotyped gender-role jobs to the ones that contribute to society and the overall economy.

According to Salloum et al. (2016), progress on gender equality in Europe is very positive. Women are extending the general entrepreneurship framework known as 3Ms (money, market, and management) to 5Ms by including motherhood and meso and macro environment (Brush et al. 2009). This can be observed through the lens of female contribution in more labor market participation and higher-level education. Regarding the gender phenomenon in the Western Balkans, Ferk (2013) analyzes the report made by the Committee on Women's Rights and Gender Equality by stating that:

> the need for women in the Western Balkans to take a prominent role in society through active participation and representation at all levels of government and in political, economic and social life. Whilst the accession countries in the Western Balkans have adopted much of the legislation required in the EU accession process, Members note that this legislation is in many cases not being effectively implemented (p. 52).

From the research standpoint, while in the developed countries this is an existing academic area, in the Western Balkans this was not a popular topic. However, the recent studies are emphasizing the importance and urgency to focus on this matter (Ferk 2013; Palalić et al. 2017, Sanfey and Milatović 2018; Stilin 2016; Zidrum and Cvitanović 2017). Therefore, there is a real need to further investigate the phenomenon called women's entrepreneurship in this region since as Širec and Močnik (2016) state "the empirical evidence on the relationship between firm profitability irrespective of the gender of the firm owner and growth is inconclusive" (p. 250).

We hope that this collection of nine chapters will reach the predetermined objectives. In this context, the first objective of the book is to describe the historical evolution of women entrepreneurship in this region and its transition from communist to post-communist and free-market economy. The book will provide an important comparative mechanism when it comes to challenges that each country faced during the process as well as how women adapted to the new roles in society. Each country from the former Yugoslavia is unique and distinctive, but at the same time have many commonalities (Dana et al. 2018; Palalić et al. 2018). By using different methods, the second objective is to analyze theoretical views and empirical evidence of women's entrepreneurship and small businesses currently promoted in each of the former Yugoslavia's republics. It treats the essential issues of economy, women entrepreneurship development, entrepreneurship challenges, entrepreneurship perspectives, entrepreneurial initiatives and innovation, policymakers for women entrepreneurship, small businesses, corporate entrepreneurship, institutional support to women entrepreneurship, and other related factors. Finally, the book presents some interesting stories, cases, and examples of women entrepreneurs.

References

Aceleanu MI, Trasca DL, Serban AC (2014) The role of small and medium enterprises in improving employment and in the post-crisis resumption of economic growth in Romania. Theor Appl Econ 21(1):87–102

Ahl H, Marlow S (2012) Exploring the dynamics of gender, feminism and entrepreneurship: advancing debate to escape a dead end? Organization 19(5):543–562

Baumol WJ (1990) Entrepreneurship: productive, unproductive and destructive. J Polit Econ 98 (5):893–921

Berry A (2002) The role of the small and medium enterprise sector in Latin America and similar developing economies. Seton Hall J Diplom Int Relat 3(1):104–119

Birkner S, Ettl K, Welter F, Ebbers I (2018) Women's entrepreneurship in Europe: research facets and educational foci. In: Birkner S et al (eds) Women's entrepreneurship in Europe: multidimensional research and case study insights. Springer, Cham, pp 3–14

Bowen DD, Hisrich RD (1986) The female entrepreneur: a career development perspective. Acad Manag Rev 11(2):393–407

Brockhaus RH (1980) Psychological and environmental factors which distinguish the successful from unsuccessful entrepreneur: a longitudinal study. Acad Manag Proc 1980(1):368–372

Brush CG, de Bruin A, Welter F (2009) A gender-aware framework for women's entrepreneurship. Int J Gender Entrepren 1(1):8–24

Chell E, Baines S (1998) Does gender affect business 'performance'? A study of microbusinesses in business services in the UK. Entrepren Reg Dev Int J 10(2):117–135

Chirwa EW (2008) Gender and performance of micro and small enterprises in Malawi. Dev S Afr 25(3):347–362

Dana LP (2010) When economies change hands: a survey of entrepreneurship in emerging markets of Europe from the Balkans to the Baltic States. Routledge, New York

Dana LP, Palalić R, Ramadani V (2018) Entrepreneurship in former Yugoslavia: an introduction. In: Palalić R, Dana LP, Ramadani V (eds) Entrepreneurship in former Yugoslavia: diversity, institutional constraints, and prospects. Springer, Cham, pp 1–7

Fayolle A (2007) Entrepreneurship and new value creation the dynamic of the entrepreneurial process. Cambridge University Press, Cambridge, UK

Ferk M (2013) Boosting Women entrepreneurship in Western Balkan countries—critical analysis and best practices. Učenje Za Poduzetništvo 3(1):49–56

Gross M, Szabo A (1992) Prema hrvatskome građanskom društvu: Društveni razvoj u civilnoj Hrvatskoj i Slavoniji šezdesetih i sedamdesetih godina 19. Stoljeća. Globus, Zagreb

Guo GC (2018) Entrepreneur as a person at crossroads: a reflection Kets de Vries (1977). In: Javadian G et al (eds) Foundational research in entrepreneurship studies: insightful contributions and future pathways. Palgrave Macmillan, Cham, pp 13–32

Gupta VK, Guo GC, Ozkazanc-Pan B (2018) Introduction. In: Javadian G et al (eds) Foundational research in entrepreneurship studies: insightful contributions and future pathways. Palgrave Macmillan, Cham, pp 1–12

Hannon D (2005) Philosophies of enterprise and entrepreneurship education and the challenges for higher education in the UK. Int J Entrepren Innovat 6(2):105–114

Hebert RF, Link AN (2006) Historical perspectives on the entrepreneur. Found Trends Entrepren 2 (4):261–408

Jerončić M (2015) Privatni i javni patrijarhat: Društveni položaj i uloga žena u Jugoslaviji tokom socijalističkog perioda. Genero 19:1–26

Kalleberg A, Leicht K (1991) Gender and organisational performance: determinants of small business survival and success. Acad Manag J 34(1):136–161

Katz JA (2003) The chronology and intellectual trajectory of American entrepreneurship education: 1876-1999. J Bus Venturing 18(2):283–300

Khalife D, Chalouhi A (2013) Gender and business performance. Int Strat Manag Rev 1(1–2):1–10

Knezović E, Bušatlić S, Riđić O (2020) Strategic human resource management in small and medium enterprises. Int J Hum Resour Dev Manag 20(2):114–139

Knowlton K, Ozkazanc-Pan B, Clark Muntean S, Motoyama Y (2015) Support organizations and remediating the gender gap in entrepreneurial ecosystems: a case study of St. Louis. Available at SSRN https://ssrn.com/abstract=2685116

Lansky M (2000) Gender, women and all the rest. Int Labour Rev 139(4):481–504

Marlow S, Henry C, Carter S (2009) Exploring the impact of gender upon women's business ownership: introduction. Int Small Bus J 27(2):139–148

Metters R (2017) Gender and operations management. Cross Cult Strat Manag 24(2):350–364

Mežnarić S (1985) Theory and reality: the status of employed women in Yugoslavia. In: Wolchik SL, Meyer AG (eds) Women, state and party in Eastern Europe. Duke University, Durham, NC, pp 214–220

Milosavljević D (1981) Organizovanje socijalističke snage i oslobođenje žene. Marksistička misao 4:61–65

Ozkazanc-Pan B (2018) Bowen and Hisrich (1986) on the female entrepreneur: 30 years of research and new directions for gender and entrepreneurship scholarship. In: Javadian G et al (eds) Foundational research in entrepreneurship studies: insightful contributions and future pathways. Palgrave Macmillan, Cham, pp 1–12

Palalić R, Ramadani V, Dana LP (2017) Entrepreneurship in Bosnia and Herzegovina: focus on gender. Eur Bus Rev 29(4):476–496

Palalić R, Dana L-P, Ramadani V(eds) (2018) Entrepreneurship in former Yugoslavia: diversity, institutional constraints and prospects. Springer, Heidelberg

Radipere S, Dhliwayo S (2014) The role of gender and education on small business performance in the South African small enterprise sector. Mediterr J Soc Sci 5(9):104–110

Ramadani V, Schneider RC (2013) Introduction. In: Ramadani V, Schneider RC (eds) Entrepreneurship in the Balkans: diversity, support, and prospects. Springer, Cham, pp 1–14

Ramadani V, Gërguri S, Dana LP, Tašaminova T (2013) Women entrepreneurs in the Republic of Macedonia: waiting for directions. Int J Entrepren Small Bus 19(1):95–121

Raposo M, do Paço A (2011) Entrepreneurship education: relationship between education and entrepreneurial activity. Psicothema 23(3):453–457

Reavley MA, Lituchy TR (2008) Successful women entrepreneurs: a six-country analysis of self-reported determinants of success—more than just dollars and cents. Int J Entrepren Small Bus 5 (3/4):272–296

Riverin N (2005) A comparison of female and male entrepreneurs—insights from GEM Canada. Paper presented at the GEM second conference, May 25, Budapest, Hungary. Available at http://web.hec.ca/creationdentreprise/CERB_Backup-12-mai-2008/pdf/2005-08GEMInsightsen.PDF. Accessed January 30, 2019

Robbins SP, Coulter M (2012) Management. Prentice Hall, Upper Saddle River, NJ

Salloum C, Azzi G, Mercier-Suissa C, Khalil S (2016) The rise of women and their impact on firms' performance. Int J Entrepren Small Bus 27(2/3):213–246

Sandberg WR, Hofer CW (1987) Improving new venture performance: the role of strategy, industry structure, and the entrepreneur. J Bus Venturing 2(1):5–28

Sanfey P, Milatović J (2018) The Western Balkans in transition: diagnosing the constraints on the path to a sustainable market economy. European Bank for Reconstruction and Development

Savlovschi LI, Robu NR (2011) The role of SMEs in modern economy. Economia, Seria Management 14(1):277–281

Schumpeter JA (1934) The theory of economic development. Harvard University Press, Cambridge, MA

Simić I (2011) Socijalizam i položaj žena u nauci, Kontinuirana edukacija - Položaj žena u nauci

Širec K, Močnik D (2016) A gender perspective of Slovenian high-growth firm's profitability. Int J Entrepren Small Bus 27(2/3):247–261

Stilin A (2016) Suvremeni trendovi u poduzetništvu. Praktični menadžment: stručni časopis za teoriju i praksu menadžmenta 7(1):39–46

Vuković K (2015) Počeci poduzetništva žena u znanstvenim i književnim djelima hrvatskih autora. 24(1):133–151

Wadhwani RD, Galvez-Behar G, Mercelis J, Guagnini A (2017) Academic entrepreneurship and institutional change in historical perspective. Manag Organ Hist 12(3):175–198

Watson J (2002) Comparing the performance of male-and female-owned businesses: relating outputs to inputs. J Small Bus 26(3):91–100

Wright M (2018) Academic entrepreneurship: the permanent evolution? Manag Organ Hist 13 (2):88–93

Zaharijević A (2017) The strange case of Yugoslav feminism: feminism and socialism in 'the East'. In: Jelača D, Kolanović M, Lugarić D (eds) The cultural life of capitalism in Yugoslavia: (Post) socialism and its other. Palgrave, Cham, pp 263–283

Zaman G, Vilceanu G (1999) Coexistence of large and small companies. Economic Tribune no. 45. Bucharest

Zidrum G, Cvitanović V (2017) Prepreke i mogućnosti razvoja ženskog poduzetništva u Republici Hrvatskoj. Obrazovanje za poduzetništvo 7(2):205–222

Emil Knezović is the Head of the Department of Economics and Management at the International University of Sarajevo. His research and teaching expertise include human resource management, entrepreneurship, small business management, and marketing. So far, he published several articles in refereed international and national journals. He has been engaged as a researcher at several projects, among which is Horizon2020 Systemic Action for Gender Equality. Before joining academia, he worked in the real estate and transport industry where occasionally he still serves as a consultant.

Ramo Palalić is the Coordinator of Leadership and Entrepreneurship Centre at the IUS. Dr. Palalić's research interests are entrepreneurship, leadership, marketing, and small and family business management. As an Assistant Professor, Dr. Palalić teaches at all three study cycles in the above areas. Apart from this, he is actively involved in business projects in the areas of entrepreneurial leadership and marketing management, in private and public organizations. He has authored and coauthored many articles in reputable international journals, several books, and many book chapters. Additionally, he is serving a few journals as reviewer/editorial board member.

Léo-Paul Dana is Professor at Dalhousie University in Canada. A graduate of McGill University and HEC-Montreal, he has served as Professor and President of the Scientific Council at Montpellier Business School and was formerly Marie Curie Fellow at Princeton University and Visiting Professor at INSEAD. He has published extensively in a variety of journals including *Entrepreneurship & Regional Development, Entrepreneurship: Theory & Practice, International Business Review, International Small Business Journal, Journal of Business Research, Journal of Small Business Management, Journal of World Business, Small Business Economics,* and *Technological Forecasting & Social Change*.

Women's Entrepreneurship in Bosnia and Herzegovina

Ramo Palalić, Emil Knezović, Azra Branković, and Azra Bičo

Abstract This chapter depicts a glance picture of women entrepreneurship in Bosnia and Herzegovina (B&H). Followed by introductory notes of the chapter, further, it is discussed the historical overview of women entrepreneurship, the current state of the women entrepreneurship in the country, as well as the entrepreneurial ecosystem of entrepreneurship pertaining to women. In a nutshell, final words are provided in this chapter.

1 Introduction

Like other Western Balkan countries, Bosnia and Herzegovina (B&H) is still in the transition phase from a political and economic perspective. Political will and economic strategies are not that much in favor of women's entrepreneurial activities. Scant literature that exists seriously threats this field and barely one can find updated data on this phenomenon. The early stage of entrepreneurship development in B&H has been profoundly researched by Dana (1999) and Dana and Dana (2003), who elaborated on the first milestones of entrepreneurship development, in which he described that small businesses were built by individuals who did not seek help from the government. They also described that women's attempts were minimal because the post-war situation did not allow women to be more involved in this process. This was mainly due to the fact that they took leadership of home issues and challenges. However, a few women who were without husbands became extraordinary brave and started some small business activities.

Moreover, women engaged in other small business activities during the post-war period such as trading of agricultural products at local bazaars. As explained by

R. Palalić (✉) · E. Knezović · A. Branković · A. Bičo
Faculty of Business and Administration, International University of Sarajevo, Ilidža, Bosnia and Herzegovina
e-mail: rpalalic@ius.edu.ba; eknezovic@ius.edu.ba; abrankovic@ius.edu.ba; abico@ius.edu.ba

R. Palalić et al. (eds.), *Women's Entrepreneurship in Former Yugoslavia*, Contributions to Management Science,
https://doi.org/10.1007/978-3-030-45253-7_2

Dana (2010) and Palalić et al. (2018a), entrepreneurship, as the private sector, was not recognized by the State (Dana et al. 2018), and yet it was resisted by the people. Like this, women's entrepreneurial activities were insignificant. However, some years later, there were some developments regarding the business activities of women in the country. For instance, these activities have been initialized by the *international community* that exists in Bosnia and Herzegovina. One of them is the European Bank for Reconstruction and Development (EBRD), which firmly supported women's activities in terms of small businesses. The EBRD extended its hand to MI-BOSPO (Microcredit Foundation) in 1996, for women entrepreneurs that needed a relatively small loan to start their business activities (EBRD 2008). Besides this, many NGOs were established to support women entrepreneurship, and lots of seminars, workshops, and roundtables have been organized to help women to take part regularly in the businesses and economic activities in the country.

The following part describes the early history and development of women entrepreneurship, with pinpointing the main facts in its early stage of modern Bosnia and Herzegovina. Moreover, the current state of women entrepreneurship is elaborated through different perspectives and indicators. Finally, the entrepreneurial ecosystem of women entrepreneurship is presented together with the future perspective of this phenomenon in B&H. The final elaboration sums up all facts and views on women entrepreneurship in this country.

2 Women Entrepreneurs: A Historical Overview

The role of women in Bosnia and Herzegovina has been dramatically changed in the last century. Due to the strong influences of patriarchal values and tradition, the role of women was marginalized before World War II (WWII) (Jerončić 2015). In this period, the main role of women was to take care of the household and children. However, the form of socialism that was presented in the Socialist Federative Republic of Yugoslavia (SFRY) started to emphasize the role of women in modern society (Šakanović 2018). This was mainly due to a very important role that women had during WWII where they equally participated in so-called "partisan leagues." In addition to their war merits, there was a need for reconstruction of the country. As Jerončić (2015) states "the idea of building a future socialist order, or accelerated processes of modernization, industrialization, and urbanization of the country, implying the need of a socialist type of society to make women more involved in the working contingent of the population, that the masses should enter the labor market" (p. 9). This was the first time that women were part of larger, more important, social inclusion. The process of women's emancipation was continued after the war through several inclusion programs, such as the ones in education and the labor market. Such programs have provided an opportunity for women to gain some kind of economic independence, which further supported women's empowerment.

The additional spur was provided by the Constitution of the Republic, which legally equalized men and women by granting voting rights (Tomšić 1981). Even though there was a positive atmosphere regarding women's emancipation during the period of Yugoslavia, there was resistance as well. This was mainly due to conservatism that was presented in many other spheres, such as marriage and abortion. According to Jerončić (2015), the new constitution was an improvement in comparison to the old one, but its practical application was questionable since the role of women in real life was still highly dependent on men. The traditional values and beliefs were supporting the general notion that the kids are best raised at their homes by their mothers. Another reason for the gap was the inefficiency of institutionalization when it comes to social care for children. This led to a double burden on women, who besides the traditional role, were enlarged by the social and business role as well (Jerončić 2015). However, the progress on women's emancipation has been continuous for the coming decades. At the beginning of the 1990s, there was equality when it comes to primary and secondary education, while there was a slight difference when it comes to higher education (Šakanović 2018). This data shows that improvement has been made regarding the role and position of women in society. However, there is a common discourse regarding the women's position in ex-Yugoslavia. In particular, some of the researchers present an argument that these reforms were not radical enough to erase the patriarchal matrix that dominated in masculinity-centric society (Tomšić 1981; Simić 2011; Jerončić 2015). The chaos and war that came at the beginning of the 1990s did not help since the progress has been stopped and dominant masculine and nationalist culture was sustained. On the contrary, some studies describe ex-Yugoslavia as a feminine culture. One of the most popular models regarding cultural dimensions that include femininity vs. masculinity as one of the dimensions is the one developed by Hofstede (1980). This dimension reflects the similarity and differences in cultural context regarding gender. For example, femininity societies are more reflected in values such as gender overlapping which makes society opportunities more equal. This reflects almost every aspect of life including the business (Hofstede 2011). While the official data for Bosnian and Herzegovina do not exist, some information can be taken from comprehensive research made by Hofstede in ex-Yugoslavia. Based on that study, Branković (2013) points out that there was a high degree of femininity present in the society of ex-Yugoslavia. However, it is very important to mention that the role of women highly differs from one region to another, as well as from rural to urban areas.

The contemporary entrepreneurship phenomenon started to exist in Bosnia and Herzegovina after the last war (1992–1995). This was a period where privatization of previously state-owned companies began. Also, after the war, the country started to transit to the capitalist economy, which opened the boundaries and spurred the competitiveness in the market. However, some form of entrepreneurship existed during Yugoslavia's time as well. Dana (2010) characterized Yugoslavia as a nationalized or state-owned economy where entrepreneurs were under rigorous taxation. As such, the form of a private-owned company existed but was highly constrained by the regulatory framework. The general notion toward such a form of business was mainly negative (Glas 1998) since it was characterized as a greedy, nonsocial approach that was favored by the self-managing socialism model implemented in the country (Palalić et al. 2018a). The emergence of entrepreneurship started at the beginning of the 1980s, where Enterprise Law recognized this type of ownership (Dana 2010). This trend was slightly interrupted during the sad happenings in the 1990s. However, the entrepreneurship fully emerged after 1995, when the country started the process of transition to a capitalist economy that is characterized by private ownership.

3 The Current State of Women Entrepreneurship in Bosnia and Herzegovina

The period after 1995 has been categorized as "a process of physical, economic and social reconstruction" (Somun-Krupalija 2011, p. iii). Together with the trend of entrepreneurship, the need for qualified and competent workforce emerged. For that reason, one of the goals of the reconstruction agenda was gender equality that was a converged economic and social aim throughout the world (Somun-Krupalija 2011). For that reason, the government implemented some important political and legal changes that aimed to improve the position of women in society (Šestić 2009). An interesting data can be exported from the STAR research in 1998 and 2002, where 16.67% of women that indicated the willingness to start their own business were in a position of an entrepreneur by 2002 (Šestić 2009). Also, there was a tremendous increase in willingness to start the business since women showed more initiative in taking the participatory role in society. According to Alice (2007), this can be observed through the role that women had in initiatives regarding the restoration of human relations and protection of human rights in the period after the war. This was supported by the legal framework in B&H that ensured equality for women and men. In particular, The Law on Gender Equality in Bosnia and Herzegovina was created in 2003 and later on revised in 2009 and 2010. This law "regulates, promotes and protects substantive gender equality and guarantees equal opportunities to all citizens, in public as well as private life, and prevents direct and indirect gender-based discrimination" (Para. 3). It reflects all sectors in society by prohibiting any kind of discrimination based on gender or sexual orientation. According to the amendments of the B&H Election Law (2018), there was a requirement of a 40% quota for less represented sex on the electoral lists for all political parties.

Even though there are some positive cases, we still do not fully understand and deal with gender concerns in society. The support for this argument can be seen in the fact that there is a serious lack of gender data on a national level. For example, there is no statistical data on the state level regarding the number of women entrepreneurs in B&H, as well as regarding the size and structure of their small businesses. In its Labor survey, the Agency for Statistics of Bosnia and Herzegovina (2017) lists only some of the self-employed people which makes impossible to concretely discuss these matters. Also, we cannot precise in what kinds of small businesses these people are engaged in. A further problem for obtaining accurate

Exhibit 1 Berberović's logo. *Source:* Berberović's web page (2019)

Exhibit 2 Berberović (Berberović is a local brand established in the year of 2013 by three ladies Sabina Berberović, Nada Berberović Dizdarević, and Emina Berberović. The exciting thing about this company is that the company is producing leather handbags featured with high quality and modern design.) handbags. Photo © 2019 Azra Bičo

statistics in this regard lays in the fact that the self-employed individuals could either be registered as sole proprietors or could be unregistered. However, the obvious increase of women's interest can be observed through labor market participation. As Efendić et al. (2017) indicate, women traditionally were involved in so-called "gender-defined jobs" that contribute to the households' budget through the informal sector. Women would usually engage in producing handmade products (Exhibits 1 and 2) or delivering certain household services.

Table 1 Comparison of working population based on gender

Year	2006		2010		2014		2018	
Indicators/gender	M	F	M	F	M	F	M	F
Activity rate (%)	54.8	32.4	56.7	33.2	55	33	53.2	31.4
Employment rate (%)	39.6	22.7	42.2	23.3	41.2	22.7	44.1	25
Unemployment rate (%)	27.6	30.0	25.6	29.9	25.2	31.2	17.2	20.3
Working population (000)	**1322**	**1410**	**1260**	**1337**	**1453**	**1529**	**1169**	**1227**
Primary school and less (%)	38.5	58.8	31.8	52.9	30.2	51.6	26.6	46.3
Secondary school (%)	53.4	36.2	59.1	39.6	58.9	39	63.2	44.3
Higher education (%)	8.1	5.0	9	7.4	10.9	9.4	10.2	9.4
Employees (%)	72.1	73.3	74.3	72.1	76.5	77.7	78.5	78.9
Self-employed persons (%)	24.9	15.8	23.2	16.8	21.8	14.4	19.6	14.3
Unpaid family workers (%)	3.0	10.9	2.4	11.1	1.7	7.9	1.9	6.8

Source: Agency for Statistics of Bosnia and Herzegovina (2019)

The economic activities performed by women were substantially lower compared to men. However, after the war, the financial pressure on households increased significantly, which almost forced women to enter the formal market. This enabled women to explore the power of networking that was comparably stronger than the ones that they had in the informal market. The power of networking had a multidimensional impact on society. Women tend to enter higher education in higher numbers, connect with other women at first and later with men as well, and using the microcredit opportunities to start their businesses. In the following part, we present the information about women's position in Bosnia and Herzegovina through official statistical data from the Agency for Statistics of B&H. We examine several factors that directly affect women's entrepreneurial activities in the country, such as employment rates, access to education, access to jobs, and the poverty level.

The data presented in Table 1 show several important indicators regarding the recent period. The biggest concern, in general, is a decrease in the working population, which is the outcome of unfavorable working conditions for both men and women. While the activity rate has been pretty constant, the employment rate of women increased in the period 2006–2018. Since the main criticism regarding the unfavorable position of women in the business is based on the lack of education and knowledge, we can see that the percentage of women completing higher education increased. This gives us an insight that the position of women should be more favorable today. However, self-employment is lower than in 2006.

Even though there were some substantial moves toward equality objective in the labor market, women are still underrepresented in many ways. For example, they are

Table 2 Employment structure based on gender

	Total			Males			Females		
Type of employees/year	2015	2016	2017	2015	2016	2017	2015	2016	2017
Employed for someone else (%)	75.8	75.6	75.4	78.2	77.2	75.2	74.3	74.7	75.6
Self-employed persons (%)	20.7	21.1	20.6	15.2	16.5	17.4	23.9	23.6	22.6
Unpaid family workers (%)	(3.5)	(3.3)	(3.9)	(6.6)	(6.3)	(7.4)	(1.7)	(1.7)	(1.9)

Source: Agency for Statistics of Bosnia and Herzegovina (2017) *Symbol: ( ) - less accurate estimate*

less represented in the labor market, have limited access to particular networks, and are discriminated against regarding financing options. This is why several recent studies focused on women in the business in Bosnia and Herzegovina by analyzing the gender influence on different performance dimensions (Palalić et al. 2017; Knezović and Musrati 2018). However, there is still a significant gap when we discuss the role, importance, and outcomes of women in business (Table 2).

Based on the data above, it can be concluded that women prefer regular employment than self-employment, as three times more women are working for someone else than themselves. Also, the number of self-employed women has been decreasing in recent years. According to the Agency for Statistics of B&H (2017), women are mostly employed in the service sector (63.2%), followed by employment in manufacturing (20%) and in agriculture (16.8%). Since there is no exact data available, based on relevant experience of women in the business, we may assume that most of them are self-employed in services.

3.1 Data on Education

According to the data obtained on Population Census, Households and Dwellings, the population of Bosnia and Herzegovina is about 3.5 million (Agency for Statistics of B&H 2018). Regarding gender, there are slightly more women (50.9%) than men (49.1%). As we analyze the educational background, one cannot neglect the fact that there is a higher share of women under the categories such as "no education," "incomplete primary education," or "completed primary education." On a rough comparative basis, it can be stated that men are more educated than women.

In Table 3, we can see that the enrollment numbers regarding gender are not significantly different. This shows that access to education on this level is almost the same. Although the number of male students in primary and secondary education is slightly higher, in higher education there is an opposite situation. The details are presented in Table 4.

From Table 4, there is an obvious indication of two facts: (1) there is no gender discrimination when it comes to the access to higher education on a gender basis and

Table 3 Pre-school, primary, and secondary education in B&H

Year	Pre-school		Primary		Secondary	
	Girls	Boys	Girls	Boys	Girls	Boys
2012/2013	8958	9859	148,585	156,296	82,242	84,420
2013/2014	9383	10,497	147,238	154,895	77,468	78,882
2014/2015	10,290	11,200	144,456	152,363	71,786	72,095
2015/2016	10,983	11,918	141,454	149,888	66,520	66,708
2016/2017	11,832	13,086	139,479	148,250	63,592	63,232

Source: Agency for Statistics of Bosnia and Herzegovina (2018)

Table 4 Students in institutions of higher education by mode of study

Year	Total		Full-time students		Part-time students	
	Females	Males	Females	Males	Females	Males
2012/2013	56,325	46,118	46,157	36,638	10,168	9480
2013/2014	55,114	44,646	45,712	35,619	9402	9027
2014/2015	53,599	42,826	45,178	34,824	8421	8002
2015/2016	52,457	41,633	45,462	34,347	6995	7286
2016/2017	50,552	39,163	43,671	31,958	6881	7205

Source: Agency for Statistics of Bosnia and Herzegovina (2018)

Table 5 Students who graduated in 2015

	Women	Men
Total	9374	6600

Source: Agency for Statistics of Bosnia and Herzegovina (2018)

Table 6 Gender comparison regarding a particular specialization

Year/gender	Masters of science and specialists		Doctors of science	
	Female	Male	Female	Male
2012	1542	1088	88	122
2013	2011	1369	112	157
2014	2001	1363	116	185
2015	2168	1468	128	157
2016	2339	1500	99	142

Source: Agency for Statistics of Bosnia and Herzegovina (2018)

(2) the enrollment of female students is higher. The higher enrollment numbers for women also affect the graduation numbers which are presented in Table 5.

Table 5 indicates that more female students graduated in comparison to male ones. The recent stats show that the rate of graduating female students outnumbered male students. This can be a consequence of a higher number of women students as well as higher success rates for women. This becomes even more interesting when we observe a particular educational area as presented in Table 6.

Besides the fact that the number of Master's holders has been increasing regardless of gender, we can see that the number of females who graduated in science fields

The Doing Business Report (2019) for B&H indicates a positive ranking when it comes to obtaining loans. B&H ranks 60th out of 190 countries. However, The Doing Business ranking considers only the regulatory and institutional frameworks, which are relatively acceptable in B&H. However, it seems that practices of lending to small and medium enterprises (SMEs) in B&H show a different picture. Recent research that has been done in the Gradačac, a municipality area of successful entrepreneurs, reported that even small companies with ideal risk profiles have difficulties to obtain loans and have to wait a lot for bank decisions. Furthermore, they have been asked to submit a large number of documents (Palalić et al. 2020). Some of the SMEs that have international experience reported that it was much faster and cheaper to obtain credit in Germany.

4.2.1 Microfinance

Microfinance has been widely available for women entrepreneurs in B&H since 1996. Microfinance is a small loan given to below-average income individuals to establish micro-businesses in order to generate income and very often escape from poverty. In the beginning, microfinance organizations mainly targeted women, as they were the part of society with lower income. This concept started by Bangladeshi economist, Dr. Muhammad Junus in the late 1970s and early 1980s and quickly spread all over the world and especially in poor countries of Latin America and Southeast Asia, promising that individual entrepreneurship will solve the poverty problem in a generation. The US government, as well as international organizations like the World Bank or United States Agency for International Development (USAID), considered microfinance to be the best way to solve the difficult post-war situation in B&H. In this way, they were providing employment and income to vulnerable categories such as returnees, demobilized soldiers, the internally displaced, and, especially, female-headed households and war widows. All these organizations gave huge amounts of money to establish the microfinance sector, expecting it to be the key driver for reconstruction and development. Drezgić (2011) quoted that the World Bank put $40 million in the Local Initiative Project, establishing 17 independent MFIs. They distributed over 50,000 microloans with an average loan of 1500 €. The World Bank claimed that the project created 100,000 jobs. USAID, UNDP, and UNHC established their microfinance programs and small microfinance institutions (MFI). Later, many international banks (ProCredit Banking Group, Hypo Alpe Adria Bank, European Bank for Reconstruction and Development) entered the microfinance market in B&H, establishing a big number of their own small MFIs. Every single municipality was served by at least two or three of the major MFIs (Drezgić et al. 2011). It is no surprise that microfinance penetration by country in 2009 shows that B&H is in second place according to the number of microfinance loans, immediately after Bangladesh (Bateman 2011). Many MFIs were specialized for women, such as the Women for Women MFI. All these institutions claimed that they created thousands of small businesses and helped thousands of B&H women to establish and operate their small businesses and thus escape poverty.

However, there is a lack of empirical evidence to support this. There are a lot of media stories about successful heroic women that succeeded to get out of poverty thanks to small microloans. There are many statements from international organizations praising microfinance and its contribution to women empowerment. But there is no actual data or research that strongly supports this argumentation. Contrary, some research (Ciprus et al. 2011) concluded that microfinance harmed women entrepreneurs in B&H and the region. Ciprus et al. argued that the experience in Southeast Europe (SEE) indicates that microfinance has failed to provide SEE women with the solution to poverty, and it has financially and socially impoverished them even further. Instead of alleviating them from poverty, women became poorer, lost their savings, and had to take several additional microloans to repay the first one or sell their houses or other assets. Držić et al. reported that in 2009 many MFIs reported a loss, even the women-only MFI, Women for Women, had serious difficulties because too many clients with multiple loans could not repay them. Because of all the failures and problems, the regulations for microfinance became much tougher and many limitations were imposed on MFIs.

Currently, there are 19 microcredit organizations in B&H, 15 of which are registered as microcredit foundations and four as microcredit companies. They are supervised by entity banking agencies. The maximum loan size which a foundation can offer is BAM 10,000 while MFIs licensed as a for-profit, microcredit companies can offer up to BAM 50,000.

4.2.2 Banking Sector

There are 24 banks in B&H, 16 registered in the Federation of Bosnia and Herzegovina and 8 registered in the Republic of Srpska (Central Bank B&H 2019). It is a big number taking into consideration that B&H is a small country consisting of 3.5 million people where the number of large companies is relatively small. So, banks have to work with small businesses. However, banks have conservative lending policies and practices. The European Investment Bank (2016) reported in its Bosnia and Herzegovina Assessment of Financing Needs Report that credit committees are usually strict, demanding real estate collateral for all but small loan sizes and requesting that the value of collateral exceed the loan amount by a large margin, usually 150% or more. The loan amounts are often lower than the amount requested by clients. There are no venture capital funds in the country which makes equity financing very difficult for SMEs.

5 Reasons for Starting Business

There are several reasons why women in B&H start their business. The first reason why women in B&H started the small businesses immediately after the war in B&H was out of necessity. Women in ex-Yugoslavia were empowered with access to free education and jobs, mainly in the state companies with proper social benefits, free health care, maternity leave, daycare centers, etc. However, this was lost because of war or privatizations of state enterprises. Many women were also displaced, refugees, or widowed. Many of them saw small businesses as a way to get some income. They chose to start microenterprises and often resorted to microfinance as the only way to get starting capital. However, the economic situation in B&H is still very difficult. There is a small number of big companies, salaries are low, and the unemployment rate is among the highest in Europe. This leads to a situation where more individuals are deciding to start their business.

Despite all these obstacles, there are some very positive cases where women own brands that are famous in local as well in the international market (Exhibits 3 and 4.)

One of the recent study performed in the context of B&H determined that the main motive for women entrepreneurs in B&H for starting a business is the desire to be the boss, rather than social status and money (Palalić et al. 2018b).

5.1 Support for Women's Entrepreneurship in B&H

Support for women's entrepreneurship has been offered by different entities, such as government and nongovernmental institutions, and international donors. At the State level, SMEs' policy is under the responsibility of the Sector for Economic Development and Entrepreneurship of the Ministry for Foreign Trade and Economic Relations. However, there are no significant activities that support women entrepreneurship. At the level of the Federation of B&H (FB&H), the Ministry of Development, Entrepreneurship, and Crafts is responsible for women entrepreneurship. They are currently engaged in developing an action plan for the development of women entrepreneurship in FB&H in the period 2018–2020 in cooperation with German

Exhibit 3 Via Media's logo. *Source*: Via Media (*Via Media* is a full-service communication agency, which is the market leader in this sector in Bosnia and Herzegovina. The company was established in 1997. It is managed by Ms. Vesna Beganović, the CEO of the company. Recently, the company has expanded its operations to the Middle East by opening its first office in Dubai. Thanks to Ms. Vesna Beganović, one of the most inspiring Bosnian lady entrepreneurs who leads the young and creative team, the company has contributed to the society employing.) web page

Exhibit 4 Via Media Facilities located in Sarajevo; photo © 2019 Azra Bičo

Technical Assistance (GIZ). In the Republic of Srpska (RS), the Ministry of Industry, Energy, and Mining produced the first draft of the Strategy for development of women entrepreneurship in RS 2018–2020, also with the support of GIZ. Gender agencies at entity levels, as well as the Gender Equality Agency of Bosnia and Herzegovina, provide some support as well. Support is provided also at the cantonal or municipality level. Chambers of commerce at the entity, cantonal, and municipality levels also offer help for women who want to start a business. Many international donors have been dealing with women entrepreneurship. Even more so, there are hardly any international donors offering support to B&H that did not deal with this topic. Many NGOs have been dealing with this topic. The Center for Women's entrepreneurship has been recently opened at the School of Economics of Sarajevo, financed by the IPA Danube transnational program. Universities in Tuzla and Banjaluka have been also dealing with this topic.

However, all this help is sporadic, targeting certain geographic regions with certain agendas and within a limited period. There is no evidence regarding the real outcome of certain projects and if the projects contributed to sustainability or even the development of women's small businesses. Web pages of these international organizations or NGOs bring stories of successful women, but there is no information that could be useful for women entrepreneurs. The general impression is that it is almost impossible for a woman who would like to start a business to get any advice on how to do it.

6 Women Entrepreneurship Ecosystem in B&H

The notion of the ecosystem was firstly introduced from a biological perspective by Tansley (1935), who defined this term as an environment in which all organisms (living and nonliving) live together and interact with each other. From an economic perspective, this term was described by Moore (1993), who pointed out that entrepreneurship cannot exist unless it has an environment in which interaction among players and forces exist. The key success of the entrepreneurial ecosystem is smooth interrelation and togetherness that will affect all players' success (Spigel 2015; Peltoniemi 2006) positively.

The entrepreneurial ecosystem is a very important ingredient in the entrepreneurship development of a country. However, the *recipe* for how to put those ingredients is crucial. The ecosystem per se alludes in an environment where all players, all kinds of beings and objects live together and somehow support each other in their lives and activities. The same philosophy applies to the context of entrepreneurship development, where different factors should have synergized its development in the long term. Therefore, different country settings and factors differently impact entrepreneurship development which is a case in B&H as well.

Different approaches to definitions of the entrepreneurial ecosystem have been presented in previous research. It is a phenomenon that consists of "interconnected group of actors" (Cohen 2006, p.), individual elements or self-regulating networks pertaining to both human beings and institutions (Isenberg 2010, 2011), "communities of agents, social structures, institutions, and cultural values that produce entrepreneurial activity" (Roundy et al. 2017, p. 99). Based on this it can be said that *the entrepreneurial ecosystem is a setup of actors like individuals, groups, private and public institutions, and organizations, integrated into legal and cultural outlook, mutually interconnected and whose role influences entrepreneurial activity and gives its positive or negative output in one country*. It represents a "symbiotic life" (Dana 2001) among those elements, which will foster the development of each element.

To analyze the entrepreneurial ecosystem, we followed Stem's (2018) framework that describes the entrepreneurial ecosystem which includes different elements and measures, such as formal institutions, entrepreneurship culture, physical infrastructure, demand, networks, leadership, talent, finance, new knowledge, and intermediate service.

Formal institutions element implies the "quality of government." This quality includes corruption level, the rule of law, government effectiveness, and voice and accountability. It is well-known that institutions in B&H are struggling with corruption. We are placed at 89 out of 99 countries (Trading Economics 2019) which suggests that the Rule of Law is still at a very low level. Additionally, government effectiveness to set up a good base for public accountability is poor since the structure of formal institutions is too complex to implement these factors properly. The changes should be from the Constitution, as the leading institution, to a municipality level of Laws. Though B&H has enacted the Law on Gender Equality in 2003, which assures women's rights in terms of employment, media, education, and the private sector. Regarding the *entrepreneurial culture*, this component is "the degree to which entrepreneurship is valued in a region." It is measured in a "number of new firms per 1000 inhabitants." The data are not available according to the World Bank (2019), but anecdotally speaking, due to certain Law regulations that suppress this "culture," this number is not exciting if not negative. Another issue, which is lately very known and obvious, is that youth is migrating to other countries, especially to Western Europe. Thousands of young families are searching to settle somewhere else rather than in Bosnia. A huge wave of migration of local people is so strong that in the long term B&H can easily lose its population and the market. So the entrepreneurship culture is affected by this trend.

Physical Infrastructure consists of the basic infrastructure that every country needs, like railroads, roads, number of passengers flights within a 90-minute drive. In the case of roads, (motorways and express roads) the country is trying to make a useful network so that can be beneficial for the whole country. Each entity has its strategy to reconstruct roads into fast roads and motorways. For instance, the Federation of Bosnia and Herzegovina (FB&H) has a strategy "2017–2020" to build certain routes of those roads ("JP Ceste FBiH" 2018[1]). Regarding air traffic, there are four airports in B&H: Sarajevo (the most frequent one), Tuzla, Banja Luka, and Mostar. Taking into consideration the number of population of B&G∗H, these four airports are quite enough to serve its residents. However, there is a space for further development in this area, especially in frequency and diversity of destinations.

The next element is a *demand* which refers to potential market demand, which is constituted from three components: purchasing power per capita, regional product, and total human population. The purchasing power per capita in 2018 was $11,500 (Trading Economics 2019), which is relatively low compared to developed countries, while the regional product is incomparable with the total human population. In this regard, it should be noted that imports still prevail over export by almost 50% (State Agency for Statistics B&H 2019). As it concerns the *networks*, it implies how businesses are connected and how they create new value. According to the National Assessment Expert (2019),[2] businesses are more-less at a small scale with internal disruptions that affect their performance in terms of innovation. For its improvements, the country needs a long journey to take *innovative leadership* in this region. Innovative products that B&H has and exports to other regions are few and even not the top ones in the ex-Yugoslavia region. This country is severely affected by many laws and regulations that many times pull back all good initiatives in terms of innovation and entrepreneurship. Thus, lots of work must be done in this regard.

[1]Available at http://www.jpautoceste.ba/wp-content/uploads/2019/03/No.pdf

[2]Digital Innovation Profile: Bosnia and Herzegovina - ICT centric innovation ecosystem snapshot, NATIONAL EXPERT ASSESSMENT, 2019, available at https://www.itu.int/en/ITU-D/Innovation/Documents/Publications/eBAT_Brochure%E2%80%93DIP%20BosniaH_431106_.pdf (04.07.2019)

Especially, the State should act as the host and show its hospitality toward innovations. The current effort is not enough, but this is also affected by a complex political system that is presented in the country.

Regarding the *talents*, we can state that Bosnia and Herzegovina is developing above the average talents, which nowadays, migrate to Western Europe to find a better job. Timely, the country's talent is fading, and this red alarm is already on. The human capital (talent) is the most critical component of the whole country's development. University education is increasing, as well as life-long learning. Youth who do not possess higher degree diplomas, they are under qualification competence or professional development to get jobs offered by the market. More women graduated from universities than men, while females tend to have degrees in business management, and males in the engineering and IT sector (MI-BOSPO, IFC, report 2008). As it concerns *finance,* SMEs have difficulties to access capital especially when it comes to obtaining loans from banks. Despite that fact, figures show that private business has grown over 20% from the year 2001. Interestingly, women are more into loans from the bank, while men borrow in personal borrowings (MI-BOSPO, IFC, report 2008). According to the same report, women in Bosnia are "better off" in getting loans compared with the region. However, like for men's businesses, taxation policies affect women's businesses too. *New knowledge* mostly implies strategies related to R&D and how much private and public sector is investing in it. In the case of B&H, it is 0.22% of GDP (Economic Tradings 2019), which is still very low compared to countries in Western Europe. The region is slightly better (Croatia 0.85%; Serbia 0.93%, North Macedonia 0.35%, Montenegro 0.37%). One of the reasons for the small number of investments is related to many problems at the political stage, where different political parties have different views, and as a result, the country is lacking behind the region.

Finally, *the intermediate service* to existing businesses in the country is relatively acceptable. Service sectors are growing rapidly, especially in the tourism sector. This sector has a positive trend, and hopefully, it will flourish more in the years to come. As it concerns the entrepreneurial ecosystem in B&H (Exhibit 5), it can be said that this model can fit the Bosnian entrepreneurial ecosystem. The situation is not promising, but there is a space for immediate and long-term improvement. Exhibit 5 represents the entrepreneurship ecosystem that impacts women entrepreneurship in B&H and has been designed by adapting the model developed by Stem (2018). In Bosnia and Herzegovina, a very important role is played by the International Community (Organization for Security and Co-operation in Europe-OSCE, Office of the High Representative-OHR, European Union-EU, European Commission-EC, etc.). These players support, suggest, help, and enforce laws that will enable female entrepreneurs to grow. For instance, networking plays a very crucial role when starting a new business. Sometimes, if discriminated against, women may face more difficulties and challenges to start and commercialize their businesses.

Formal institutions have done positive things regarding female entrepreneurial activities in terms of laws. Entrepreneurial culture is still an embryo, which needs treatment. Culturally, this region was isolated regarding women entrepreneurship, compared to the rest of Europe. The "Yugopluralist" model did not recognize the

Exhibit 5 Women entrepreneurship ecosystem in Bosnia and Herzegovina. *Source:* Authors' compilation based on Stem's framework (2018)

private sector as a potential power for economic development (Palalić et al. 2018a; Dana 2010). The current physical infrastructure is slowly developing and it will take time when it will be at disposal for entrepreneurship, as well as women's businesses. Purchasing power per capita, regional product, and total population reflected in demand are playing an important constraint in women's prospective businesses. How much of premium products, that require added values (via new knowledge) obtained through innovation, will be willingly purchased, depends on customers' purchasing power. From a financial standpoint, we can state that financing is relatively available for any kind of small business through the local banks, which makes it easier for prospective businesswomen to start their businesses. New ideas and new values are set off by properly educated people (talents) in organizations. Females outnumbered males in terms of education, especially in business and management, which is a good base for future businesswomen. In this regard, some studies even show that women are more entrepreneurial oriented compared to men (Palalić et al. 2017).

The ecosystem of women entrepreneurship itself in Bosnia and Herzegovina is not well developed. However, there is a relatively good foundation that can be improved and advanced to will nurture this phenomenon in this country. By following the elements presented in Stem's (2018) model, a country can develop a healthy ecosystem that can help and enhance women entrepreneurship development in Bosnia and Herzegovina.

7 Toward the Future

Today, there is a huge question of whether Bosnia and Herzegovina has a feminine or masculine culture. Some happenings such as war and the difficult post-war period did not contribute to further development of feminine characteristics. This conclusion is related to the data regarding access to education and access to jobs where girls and boys in Bosnia and Herzegovina have the same access to education, but regarding the actual industry presence, female unemployment is higher. However, there is a similar or even bigger number of female medical doctors, educators, judges, researchers, and civil servants. Recent research on women entrepreneurship leadership in B&H supported the findings of the previous research regarding motives for starting a business between men and women (Palalić et al. 2018b). The research found that motives for starting a business do not differ a lot between men and women and that women in small business seek a life–work balance.

Women entrepreneurship phenomenon in Bosnia and Herzegovina is a challenge for the State as well as for prospective women entrepreneurs. Although the State claims that they support, promote, and cherish female entrepreneurship, it is still at a low development scale. The women entrepreneurship in B&H is relatively new. However, after the war in the 1990s, the true entrepreneurs were mostly men. Women had to take care of family issues and support their men in daily entrepreneurial activities. Apart from this, some women, who were widows, for instance, they started to think and act entrepreneurially with their vision of future business prospects. At that time the whole industry infrastructure has been destroyed so the basis of entrepreneurship has not given any sign of life. In other words, the entrepreneurship ecosystem, especially the women entrepreneurship ecosystem, was not there at all. The only tools for entrepreneurs were motivation and few pennies to start a business regardless of what sector an entrepreneur is going to be in. The current entrepreneurship ecosystem is not in favor either of men and women.

By the law, Bosnia and Herzegovina provide equal rights to men and women. However, due to the lack of available data, the general notion is that there are more male entrepreneurs are in the country than women. What could be the reason why women entrepreneurs are less than men ones? This could be explained from different perspectives. Anecdotally speaking, women will say that their opportunities are comparatively lower while men will say that all of us have opportunities. The second question could be whether men and women entrepreneurs are equal from the cultural perspective. The lack of availability of reliable statistical data on women entrepreneurship is a big problem for B&H. The Agency for Statistics of B&H has limited data. The problem is that B&H has a much-decentralized structure. Bosnia and Herzegovina has institutions at the State level, as well as the entity levels (at the level of FB&H and RS). In addition, there is a district with a special status—"Brčko" District (BD), which functions as a separate administrative unit. FB&H is divided into ten cantons. Cantons are divided into municipalities. FB&H has 79 municipalities. RS has 62 municipalities. All these levels have some data regarding women entrepreneurship. However, there is no centralized database at the State level. Also, it is very important to emphasize that just a few research studies are dealing with women entrepreneurship in B&H. They are all limited in scope. Answer on this question requires more in-depth research with well-grounded data and facts, which at this point in time cannot be implemented, but it is one of the future research possibilities.

To summarize, women entrepreneurship has the future. Statistical data show that there are more women than men in Bosnia. However, regarding the self-employment, there are more men classified as self-employed. In higher education, women prevail compared to men (at the first and second cycle). Building a stronger and favorable landscape for prospective women entrepreneurs is imperative, and education, knowledge, and finance are relatively available, which can support the growth. Most importantly, the State should support women entrepreneurship development in the long term. This should be reflected in the contribution of building a smooth entrepreneurship ecosystem that will enable women entrepreneurs to observe that possibility and think entrepreneurially.

When speaking in favor of the future entrepreneurship, especially of women's entrepreneurship, a systematic approach to this issue is the only solution as previously discussed by Palalić et al. (2018c). The State has to take a more proactive role to create a favorable women's entrepreneurship ecosystem. It is necessary to have a government center at the State level whose focal point should be all issues regarding women entrepreneurship. It has to be supported by adequate budget, partnerships, and staff. Various projects supported by the international community dealt just with one topic from the whole specter of women entrepreneurship, like, for instance, making a business plan, lasted a limited time, had a limited budget, hired people for a limited time, and disappeared after that. It is obvious that the sustainability of such projects was neglected. All projects proposed by the international community or NGOs should be coordinated through this center. Women entrepreneurs should have the possibility to call or come to the center and get any advice for a startup or later for the development of their small businesses. This center should have a good web page (or e-platform) that could offer real help. The center also has to help with networking.

The center should regularly collect and have all data regarding women entrepreneurship. Various training regarding targeting the specific needs of women entrepreneurs should be provided. The center for women entrepreneurship should promote women entrepreneurship and encourage women to participate in entrepreneurial activities that could generate high income and living standards. The financial flow from donors is not predictable and usually too small for the number of start-ups. It is also necessary to have a development bank for support of small business, generally and specifically for women. It should also be the responsibility of government institutions to create a favorable environment for small businesses. The current constraints (ecosystem components) are not along the same line so that male or female future entrepreneurs would alternatively think of this journey. Simply, many "bad factors" destroy an entrepreneurial spirit and an idea of being an employer (Palalic 2017; Palalic et al. 2017; Palalić and Bičo 2018), so is for potential women entrepreneurs.

References

Alice L (2007) Monitoring implementation of UN SCR 1325 in Bosnia and Herzegovina. Udruženje Žene Ženama, Sarajevo, Bosnia and Herzegovina

Bateman M (2011) Introduction: looking beyond the hype and entrenched myths. In: Bateman M (ed) Confronting microfinance undermining sustainable development. Kumarian, Sterling, VA

Berberović (2019). https://www.facebook.com/DesignbyBerberovic/. Access date on 14.11.2019

Branković A (2013) Femininity cultural dimension in Bosnia and Herzegovina. In: International conference on education, culture and identity (ICECI 2013). International University Sarajevo, Bosnia and Herzegovina

Ciprus V, Hughes L, Vukojevic M (2011) Gender and microfinance in Southeastern Europe: a critical view. In: Bateman M (ed) Confronting microfinance undermining sustainable development. Kumarian, Sterling, VA

Cohen B (2006) Sustainable valley entrepreneurial ecosystems. Bus Strateg Environ 15(1):1–14

Dana LP (1999) Business and entrepreneurship in Bosnia-Herzegovina. J Bus Entrepren 11(2):105

Dana LP (2001) The education and training of entrepreneurs in Asia. Educ Train 43(8/9):405. ABI/INFORM Global

Dana LP (2010) When economies change hands: a survey of entrepreneurship in the emerging markets of Europe from the Balkans to the Baltic States. Routledge, New York

Dana LP, Dana T (2003) Management and enterprise development in post-communist economies. Int J Manag Enterprise Dev 1(1):45–54

Dana LP, Palalić R, Ramadani V (2018) Entrepreneurship in former Yugoslavia: an introduction. In: Palalić R, Dana LP, Ramadani V (eds) Entrepreneurship in former Yugoslavia: diversity, institutional constraints, and prospects. Springer, Cham, pp 1–7

Doing Business Report (2019). https://www.doingbusiness.org/content/dam/doingBusiness/media/Annual-Reports/English/DB2019-report_web-version.pdf. Access date on 24.10.2019

Drezgić S (2011) Public investments and regional income convergence: empirical analysis of Croatian regions. Socialiniai tyrimai 3(24):43–55

Drezgić S, Pavlovic Z, Stojanov D (2011) Microfinance saturation in Bosnia and Herzegovina: what has really been achieved for the poor? In: Bateman M (ed) Confronting microfinance undermining sustainable development. Kumarian, Sterling, VA

EBRD (2008). www.ebrd.com. Access date on 10.09.2019

Economic Tradings (2019). https://tradingeconomics.com/countries. Access date on 24.10.2019

Efendić N, Obad O, Prica I, Škokić T, Krasniqi V, Gavrilović D (2017) Women's entrepreneurship between production and reproduction. Working paper, INFORM

Fayolle A (2007) Entrepreneurship and new value creation: the dynamic of the entrepreneurial process. In: EBHA conference, Barcelona, Spain, 16–18 Sept 2004. Cambridge University Press

Glas M (1998) Eastern Europe: Slovenia. In: Morrison AJ (ed) Entrepreneurship: an international perspective. Heinemann, Oxford, pp 108–124

Hisrich RD, Petković S, Ramadani V, Dana LP (2016) Venture capital funds in transition countries: insights from Bosnia and Herzegovina and Macedonia. J Small Bus Enterprise Dev 23 (2):296–315

Hofstede G (1980) Culture's consequences: international differences in work-related values. Sage, Beverly Hills, CA

Hofstede G (2001) Culture's consequences: comparing values, behaviours, institutions and organizations across nations. Sage, Thousand Oaks, CA

Hofstede G (2011) Dimensionalizing cultures: the Hofstede model in context. Online Readings Psychol Cult 2(1). https://doi.org/10.9707/2307-0919.1014

Hofstede G, Hofstede GJ, Minkov M (2010) Cultures and organizations: software of the mind, 3rd edn. McGraw Hill, New York

Ilgün E, Coşkun A (2009) Foreign direct investments in Bosnia and Herzegovina: banking sector example

Isenberg D (2010) How to start an entrepreneurial revolution. Harv Bus Rev 88(6):40–50

Isenberg D (2011) The entrepreneurship ecosystem strategy as a new paradigm for economy policy: principles for cultivating entrepreneurship. Babson Entrepreneurship Ecosystem Project, Babson College, Babson Park, MA

Ivy RL (1996) Global perspectives: small scale entrepreneurs and private sector development in the Slovak Republic. J Small Bus Manag 34(4):77

Jerončić M (2015) Privatni i javni patrijarhat: Društveni položaj i uloga žena u Jugoslaviji tokom socijalističkog perioda. Genero 19:1–26

Julien PA (1993) Small businesses as a research subject: some reflections on knowledge of small businesses and its effects on economic theory. Small Bus Econ 5(2):157–166

Knezović E, Musrati M (2018) Empowering leadership, psychological empowerment and employee creativity: a gender perspective. Int J Innovat Creativity Change 4(2):51–72

MI-BOSPO (2008). https://mi-bospo.org/index.php/ba. Access date on 24.10.2019

Moore JF (1993) Predators and prey: a new ecology of competition. Harv Bus Rev 71(3):75–83

Omercevic S (2012) The most common symptoms and causes of crises in small and middle companies. In: 2nd Redete international scientific conference: economic development and entrepreneurship in transition economies: a search for new paradigms, Banja Luka, 25–27 Oct 2012

Palalic R (2017) The phenomenon of entrepreneurial leadership in gazelles and mice: a qualitative study from Bosnia and Herzegovina. World Rev Entrepren Manag Sustain Dev 13 (2/3):211–236

Palalić R, Bičo A (2018) Entrepreneurship in Bosnia and Herzegovina. In Palalić R, Dana LP, Ramadani V (eds) Entrepreneurship in former Yugoslavia: diversity, institutional constraints and prospects. Springer, Cham, pp 9–35

Palalić R, Ramadani V, Dana LP (2017) Entrepreneurship in Bosnia and Herzegovina: focus on gender. Eur Bus Rev 29(4):476–496

Palalić R, Dana LP, Ramadani V (2018a) Entrepreneurship in former Yugoslavia: diversity, institutional constraints and prospects. Springer, Cham

Palalić R, Ramadani V, Dana LP, Ratten V (2018b) Gender entrepreneurial leadership in family business: a case study from Bosnia and Herzegovina. In: Ratten V, Dana LP, Ramadani V (eds) Women entrepreneurship in family business. Springer, New York

Palalić R, Dana LP, Ramadani V (2018c) Entrepreneurship in former Yugoslavia: toward the Future. In: Palalić R, Dana LP, Ramadani V (eds) Entrepreneurship in former Yugoslavia: diversity, institutional constraints, and prospects. Springer, Cham, pp 147–151

Palalić R, Branković A, Bičo A (2020) Entrepreneurial mindset and SMEs' sustainability. Springer, Cham

Peltoniemi M (2006) Preliminary theoretical framework for the study of business ecosystems. Emergence 8(1):10–19. Lawrence Erlbaum, Mahwah, NJ

Petković S (2010) Small and medium-sized enterprises in the function of economic performance (projected on the Republic of Srpska). Unpublished doctoral dissertation, Faculty of Economics, University of Banja Luka, Banja Luka

Petričević O, Danis WM (2007) Bosnia and Herzegovina: navigating a turbulent business environment. Thunderbird Int Bus Rev 49(4):417–443

Pilav-Velić, Mangafić (2016) Study on Women's Entrepreneurship in BIH. Centar za zensko preduzetnistvo i inovacije, Sarajevo

Ramadani V, Dana LP (2013) The state of entrepreneurship in the Balkans: evidence from selected countries. In: Ramadani V, Schneider RC (eds) Entrepreneurship in the Balkans. Springer, Berlin, pp 217–250

Ramadani V, Gërguri S, Dana LP, Tašaminova T (2013) Women entrepreneurs in the Republic of Macedonia: waiting for directions. Int J Entrepren Small Bus 19(1):95–121

Ramadani V, Rexhepi G, Gërguri-Rashiti S, Ibraimi S, Dana LP (2014) Ethnic entrepreneurship in Macedonia: the case of Albanian entrepreneurs. Int J Entrepren Small Bus 23(3):313–335

Roundy PT, Brockman BK, Bradshawb M (2017) The resilience of entrepreneurial ecosystems. J Bus Ventur Insights. https://doi.org/10.1016/j.jbvi.2017.08.002

Šakanović D (2018) Emancipacija bosanskohercegovačke žene u komunizmu. Available at https://www.academia.edu/37943626/Emancipacija_bosanskohercegova%C4%8Dke_%C5%BEene_u_komunizmu

Šestić M (2009) Women in Bosnia and Herzegovina and starting their own business. J Women Entrepren Educ 2009(1–2):51–59

Simić I (2011) Socijalizam i položaj žena u nauci. Kontinuirana edukacija—Položaj žena u nauci

Somun-Krupalija L (2011) Gender and employment in Bosnia and Herzegovina—a country study. Working paper, Bureau for Gender Equality, International Labour Organization, Geneva

Spigel B (2015) The relational organization of entrepreneurial ecosystems. Entrepren Theor Pract 41(1):49–72

Stem E (2018) Measuring entrepreneurial ecosystems. In: O'Connor A, Stam E, Sussan F, Audretsch DB (eds) Entrepreneurial ecosystems. Place-based transformations and transitions. Springer, New York, pp 173–196

Tansley AG (1935) The use and abuse of vegetational concepts and terms. Ecology 16(3):284–307

Tomšić V (1981) Žena u razvoju sociajlističke samouprave Jugoslavije. Novinsko-izdavačka radna organizacija—Jugoslovenska stvarnost, Beograd, Jugoslavija

Websites

Agency for Statistic of Bosnia and Herzegovina (2015) Household budget survey in B&H. Agency for statistics of Bosnia and Herzegovina, Sarajevo

Agency for Statistic of Bosnia and Herzegovina (2016) Labor Force Survey. Sarajevo: Agency for statistics of Bosnia and Herzegovina

Agency for Statistic of Bosnia and Herzegovina (2017) Labor Force Survey. Sarajevo: Agency for Statistics of Bosnia and Herzegovina

Agency for Statistic of Bosnia and Herzegovina (2018) Women and men in Bosnia and Herzegovina. Thematic Bulletin 3. Agency for statistics of Bosnia and Herzegovina, Sarajevo

Agency for Statistics of Bosnia and Herzegovina (2019) Compiled data from labor force surveys. Available at http://www.bhas.ba/index.php?option=com_content&view=article&id=113=ba&Itemid=&lang=en. http://bhas.gov.ba/?lang=en. Access date on 25.06.2019

Agency for Statistics of Bosnia and Herzegovina. http://www.bhas.ba/index.php?option=com_publikacija&view=publikacija_pregled&ids=2&id=11&n=Nati&Itemid=&lang=en. Accessed 20.06.2019

Central Bank of Bosnia and Herzegovina (2019) Banks in BH. https://cbbh.ba/Content/Read/7?lang=en. Access date 15.07.2019

Digital Innovation Profile: Bosnia and Herzegovina—ICT centric innovation ecosystem snapshot. National Expert Assessment, 2019. Available at https://www.itu.int/en/ITU-D/Innovation/Documents/Publications/eBAT_Brochure%E2%80%93DIP%20BosniaH_431106_.pdf. 04.07.2019

Election law of Bosnia and Herzegovina—consolidated text (2018) https://www.izbori.ba/Documents/documents/ZAKONI/BiH_Election_Law_last_consolidated_version_2018.pdf. Access date: 15.07.2019

European Bank for Reconstruction and Development—EBRD (2019) Business Environment and Enterprise Performance Survey—BEEPS. http://ebrd-beeps.com/countries/bosnia-and-herzegovina/. Access date: 15.07.2019

European Bank for Reconstruction and Development. https://www.ebrd.com/news/2008/helping-small-businesses-grow.html. Access date on 25.06.2019

European Commission Directorate General for Enterprise and Industry (2007) Report on the implementation of the European charter for small enterprises in the Western Balkans. SME Policy Index 2007

European Investment Bank (2016) Bosnia and Herzegovina assessment of financing needs of SMEs in the Western Balkans countries. Country report B&H. Business and Finance Consulting, Zurich

International Finance Corporation (IFC) (2010) Scaling-up SME access to financial services in the developing world. Available at www.gpfi.org/sites/default/files/documents/G20_Stocktaking_Report_0.pdf

Javne autoceste FBiH. http://www.jpautoceste.ba/wp-content/uploads/2019/03/No.pdf. Accessed on 3.7.2019

Labor Force Surveys (2015) Retrieved from http://www.bhas.ba/

Labor Force Surveys (2016) Retrieved from http://www.bhas.ba/

Law on Gender Equality in Bosnia and Herzegovina (2010) Available from https://arsbih.gov.ba/english/law-on-gender-equality-in-b-h/

OECD (2004) Women's entrepreneurship: issues and policies. OECD, Paris

The Law on Gender Equality in Bosnia and Herzegovina—consolidated text ("Official Gazette of Bosnia and Herzegovina", no. 32/10)

Trading Economics. https://tradingeconomics.com/bosnia-and-herzegovina/corruption-rank. Accessed on 3.7.2019

World Bank (2016) Doing business 2017: equal opportunity for all—Bosnia and Herzegovina. Doing business 2017. World Bank Group, Washington, DC. Accessed 11.11.2017

World Bank (2019) Doing business. Economy profile Bosnia and Herzegovina. https://www.doingbusiness.org/content/dam/doingBusiness/country/b/bosnia-and-herzegovina/BIH.pdf. Access date 15.07.2019

World Bank. http://iab.worldbank.org/Data/ExploreEconomies/bosnia-and-herzegovina#starting-a-foreign-business . Accessed 20.06.2019

Ramo Palalić is the Coordinator of Leadership and Entrepreneurship Centre at the IUS. Dr. Palalić's research interests are entrepreneurship, leadership, marketing, small and family business management. As an Assistant Professor, Dr. Palalić teaches at all three study cycles in the above areas. Apart from this, he is actively involved in business projects in the areas of entrepreneurial leadership and marketing management, in private and public organizations. He has authored and coauthored many articles in reputable international journals, several books, and many book chapters. Additionally, he is serving a few journals as reviewer/editorial board member.

Emil Knezović is the Head of Department of Economics and Management at the International University of Sarajevo. His research and teaching expertise include human resource management, entrepreneurship, small business management, and marketing So far, he published several articles in refereed international and national journals. He has been engaged as a researcher at several projects, among which is Horizon2020 Systemic Action for Gender Equality. Before joining academia, he worked in the real estate and transport industry where occasionally he still serves as a consultant.

Azra Branković is currently engaged as Assistant Professor at the International University of Sarajevo, Bosnia and Herzegovina at the Department of International Business and Finance. She is teaching Business Communication, International Marketing, International Business, Business Ethics, Entrepreneurship and Small Business Development, and Human Resource Management. Her academic experience of many years includes the University of Sarajevo, Department of Economics and Business; the Athens University of Economics and Business, Athens, Greece; the University Bocconi, Milan, Italy; the Academy of Economics, Krakow, Poland. Dr. Branković's professional career also includes work for the Italian company Ferrero as International Manager, where she was in charge of developing business in Poland. Further, she was engaged by the Organization for Security and Cooperation in Europe as the Chief of Supply, and by the government of Mecklenburg County, North Carolina, USA. Dr. Branković has been living in Bosnia and Herzegovina for the last 15 years, working with the Parliamentary Assembly as Head of the Research Center, and for the Council of Ministers as Expert Adviser for public administration reforms. In addition, Dr. Branković has been a member of several Steering Boards on EU projects.

Azra Bičo has graduated from Bachelor of Economics and Management in 2010, Department of Economics and Management, Faculty of Business and Administration, International University of Sarajevo. She attained her MA in 2014, from the same Department. Currently, she is a Senior Assistant and Ph.D. Candidate at the Department of Economics and Management. Azra Bičo has authored/coauthored several articles published in reputable journals, book chapters in books published by famous publishers, as well as conference papers. She is lecturing and assisting several courses in economics: Macroeconomics, Microeconomics, Labor Economics, International Economics, and Growth and Development. Her research interests include Labor Economics, Macroeconomics, Gender studies related to Labor Economics, and Entrepreneurship.

Women's Entrepreneurship in Croatia

Mihaela Mikic and Maja Has

Abstract This chapter is dedicated to women entrepreneurship in the Republic of Croatia. Considered from a historical perspective or its current challenges, women entrepreneurship distinguishes itself as a vital part of the national economy. On their path to becoming entrepreneurs, women are faced with numerous obstacles and are motivated by various factors. By discovering and committing to analyze these problems and motivations, we are able to provide support programs, which will be effective in further developing women entrepreneurship.

1 Introduction

Entrepreneurship supports the creation of new jobs and economic growth. It is important for the development of competition, personal potentials, and general social interests (European Commission 2003). Regardless of whether entrepreneurs are male or female, they represent a key initiator of economic growth, generator of creation of new jobs, and provider of new products and services. There is a large pool of contemporary definitions of entrepreneurship and entrepreneurs, all of which include initiative, organizing, and reorganizing of social economic mechanisms in order to get practical results, and acceptance of risk and failure (Renko 2000). An entrepreneur is deliberating, improving old and creating new. He or she is an explorer who is aware of risk and uncertainty, unpredictability and the numerous problems he or she is facing. Whether an entrepreneur is male or female, the same result is expected, contribution to economic development of society.

M. Mikic (✉)
Faculty of Economics and Business, University of Zagreb, Zagreb, Croatia
e-mail: mmikic@efzg.hr

M. Has
European Business School Zagreb, Zagreb, Croatia
e-mail: maja.has@zrinski.org

R. Palalić et al. (eds.), *Women's Entrepreneurship in Former Yugoslavia*, Contributions to Management Science,
https://doi.org/10.1007/978-3-030-45253-7_3

Numerous researches have contributed to affirmation of women entrepreneurship as a field. They have showed that women are the fastest growing entrepreneurial population and that entrepreneurial ventures started by women are significant in the number of created jobs, sale growth, and innovation (Casson et al. 2006). Women entrepreneurs are of special significance for transitioning countries' economies. They tend to employ other women more frequently, which helps reduce the effect of discrimination against women in the labor market. Also, by reducing female unemployment, women entrepreneurs can assist in fighting the trafficking of women, and female business owners serve as role models for younger generations by demonstrating new opportunities and encouraging other potential women entrepreneurs (Welter et al. 2004).

Women entrepreneurship has big potential. To support this thesis we can state numerous examples of successful women entrepreneurs, showing and proving that women are capable of achieving high business performance results. Programs for supporting women entrepreneurship should not be focused only on increasing the number of businesses founded by women, but also on increasing business performance and growth potentials of their businesses.

2 Women Entrepreneurs: A Historical Overview

Although there is no doubt that women entrepreneurs and entrepreneurship are present in Croatia from the beginning of economic activity, available data shows significant female entrepreneurial activity from the late nineteenth century. At this time, the economy is characterized by liberalization, crises, and adjustment of the legislative framework to free market principles in order to encourage the founding of new business (Vuković 2015). In Croatia adjustment of the legislative framework was accomplished by passing the Craft[1] law in 1859, which secured freedom of doing business (concessions still being present in certain industries) and access to the free market, therefore formally facilitating the entrance of both males and females in entrepreneurship (Gross and Szabo 1992).

Women confronted with new social and economic conditions and high unemployment were trying to find solutions in self-employment. Toward the end of nineteenth and during the beginning of twentieth century women entrepreneurs in Zagreb represented in average 35% of owners of large or small craft workshops and industrial businesses, a majority being in the following business activities: sewing craft, saloon and inn management, barbershops and hairstyling salons. Moreover, women were also present in trade with a share of 28%, especially in the food and drink sector (Szabo 1984). Furthermore, a large number of women secured their own existence in small crafts and trade by being the only employees in their businesses

[1] In Croatian the word *obrt* is best translated as "craft" and represents a legal form of business (sole proprietorship).

(Stipetić 2012). Due to the lack of money, women chose business activities with low entry barriers. Rare examples of women entrepreneurs in manufacturing were the result of inheritance from either a husband or parents (Vuković and Šmaguc 2015).

Small representation of women in most business activities can be explained by gender determinant policy, which defines men as strong, smart and rational enough for economic and politic activities, whereas women are described as intuitive, sensible, altruistic, and emotional characteristics which are deemed negative for public activity (Davidoff 2003).

Although partial data is not available for the majority of the twentieth century, we can still conclude that women entrepreneurship includes different categories from self-employment, founding new entrepreneurial ventures, managing inherited family business, helping to sustain family business, business partnerships, and emotional support to newly employed family members (Vuković 2015). According to the same source, these women entrepreneurs were either members of the nobility, members of the higher middle class, as well as members of the lower economic layers of society.

In the modern Croatian state women entrepreneurship was recognized with the *Strategy of Development of Women Entrepreneurship 2010–2013*, initiated by the Ministry for Economy, Work and Entrepreneurship (see Sect. 6). The Ministry recognized a need for this strategy based on the initiative of the Croatian Association of Businesswomen—Circle and National Policy for the Promotion of Gender Equality 2006–2010. The purpose of this strategy was supporting the development of an entrepreneurial environment and achieving social cohesion and justice, regional development levering and highlighting the role of education, science and market of financial services, with the purpose of strengthening women entrepreneurship. Finally, several institutions participated in formulating this strategy, including the Ministry for Economy, Work and Entrepreneurship, the Ministry of Family, Veterans and Intergenerational Solidarity, the Office for Gender Equality, the Croatian Chamber for Economy, the Croatian Employers' Association and the Croatian Association of Businesswomen—Circle. The new strategy, for the period 2014–2020 is a continuation of the previous one and is mostly an adaptation to European regulations and policies.

Today in the Republic of Croatia there is a significant number of NGOs supporting the development of women entrepreneurship, such as Croatian Association of Businesswomen—Circle, Women in Adria, International Network of Businesswomen, Association of Croatian Women Entrepreneurs, and Women Entrepreneurial Center. All of them work on the development of women entrepreneurship through networking, promotion of good practice examples, organizing workshops, providing information about business opportunities and financial support programs.

A specific example of a good practice is Amulet Studio and its owner Tihana Šmitran. She has been awarded Start-Up Women Entrepreneur of the Year in 2017. In 2019 she was a member of the US Department of State's *Professional Fellow Program* for her achievements and global results-oriented leadership, with proven success in new markets identification and innovations, while aiming to raise awareness on global challenges worldwide. Tihana Šmitran is highly educated, a member

Exhibit 1 &black&white. *Source:* Tihana Šmitran

of Women in Adria association and often uses available financing from women entrepreneurship support programs for her business needs.

Mrs. Smitran's business is based on creating digital content such as animations, infographics, and eye-catching visuals for the purpose of building up brands, handling marketing campaigns including their social media and web pages, and optimizing the company's internal communications. Amulet Studio also engaged in producing an original animated series. The first series, named *&Black&White,* is an artistic cartoon that engages with shapes in black and white contrast (Exhibit 1). It is promoted for children and adults of all ages. It has recently received second place at the Los Angeles Animation Festival for Best Short Animated Series. This animated series is the first independently financed animated project in Croatia in the last 40 years.

Mrs. Smitran's new project is named *MaNaBu*, an educational platform that helps kids aged 5–9 years to understand global challenges based on 17 UN Sustainable Development Goals, by using edutainment media and tools (Exhibit 2). The *MaNaBu* edutainment platform consists of series, songs, and games with the mission of helping children discover the true values of life and encourage them to become positive leaders of tomorrow. The project team includes an Oscar Award Nominee team, media experts, educators, and IT experts from all around the world.

What can we learn from historical and modern examples of good practice? Only with further investment in education and programs for the support of the development of women entrepreneurship can we open paths for more effective policies, which will result in more positive and inclusive economic effects.

Exhibit 2 MaNaBu. *Source:* Tihana Šmitran

3 The Current State of Women Entrepreneurship in Croatia

In the 1990s, the Republic of Croatia made the transition from a planned to a market economy. During this period, numerous social and economic changes took place that affected the country's economy, entrepreneurship, and society as a whole. With the ending of the war, transition and privatization problems in Croatia neglected the needs of the small business sector for a relatively long time. The adoption of the *Small Business Development Promotion Act* in 2002 was a very important step, which established the basis for support and development of small and medium sized companies, and the establishment of the Croatian Small Business Agency (Alpeza et al. 2018). Although entrepreneurship has been characterized as a male activity, in the past few years there is increased discussion about women entrepreneurs.

According to the existing statistical data, a large underrepresentation of women in entrepreneurship is evident. The causes of large differences in entrepreneurial activities between women and men in Croatia lie in the consistency of obstacles to the development of women entrepreneurship, and an inadequacy of programs and measures devoted to the development and strengthening of women entrepreneurship (CEPOR 2016). Existing programs oriented to women entrepreneurship promotion and strengthening are a positive step forward, but there is room for improvement. According to the Country Assessment Notes for Croatia prepared by the OECD and European Commission (2018), growth-oriented women entrepreneurs are not well-served by existing programs as the financial instruments are not appropriate, and little training, business advice or mentoring are available. There is also a need to provide more comprehensive support for women entrepreneurs with family responsibilities, such as childcare. In this chapter, the most important indicators of women's entrepreneurial activity are presented, as well as basic economic and social indicators related to entrepreneurship development.

3.1 Position of Women in Economy and Society

Women play a significant role in society and its development. The position of women in society has been changing since Croatia gained its independence. Although some progress has been noted, there are still gender inequalities that are evident in certain economic and social categories such as the labor market, employment and earnings, education, career progression, politics, and judiciary. This subchapter provides an overview of selected social and economic indicators that affect entrepreneurship and its development.

According to the data presented in Table 1, women in Croatian society have a majority share in total population, graduates from institutions of higher education, and pension beneficiaries. The situation is disproportional in favor of men in the sectors of justice affairs and political governance. The Ombudswomen for Gender Equality conducted a quantitative analysis on the representation of women and men in managerial positions in business entities in the Republic of Croatia. This research confirmed the thesis that women are extremely underrepresented in governing bodies of companies in Croatia. According to the research, women account for 25.4%, and men for 74.6% of all management board members in governing bodies of companies that participated in the study. Furthermore, women are represented with 22.7% in supervisory boards of companies, and with just 9.4% in the position of president of the management board of companies that participated in the research (CEPOR 2016).

The existence of certain gender inequalities in Croatia is consistent with the Global Gender Gap Report and Gender Equality Index. In 2018, the Global Gender Gap Report covered 149 countries and Croatia ranked as 59th (World Economic Forum 2018). According to the report, in terms of gender equality Croatia has the

Table 1 Selected social and economic indicators

Category	Women	Men
Population (%)[a]	51.7	48.3
Graduates from institutions of higher education (%)[a]	59.7	40.3
Pension beneficiaries (%)[b]	54.2	45.8
Constitutional court judges (%)[b]	23.1	76.9
Government ministers (%)[c]	20.0	80.0

Source: Croatian Bureau of Statistics (2019b)
[a]2017
[b]2018
[c]2016

Table 2 Registered unemployed persons (average) from 2016 to 2018

Registered unemployed persons		Year 2016	2017	2018
Unemployed persons	Total	241.860	193.967	153.542
	Men	107.947	83.144	66.403
	Women	133.913	110.823	87.139
Unemployed persons without work experience	Total	42.935	31.985	24.144
	Men	19.297	13.665	9.936
	Women	23.638	18.320	14.208

Source: Croatian Employment Service (2019)

Table 3 Working-age population, by activity and gender from 2015 to 2018

	Year							
	2015		2016		2017		2018	
Indicators[a]	W	M	W	M	W	M	W	M
Activity rate (%)	46.9	59.1	45.4	57.8	45.6	58.2	45.5	57.4
Employment/population ratio (%)	39.0	50.0	39.2	50.5	40.2	52.0	41.3	53.0
Unemployment rate (%)	16.9	15.6	13.8	12.6	11.9	10.6	9.3	7.6

Source: Croatian Employment Service (2019)
[a]Activity rate represents the labor force as a percentage of the working-age population. Employment/population ratio represents persons in employment as a percentage of working-age population. Unemployment rate represents unemployed persons as a percentage of the labor force

best standing in the field of educational attainment (enrolment in secondary and tertiary education), professional and technical workers, and health and survival (sex ratio at birth, healthy life expectancy), while it is the worst in the field of wage equality for same or similar work. According to the last results on the Gender Equality Index, Croatia ranked 22nd in the EU with 55.6 out of 100 points. The score is 11.8 points lower than the EU's score (EIGE 2019). Croatia's scores are highest in the domains of health and money, while gender inequalities are most pronounced in the domain of power.

By comparing the status of women and men in Croatia, a consistent difference in employment and unemployment is observed (Table 2). According to the official statistic data, of the total number of unemployed persons in 2018, 56.8% were women. Furthermore, women were 58.8% of the total number of unemployed persons without work experience.

Table 3 presents relevant indicators related to the labor market in Croatia. While the activity rate and employment ratio have been pretty constant, the unemployment rate of women decreased in the period 2015–2018. Regardless of the decrease, unemployment rate for women was greater than the unemployment rate for men. In 2018 the unemployment rate for women was 1.7% higher than that of men. Based on the above data, it can be concluded that women face more problems tackling long-term unemployment.

Table 4 Population aged 15 years and over, by educational attainment and gender, by census 2011

Educational attainment[a]	Gender		
	Women	Men	Total
Basic education or less (%)	37.2	23.8	30.8
Upper secondary education (%)	45.9	60.0	52.6
Higher education (%)	16.7	16.0	16.4

Source: Croatian Bureau of Statistics (2019a)
[a]Difference to 100.0% refers to unknown educational attainment

According to the latest available data on educational attainment by gender, 37.2% of women in Croatia attain basic education or less, 45.9% attain secondary education and 16.7% achieve higher education (Table 4). Analysis of educational structure of the population by gender based on Croatian Bureau of Statistics data (2019a) indicates interesting findings related to higher education. In the academic year 2017/2018 there were 159.638 students enrolled, of which 57% were women. Female students represented the majority in all faculties, except for engineering. In the academic year 2017/2018 there were women were 54.3% of enrolled students in doctoral studies. Of the fields which have been analyzed, higher education is one of the few in which higher proportion of women than men is noticed.

3.2 Position of Women in Entrepreneurial Activity

Croatia has been involved in *GEM—Global Entrepreneurship Monitor* since 2002. GEM, as the world's largest study of entrepreneurship research, enables analysis of the difference in business venture start-up activity between women and men. The level of activity in starting business ventures at the national level is measured by the TEA index[2] (CEPOR 2018). In Tables 5 and 6, relevant data on entrepreneurial activity by gender according to GEM reports is presented.

Based on the above data, it can be observed that in the period of 2014–2018 the share of men in business venture start-up activities was higher than the share of women. In 2018, ratio TEA Men/TEA Women was 1.7 which indicates 1.7 times higher activity of men in business venture start-up in relation to women. Although certain positive changes are visible in all the observed years, this ratio in Croatia is worse than the average of all countries involved in the GEM research. In 2018, of all men who started a business venture, 63.3% did so because of a perceived opportunity, compared to 59.6% women. On the other hand, of all men who started a business venture, 32.4% did so out of necessity, compared to 32.2% of women (CEPOR 2019).

[2]TEA (Total Early Entrepreneurial Activity) index represents the number of entrepreneurially active people (it combines the number of people who are starting an entrepreneurial venture and the number of people who are owners or owners/managers of enterprises younger than 42 months) per 100 examinees that are 18–64 years old.

Table 5 Entrepreneurial activity by gender from 2014 to 2018, measured by the TEA index (%)

	Year									
	2014		2015		2016		2017		2018	
Indicators	GEM average	Croatia	GEM average	Croatia	GEM average	Croatia	GEM average	Croatia	GEM average	Croatia
TEA Women	11.3	4.8	11.1	5.7	10.0	5.6	10.5	6.4	10.4	7.1
TEA Men	14.9	11.3	15.4	9.7	14.6	11.2	14.4	11.5	14.7	12.1
TEA Men/TEA Women	1.3	2.4	1.6	1.7	1.6	2	1.5	1.8	1.6	1.7

Source: CEPOR—SMEs and Entrepreneurship Policy Center (2019)

Table 6 Entrepreneurial activity by gender and age structure from 2016 to 2018, measured by the TEA index (%)

	Year					
	2016		2017		2018	
Age group	Women	Men	Women	Men	Women	Men
18–24	5.4	11.7	6.4	14.9	8.5	14.8
25–34	8.7	16.9	7.5	17.9	14.7	23.0
35–44	9.5	13.5	10.0	12.9	7.2	15.6
45–54	3.6	9.5	6.3	7.9	3.9	6.0
55–64	1.4	4.5	1.9	5.0	2.5	2.1

Source: CEPOR—SMEs and Entrepreneurship Policy Center (2019)

According to the World Bank Group (2019b), Croatia is characterized by limited self-employment and particularly low entrepreneurial activity among women. In 2017, Croatia had one of the lowest entrepreneurship rates within the EU-28, both for women and men. Furthermore, women were significantly under-represented in entrepreneurial activities, with gender gaps that are larger than EU average.

The Female Entrepreneurship Index (FEI) measures the development of high potential female entrepreneurship worldwide. According to the last Female Entrepreneurship Index rankings for the 77-country sample, Croatia took the 31st place with 49.9 points (Global Entrepreneurship and Development Institute 2015). Equal rights, executive status, and secondary education were highest rated indicators, while R&D expenditure and opportunity recognition were the lowest scored indicators.

Table 6 presents entrepreneurial activity by gender and age structure measured by TEA indexes. Data shows that men are the most entrepreneurially active in the 25–34 age group, and women in the 35–44 age group (except in 2018, when the most entrepreneurially active women were in the age group 25–34). According to gender, the biggest difference in entrepreneurial activity is observed in 18–24 and 25–34 group. This can be explained by the role of women have in maternity, but also other factors which affect the more equal organization of family life such as nurseries, kindergartens, meals in school and in the workplace, maternity leave for fathers, and cultural attitude toward the role of women in the family (CEPOR 2018). These are important factors that place women entrepreneurial activity in the wider social and cultural concept, and policy makers should focus on these factors when defining policies which promote women entrepreneurship.

In 2012, according to the European Commission (2014), women entrepreneurs in the EU-28 tended to be better educated than men entrepreneurs. Women entrepreneurs in EU-28 attained on average level 2.1 and men entrepreneurs level 2.0, indicating that women were slightly more highly educated than men entrepreneurs. Based on the same report, the data for Croatia was different, since Croatian male entrepreneurs attained educational level 1.89, and women entrepreneurs on average level 1.79.

Table 7 Company ownership structure by gender from 2016 to 2018

Indicators	Ownership structure	Year 2016	2017	2018
Share in total number of enterprises that submitted annual financial reports (%)	Founded by women	21.8	21.9	22.0
	Founded by men	55.8	56.7	57.9
Share of total income of enterprises that submitted annual financial reports (%)	Founded by women	4.7	4.4	4.5
	Founded by men	28.6	27.8	29.0
Share of employment of total employed persons in enterprises that submitted annual financial reports (%)	Founded by women	8.2	8.2	8.2
	Founded by men	34.8	34.2	35.4

Source: Financial Agency (2019)
Difference to 100.0% refers to other founders such as legal entities

Analysis of data on entrepreneurial activity in Croatia by gender, based on data collected by the Financial Agency (FINA) Register of Annual Financial Statements, indicates that the share of women enterprise owners in total number of enterprises is significantly lower than the share of men enterprise owners (Table 7). Significant differences which demonstrate underrepresentation of women in entrepreneurial activities can also be observed through the following indicators, income and employment. In 2018, enterprises owned by women which submitted annual financial reports, participated in the total income of Croatian enterprises with only 4.5%, and with 8.2% in the total number of employed persons.

Observed by activities, enterprises with majority women ownership are dominant in the (S) area of activity—other service activities[3] with share of women entrepreneurs of 57.2% in 2018. This is followed by activity in the area of education (P) with 41.1%; then area of human health and social work activities (Q) with 39.9%; and the area of professional, scientific, and technical activities (M) with 39.9% (Financial Agency 2019). These data are consistent with the European Commission statistical data on women entrepreneurs in Europe. According to European Commission, in 2008 and in 2012, a higher proportion of women than men entrepreneurs in EU-28 were active in the sector groups of human health and social work activities, education, and other services. In 2012, 60% of the entrepreneurs active in human health and social work activities were women, 65% in other services sector and 55% in education (European Commission 2014). Men on the other hand were much more likely to operate in the business sectors of construction, transport and storage, water supply, information and communication, and manufacturing. According to OECD's

[3]Accoridng to National Classification of Activities 2007, this area (as a residual category) includes activities of membership organisations, repair of computers and personal and household goods and other personal service activities not elsewhere classified in the classification

Table 8 Users of grants for self-employment from 2016 to 2018

Users	Year		
	2016	2017	2018
Total	2.333	3.583	6.485
Men	1.262	1.982	3.939
Women	1.071	1.601	2.546

Source: Croatian Employment Service (2019)

Table 9 Persons in employment, by status in employment and gender from 2015 to 2018

Indicators	Year							
	2015		2016		2017		2018	
	W	M	W	M	W	M	W	M
Persons in paid employment (%)	87.7	81.4	89.5	83.2	90.1	85.6	90.0	86.1
Self-employed persons (%)	9.5	17.4	8.5	15.9	8.3	13.4	8.3	12.9
Unpaid family workers (%)	(2.8)	((1.2))	(2.0)	((0.9))	((1.6))	((1.0))	((1.7))	((0.9))

Source: Croatian Employment Service (2019)

Policy Brief on Women's Entrepreneurship (OECD and European Union 2017b), women's entrepreneurial ventures are less oriented toward high growth and job creation. These findings are in line with the data presented above, which shows that enterprises owned by women mostly operate in activities which do not have high profit potential (education, social work, etc.).

Starting business ventures out of necessity is one of the ways out of unemployment. Croatian Employment Service provides financial support to its users through grants for self-employment. Grants are a measure of active employment policy intended for people registered in the unemployment register who have an entrepreneurial idea (CEPOR 2018). In the last 3 years the number of grant users for self-employment is in increase, which is the result of the implementation of a series of active employment policy measures by the Ministry of Labor, the Pension System and the Croatian Employment Service. Based on the data in Table 8, it can be observed that the number of users of grants for self-employment increases in the period 2016–2018. In 2018, male users participated with 60.7%, while female users participated with 39.3%. In 2016 and 2017, the difference in proportion by gender was less pronounced.

In Croatia, the proportion of workers who are self-employed has declined in recent years. The proportion of working women who were self-employed declined from 9.5% in 2015 to 8.3% in 2018 (Table 9).

The main reasons for the smaller inclusion of women in the labor market remain parenthood and eldercare. In Croatian society, women still play a dominant role in managing family life, and many women maintain an attitude that career cannot be balanced with motherhood. Based on the data above, it can be concluded that women prefer regular employment than self-employment. A possible explanation for this observation is that women still do not recognize self-employment and managing one's own company as good opportunities to build a career.

4 Main Obstacles to Women Entrepreneurship in Croatia

The main obstacles that represent the base problem in development of women entrepreneurship are (Ministry of Entrepreneurship and Crafts 2014):

- Women represent the majority of unemployed persons.
- There is continuous gap between the representation of men and women in entrepreneurial activity.
- There is low representation of women in key management positions within companies.

High rates of female unemployment are the result of multiple barriers to access the labor market. One such barrier is mobility, since women are usually unable or unwilling to migrate. Also, women are often included in vulnerable groups because of lower education and skill level which make them noncompetitive in the formal labor market. However, stigma and social norms are still a major factor (World Bank Group 2019a). The decline in presence of women in the hierarchy pyramid is also present outside the business sector, additionally supporting the conclusions on the existence of stereotypes, which reinforce the balance which women must make between the burden of profession and family life (Keser 2014). Although these obstacles cannot be applied to the same degree for self-employment and entrepreneurship, the continuous gap between the representation of men and women persists.

Main obstacles are closely related, yet vary widely, making them difficult to eliminate. Each obstacle requires a different solution and resources for its support, such as time, public will, financial sources, institutional support, etc. According to the *Strategy of Development of Women Entrepreneurship 2014–2020* the main obstacles that women entrepreneurs face in Croatia can be grouped into three categories. These are structural, economic, and "soft" obstacles (Ministry of Entrepreneurship and Crafts 2014).

Structural obstacles are the most challenging. They are the result of cultural heritage and social values, lack of political will in constant and persistent implementation and application of the political-regulatory framework, and lack of infrastructure support for family life. Structural obstacles are stereotypes toward women in the field of science and technology, traditional views on the role of women in society, educational choices that women make which then reduce their abilities to initiate businesses in high technology sectors, lack of support for women with two roles which are family and business, and the political-regulatory framework and its purpose of supporting gender equality (Ministry of Entrepreneurship and Crafts 2014). When women choose to enter traditionally male industries, their success is limited by the lack of perceived credibility from their peers and clients. For this reason, it is not uncommon for women to partner up with a husband or male relative, just so that the company has a male face in its professional dealings (Sulejmanović 2008).

Cultural norms place the burden of taking care of children and the elderly on women, which further restricts their role (World Bank Group 2019a). The Croatian political culture of the past 10–15 years highlighted the role of the church and decreed that women's place was primarily in the house, a fact which considerably worsened the status of women and discouraged them to attempt at improving their own status in society through entrepreneurship, work, and career advancement (Leinert-Novosel 2000).

Economic obstacles represent difficulty to access financial resources, lack of market information, limited bargaining power, unequal access to productive resources and services, and lack of business networking which is associated with difficulties in obtaining necessary information. For example, because of the difficulties in gathering financial resources, there is a necessity for providing special support programs and creating strategic partnerships of different government programs and commercial banks for the support of promising entrepreneurial projects initiated by women. An example would be a tax policy which is used to support alternative sources of finance, such as business angels. The reasons for which women lack business networking stem from dated stereotypes of masculinity and femininity, in which men are deemed dominant to women and brave when it comes to building networks, whereas women are viewed as more cautious, tending to build networks with trusted people, such as family and friends (Palalic et al. 2017b).

"Soft" obstacles represent the lack of advice; mentorship; lack of access to entrepreneurial networks; women's perception of their lack of self-confidence, capacity to take risk and training; education and professional qualifications for high technology ventures (Ministry of Entrepreneurship and Crafts 2014). Usually, when women decide to become entrepreneurs they are handicapped by the lack of financial literacy and business-related skills. There is an absence of structured and continuous support in the entrepreneurial ecosystem, as well as effective and affordable business development services that would encourage women to take on entrepreneurial roles in either starting or continuing in business (World Bank Group 2019a).

Even though support programs are available, they usually have limitations. First is their limited scope of reach. Rural and vulnerable women may not be approached by these programs because of their demand for smaller loans or more women-centric financial products. Second is the perception that procedures are complicated. In order to use financial support programs for the development of products and services, the applicant needs to submit a business plan which includes a detailed financial plan. Most of the women entrepreneurs lack formal business and financial knowledge, and therefore without adequate support this barrier can be debilitating for potential women entrepreneurs. The World Bank Group (2019a) assesses that 26 minority groups, including women, continue to be excluded from support programs, pointing out that the instruments do not meet the needs of excluded groups.

Entrepreneurial activity is dependent upon whether individuals can identify with the characteristics and behaviors that are associated with entrepreneurship. These characteristics are usually strongly linked to masculine characteristics, such as autonomy, perseverance, high energy levels, self-confidence, and decisiveness. The domination of these characteristics leads to the creation of a perceived male norm of entrepreneurship, which negatively effects the entrepreneurial self-perception of women (Keser 2014).

Unfortunately, according to Keser (2014), this norm pervades the current educational system as a whole. The effects of this norm can be seen specifically in universities, as male students have a higher level of entrepreneurial orientation than female students (Bilić et al. 2011). Therefore, in order to encourage egalitarian practices, educational institutions should provide students with examples of good practice of women entrepreneurs. By encouraging female students to recognize their self-efficacy, universities can convert their cultural capital into social capital by bridging it between distant actors of society, leading finally to the conversion of social capital into economic capital (Vuković et al. 2017).

5 Motives for Engaging in Entrepreneurial Activities

Individuals engage in entrepreneurship for two main reasons: opportunity and necessity. The first reason represents starting a new business to exploit a perceived business opportunity and the second is being pushed into entrepreneurship because all other options of getting employment are either absent or unsatisfactory (Kedmenec et al. 2014). Throughout history, women were often by necessity, but also sometimes by free choice, looking for the means of earning income for securing survival or better living conditions (Vuković 2015). Hard to reach population groups (women, older men and youth) often resort to self-employment due to a lack of formal employment opportunities (OECD and European Union 2017a). Schumpeter saw the entrepreneur as a hero and agent of change. Today, we are distanced from this point of view because the subjects of entrepreneurship are now identified as business active women who under the influence of life, economic and social circumstances decided to seize opportunity or were just forced to rely on personal strengths in securing their own existence (Vuković 2015).

Females included in TEA who claim to be driven by necessity in the period 2012–2016 in Croatia is 43%, which means that 43% of women entering entrepreneurship did not have other employment opportunities (OECD and European Union 2017a). The data for the same period shows that necessity is the motive for 35% of men. When compared with EU average, we notice that women in the European Union (EU-27) enter entrepreneurship from necessity only in 23% of cases, and the overall average (for all entrepreneurs) is only 22%. Presented data show that opportunity, as a motive for entering entrepreneurship in Croatia, is not as strong as in other European countries.

In the period 2012–2016 in Croatia only 17% of women entrepreneurs started their businesses offering products and services new to some or all customers, compared to EU average of 28% (OECD and European Union 2017a). In the same period, men in Croatia had the share of offering new products and services of 28%. The overall average for EU-27 countries and all entrepreneurs in the same period was 29%.

If we look beyond the motives of necessity and opportunity, we can see that women, like men, enter entrepreneurship for a variety of reasons: extrinsic, intrinsic, or transcendental nature. Intrinsic motivation refers to doing an activity for its inherent enjoyment rather than for some separable outcome, a person acts for the fun, challenge, or satisfaction entailed, and not due to the external outcome, pressure, or reward (Deci and Ryan 2010). According the same source, extrinsic motivation refers to doing an activity in order to attain some separable outcome, such as earning a reward or avoiding punishment. In the case of entrepreneurship, this type of behavior could be described as profit-based motivation of starting business. Transcendence nature motives (spirituality) goes far beyond the intrinsic tendencies to fulfill self-centered psychological needs and beyond the orientation on extrinsically regulated material aspects of life (Górnik-Durose et al. 2017).

According to Heilman and Chen (2003) women are connected to motivations reliant on an intrinsic and transcendental nature, while men are driven to business creation for primarily extrinsic reasons. When women are creating a new business based on intrinsic factors, they are motivated by desire for independence, self-realization, internal control, perseverance and an interest in taking up the challenges posed by creating a new firm, the opportunity to develop their skills and experience, and the chance to influence their own destinies (Akehurst et al. 2012). The most common transcendence motive is flexible job opportunity that allows women to combine professional and family life by setting their own working hours (Scott 1986). This is important because it shows the advantage of running one's own business and its compatibility with the demanding role in family life women have, especially in child rearing.

When a woman is making decisions about engaging in entrepreneurship she is also influenced by informal and formal institutions (Aidis et al. 2005). Informal institutions represent the invisible "rules of the game" made up of norms, values, acceptable behaviors, and codes of conduct. The formal institutions are visible "rules of the game" such as laws, which can be altered quickly to adapt to changing economic circumstances (North 1990). Informal institutions can influence perceptions of entrepreneurial opportunities, which change the extent to which women entrepreneurship is able to develop, and formal institutions can create opportunities for entrepreneurship, such as the types of enterprises in which women can engage (Welter and Smallbone 2003).

6 Support Programs for Women Entrepreneurship Development

Encouraging women entrepreneurs does not only have social benefits based on gender equality, but also significant economic benefits. According to *Policy Brief on Women's Entrepreneurship* (2017), the challenges that women identify in starting a business include discouraging social and cultural attitudes, lower levels of entrepreneurship skills, greater difficulty in accessing start-up financing, smaller and less effective entrepreneurial networks, and policy frameworks that discourage women entrepreneurship.

Therefore, it is important to implement a variety of measures to encourage women entrepreneurship and empowerment of women in society. Oberman Peterka et al. (2016) pointed out that women entrepreneurship can be successfully encouraged through the following activities: intensifying lobbying activities of professional women's organizations and nonprofit associations; organizing the exchange of experience between already successful women entrepreneurs and beginner women entrepreneurs; various programs for encouraging women entrepreneurship through training, education, guarantees for obtaining bank loans for starting businesses by women; encouraging the networking of women entrepreneurs through local and regional development networks; providing free or subsidized consulting services of foreign or local consultants to female entrepreneurs. Ramadani et al. (2013) propose the following measures for the development of women entrepreneurship: extending credits to support women entrepreneurship, establishing funds which provide loans, providing training, developing special programs, offering support to microenterprises, establishing a database of women entrepreneurs and introducing policies for women entrepreneurs. Also, Palalic et al. (2017a) suggests that women, especially those without entrepreneurial experience, need to be involved more in entrepreneurship development programs organized and implemented by the state and its agencies.

The government of the Republic of Croatia adopted in 2014 the national *Strategy of Women Entrepreneurship Development in the Republic of Croatia 2014–2020* (hereinafter: the Strategy). The Strategy is based on the EU Strategic Framework, Small Business Act, Women's Charter and the Europe 2020 Strategy, whose aims are to achieve smart, sustainable, and inclusive growth, implying wide and efficient acceleration of women's economic potential (Ministry of Entrepreneurship and Crafts 2014). The strategy addresses the following four strategic objectives: improving alignment and networking of public policies, improving systematic support to women in entrepreneurship, introducing women entrepreneurship to the overall institutional infrastructure, and promoting women entrepreneurship.

Furthermore, the strategic objectives are complemented with specific measures, implementation activities, and the Action Plan that includes performance indicators for measuring the implementation effectiveness of the Strategy. The expected result of the application of this strategic document was to increase the number of women starting a business venture, and the number of women who are owners of growing business ventures, in order to achieve the EU average as measured by the TEA indicator (Ministry of Entrepreneurship and Crafts 2014). According to previously reported data on entrepreneurial activities among women, it cannot be confirmed that this goal was achieved. Furthermore, the publication of *Inclusive Entrepreneurship Policies: Country Assessment Notes* (2018) reported that publicly available reports on implementation results do not exist, making it difficult to draw conclusions about the effects of strategies.

In recent years, Croatia implemented a number of programs and projects aimed at encouraging the development of women entrepreneurship. One of the major programs was *Entrepreneurial Impulse Program—Project Women Entrepreneurship for the promotion of entrepreneurship and crafts*, implemented by the Ministry of Entrepreneurship and Crafts. This program offered measures and instruments for encouraging the development of the small and medium enterprise sector, focused on achieving strategic goals related to the development of entrepreneurship at the national level. In the period 2011–2015, 5372 grants representing 39.3% of all those awarded and totaling an amount of HRK 142 million, were administered for the purpose of encouraging women entrepreneurship (CEPOR 2016).

In 2011, the Croatian Bank for Reconstruction and Development (HBOR) started the implementation of a program for crediting women entrepreneurs. The objective of this program was to encourage funding through loans with a 2% interest rate and development of enterprises that are owned by women (HBOR 2019). In the period 2011–2017, a total of 502 loans intended for entrepreneurial ventures for women were approved, in total value of over HRK 170.1 million (CEPOR 2016, 2018).

Since 2011, the European Bank for Reconstruction and Development has been implementing *Croatia Women in Business Program*, aimed at women-led small and medium sized enterprises. The program provides financing through partner banks and several nonfinancial instruments aimed at strengthening women in entrepreneurship like business consulting, education, workshops, and mentoring (EBRD 2019). According to CEPOR (2018), in cooperation with local consultants, in 2016 and 2017, EBRD implemented and cofinanced 52 consulting projects with women entrepreneurs.

In addition to the specific measures, programs and funding instruments mentioned above, there are also entrepreneurship support institutions at the national and the local level, which encourage women entrepreneurs to accomplish their entrepreneurial projects. Some cities contribute to the development of entrepreneurship by establishing entrepreneurial centers, incubators, and development agencies. Furthermore, associations play an important role in promoting women's entrepreneurship and serve as inspiration for all women who want to become entrepreneurs.

The Center for Education, Counselling and Research—CESI is a nonprofit association committed to promoting women's social status and achieving gender equality. In 2015, CESI launched the *FREE—Rural Women and Entrepreneurship projects* with the goal of supporting women from rural areas who want to start their own enterprise or to support women who have already started one. The project is financially supported by the European Commission, and in addition to Croatia, includes partner-countries Iceland, the United Kingdom, Lithuania, and Bulgaria

(CESI 2019). According to the needs of a target group of women, activities for strengthening skills, competencies, networking, supporting enterprise growth by encouraging creativity, encouraging start-ups, and growth of existing enterprises were designed.

The network of business women "Women in Adria" operates through a web portal, social networks, and organization of networking events with the aim of networking and exchanging experiences of women entrepreneurs and business women. Since 2012, a series of networking events has been organized with the purpose of exchanging ideas and experiences, as well as award ceremonies for best women entrepreneurs (CEPOR 2018). Similar activities are undertaken by the *Virtual Women's Entrepreneurial Center* and *Aurora*, both of which are digital platforms. The main goals of these centers are the promotion of successful entrepreneurial stories among women, the exchange of experiences, and the creation of business contacts.

As we can see in this chapter, the Republic of Croatia recognized women entrepreneurship as a vital part of the Croatian Economy, both from an economic and social perspective. The various implemented programs in Croatia have allowed for positive change for women entrepreneurship. However, there continues to be room for improvement and advancement in the field, especially in better adjustment of the support instruments which must meet real needs of all women entrepreneurs.

7 Conclusion

Lately, there has been more research in the field of women entrepreneurship and its development, but overall it is still an under-researched area of entrepreneurship. From the historical perspective to the present day, women have had a significant role in Croatian society. This role has changed over time under the influence of various social, cultural, and economic factors. Although specific progress has been noted, the data indicate that there are still gender inequalities, which is evident in certain economic and social categories.

In the modern Croatian state, women entrepreneurship was recognized with the *Strategy of Development of Women Entrepreneurship*, prepared for two time periods, 2010–2013 and 2014–2020. The Strategy addresses the following four strategic objectives of development of women entrepreneurship: improving alignment and networking of public policies, improving systematic support to women in entrepreneurship, introducing women entrepreneurship to the overall institutional infrastructure, and promoting women entrepreneurship.

Based on data presented in previous chapters, it can be concluded that women in Croatia are underrepresented in entrepreneurial activities. Significant differences which indicate underrepresentation of women in entrepreneurial activities can be observed in the following indicators: share of women enterprise owners in total number of enterprises, TEA (Total Early Entrepreneurial Activity) indexes, unemployment rate, self-employment rate, opportunity as motive for entering entrepreneurship, etc. Although there are certain improvements which have been observed over the past few years, compared to other EU countries Croatia is still far behind.

In recent years, several programs and projects were implemented with the aim of encouraging the development of women entrepreneurship. These are mainly related to the financing of women's entrepreneurial ventures and counseling services. Furthermore, there is a significant number of NGOs supporting the development of women entrepreneurship, all of which work on the development of women entrepreneurship through networking, promoting good practice examples, organizing workshops, providing information about business opportunities and financial support programs.

To conclude women entrepreneurship in Croatia has big potential. To support this thesis we can offer numerous examples of successful women entrepreneurs, which prove that women are capable of achieving high business performance results. Positive examples of women entrepreneurs in Croatia can certainly serve as guidelines for designing new support programs. Such programs should not only be focused on increasing the number of businesses founded by women, but should also increase business performance and growth potentials of their businesses. Finally, policy makers and relevant institutions should take into account wider social and cultural concepts of women entrepreneurship, in order to assist society to move beyond outdated and problematic stereotypes.

References

Aidis R, Welter F, Smallbone D, Isakova N (2005) Female entrepreneurship in transition economies: the case of Lithuania and Ukraine. Working paper, University College London, London

Akehurst G, Simarro E, Mas-Tur A (2012) Women entrepreneurship in small service firms: motivations, barriers and performance. Serv Indust J 32(15):2489–2505. https://doi.org/10.1080/02642069.2012.677834

Alpeza M, Oberman Peterka S, Has M (2018) Entrepreneurship in Croatia. In: Palalić R, Dana LP, Ramadani V (eds) Entrepreneurship in former Yugoslavia: diversity, institutional constraints and prospects. Springer, Cham, pp 37–50

Bilić I, Prka A, Vidović G (2011) How does education influence entrepreneurship orientation? Care study of Croatia. Management 16(1):115–128

Casson M, Yeung B, Basu A (2006) The Oxford handbook of entrepreneurship. Oxford University Press, New York

Center for Education, Counselling and Research—CESI (2019) Available at http://www.cesi.hr/en/project-free-rural-women-and-entrepreneurship/. Accessed 14.12.2019

CEPOR—SMEs and Entrepreneurship Policy Center (2016) Small and medium enterprises report – Croatia 2015 including the results of GEM—global entrepreneurship monitor research for Croatia for 2014. CEPOR, Zagreb

CEPOR—SMEs and Entrepreneurship Policy Center (2018) Small and medium enterprises report – Croatia 2018 including the results of GEM—global entrepreneurship monitor research for Croatia for 2017. CEPOR, Zagreb

CEPOR—SMEs and Entrepreneurship Policy Center (2019) Small and medium enterprises report – Croatia 2019. CEPOR, Zagreb
Croatian Bank for Reconstruction and Development (2019) Available at https://www.hbor.hr/tema/mladi-zene-pocetnici/. Accessed 14.12.2019
Croatian Bureau of Statistics (2019a) Labour force in the Republic of Croatia, 2018 annual average [online]. Croatian Bureau of Statistics. Available at https://www.dzs.hr/Hrv_Eng/publication/2019/09-02-07_01_2019.htm. Accessed 12.12.2019
Croatian Bureau of Statistics (2019b) Women and men in Croatia, 2019. Croatian Bureau of Statistics, Zagreb
Croatian Employment Service (2019) Available at https://statistika.hzz.hr/. Accessed 13.12.2019
Davidoff L (2003) Gender and the "great divide": public and private in British gender history. J Women Hist 15(1):11–27. https://doi.org/10.1353/jowh.2003.0020
Deci EL, Ryan RM (2010) Intrinsic motivation. Corsini Encyclopedia Psychol. https://doi.org/10.1002/9780470479216.corpsy0467
European Bank for Reconstruction and Development (2019) Available at https://www.ebrd.com/croatia.html. Accessed 13.12.2019
European Commission (2003) Green paper entrepreneurship in Europe. Available at https://web.archive.org/web/20040611050753/http://www.europa.eu.int:80/comm/enterprise/entrepreneurship/green_paper/index.htm. Accessed 10.12.2019
European Commission (2014) Statistical data on women entrepreneurs in Europe. European Commission—Directorate-General for Enterprise and Industry, Brussels
European Institute for Gender Equality—EIGE (2019) Gender equality index 2019 work—life balance. EIGE, Vilnius
Financial Agency—FINA (2019) Analysis of the share of women entrepreneurs in the ownership structure of trading companies. FINA, Zagreb
Global Entrepreneurship and Development Institute (2015) The female entrepreneurship index (FEI). An analysis of the conditions that foster high-potential female entrepreneurship. Global Entrepreneurship and Development Institute
Górnik-Durose M, Jach Ł, Langer M (2017) Intrinsic—extrinsic—transcendent. A triarchic model of goal contents: introduction and validation. Curr Issues Pers Psychol 5. https://doi.org/10.5114/cipp.2017.66890
Gross M, Szabo A (1992) Prema hrvatskome građanskom društvu: Društveni razvoj u civilnoj Hrvatskoj i Slavoniji šezdesetih i sedamdesetih godina 19. stoljeća. Globus, Zagreb
Heilman ME, Chen JJ (2003) Entrepreneurship as a solution: the allure of self-employment for women and minorities. Hum Resource Manag Rev 13:347–364
Kedmenec I, Tominc P, Rebernik M (2014) Gender differences in the usage of resources in the entrepreneurial opportunity identification process in Slovenia and Croatia. Econ Res Ekonomska istraživanja 27(1):366–377. https://doi.org/10.1080/1331677X.2014.966973
Keser J (2014) Importance of women and women entrepreneurs education for new technologies: an analysis of policy documents. Available at https://hrcak.srce.hr/file/198630
Leinert-Novosel S (2000) Žena na pragu 21. stoljeća: između majčinstva i profesije. Ženska grupa TOD, Zagreb
Ministry of Entrepreneurship and Crafts (2014) Strategy of development of women entrepreneurship 2014.-2020. Available at http://www.europski-fondovi.eu/sites/default/files/dokumenti/SRP%C5%BD%20%202014%20-%202020.pdf. Accessed 14.12.2019
North DC (1990) Institutions, institutional change and economic performance. Cambridge University Press, Cambridge
Oberman Peterka S, Koprivnjak T, Zvijerac M (2016) Women and entrepreneurship in Croatia—stereotypes, impediments, incentives. In: 5th international scientific symposium economy of Eastern Croatia—vision and growth. Faculty of Economics in Osijek—J. J. Strossmayer University of Osijek, Osijek, pp 276–287

OECD and European Union (2017a) Inclusive entrepreneurship trends and policies in Croatia. In: The missing entrepreneurs 2017: policies for inclusive entrepreneurship. OECD, Paris. https://doi.org/10.1787/9789264283602-17-en
OECD and European Union (2017b) Policy brief on women's entrepreneurship
OECD and European Union (2018) Inclusive entrepreneurship policies: country assessment notes. Croatia
Palalic R, Ramadani V, Dana LP (2017a) Entrepreneurship in Bosnia and Herzegovina: focus on gender. Eur Bus Rev 29(4):476–496
Palalic R, Ramadani V, Dana LP, Ratten V (2017b) Gender entrepreneurial leadership in family business: case study from Bosnia and Herzegovina. In: Ratten V, Dana LP, Ramadani V (eds) Women entrepreneurship in family business. Routledge, Oxfordshire, pp 208–226
Ramadani V, Gërguri S, Dana LP, Tašaminova T (2013) Women entrepreneurs in the Republic of Macedonia: waiting for directions. Int J Entrepren Small Bus 19(1):95–121
Renko S (2000) Malo poduzetništvo: izvor ekonomskog progresa Republike Hrvatske. Ekonomski pregled 51(5–6):495–508. Available at https://hrcak.srce.hr/65484
Scott CE (1986) Why more women are becoming entrepreneurs? J Small Bus Manag 24(4):36–44
Stipetić V (2012) Dva stoljeća razvoja hrvatskoga gospodarstva (1820-2005). HAZU, Zagreb
Sulejmanović L (2008) Female entrepreneurship in Croatia report. World Bank and Harvard Business School. Available at http://siteresources.worldbank.org/EXTECAREGTOPGENDER/Resources/FemaleEntrepreneurshipCroatia.pdf?resourceurlname=FemaleEntrepreneurshipCroatia.pdf. Accessed 10.12.2019
Szabo A (1984) Regionalno porijeklo i socijalna struktura stanovništva grada Zagreba između 1880-1910. godine. Radovi Zavoda za hrvatsku povijest 17(1):101–120
Vuković K (2015) Počeci poduzetništva žena u znanstvenim i književnim djelima hrvatskih autora. Društvena istraživanja 2(1):133–151. https://doi.org/10.5559/di.24.1.07
Vuković K, Šmaguc T (2015) Društveni kontekt izbora zanimanja žena u Hrvatskoj u razdovlju od kraja 19. do početka 21 stoljeća. Ekonomska misao i praksa 1:297–310. Available at hrcak.srce.hr/140304
Vuković K, Kedmenec I, Postolov K, Jovanovski K, Korent D (2017) The role of bonding and bridging cognitive social capital in shaping entrepreneurial intention in transition economies. Management 22(1):1–33. https://doi.org/10.30924/mjcmi/2017.22.1.1
Welter F, Smallbone D (2003) Entrepreneurship and enterprise strategies in transition economies: an institutional perspective. In: Kirby D, Watson A (eds) Small firms and economic development in developed and transition economies: a reader. Ashgate, Aldershot, Hampshire, UK, pp 95–114
Welter F, Smallbone D, Isakova N, Aculai E, Schakirova N (2004) Women entrepreneurs in the Ukraine, Republic of Moldova and Uzbekistan: results of a comparative study. In: UNECE (ed) Access to financing and ICT: women entrepreneurs in the ECE region. United Nations, Geneva, pp 39–52
World Bank Group (2019a) Croatia country gender assessment: investing in opportunities for all. Available at http://pubdocs.worldbank.org/en/695541553252905811/WB-Croatia-gender-equality-22032019.pdf. Accessed 18.12.2019
World Bank Group (2019b) Investing in opportunities for all. Croatia country gender assessment. World Bank Group—Croatia Country Office
World Economic Forum (2018) The global gender gap report 2018. World Economic Forum, Cologny/Geneva

Mihaela Mikic is an Assistant Professor at the Department for Managerial Economics, Faculty of Economics and Business, University of Zagreb, Zagreb, Croatia, where she teaches Entrepreneurship, Business Plan, Fundamentals of Entrepreneurship and Small Business Management. Her research interests include: Entrepreneurship, Social Entrepreneurship, Women Entrepreneurship, Internationalization, Small Business Management, and Small Business Financing. She is an author of several articles published in refereed international journals and two books. Additionally, she is serving a few journals as reviewer/editorial board member.

Maja Has is the Head of Undergraduate Professional Study of Entrepreneurship Economics at the European Business School Zagreb, where she teaches different courses on Entrepreneurship, Family Entrepreneurship, Integral Business Management, and Business Planning. Currently, she is a Ph.D. candidate at the Faculty of Economics and Business, University of Zagreb. She has authored/coauthored several articles published in refereed international and national journals, as well as conference papers. Her research interests include Entrepreneurship, SME Sector Development, New Venture Creation, and Small Business Management.

Women's Entrepreneurship in Kosovo

Nora Sadiku-Dushi, Veland Ramadani, Dianne H. B. Welsh, and Ramo Palalić

Abstract This chapter offers insights into women entrepreneurship in the Republic of Kosovo. The chapter initially provides the historical and demographic overview of Kosovo. The study continues by presenting the current state of women entrepreneurship through the available data. Further government policies for women entrepreneurship promotion followed by the local and international organizations that support women entrepreneurship are discussed. And, in the end, the chapter takes a look at the development of women entrepreneurship in the future.

1 Introduction

After the Yugoslavia breakdown, similar to other ex-Yugoslavian republics also the Republic of Kosovo has broken off from the Federal Republic of Yugoslavia (at that time consisting of the Republics of Serbia and Montenegro) after an armed conflict that lasted from February 1998 until June 11, 1999 (Independent International Commission on Kosovo 2000). On February 17, 2008, Kosovo declared its independence, becoming Europe's newest state (Rohan 2018). Even though Kosovo declared independence there are still countries that do not recognize Kosovo as a

N. Sadiku-Dushi
University for Business and Technology, Prishtina, Kosovo
e-mail: nora.sadiku@ubt-uni.net

V. Ramadani (✉)
South-East European University, Tetovo, North Macedonia
e-mail: v.ramadani@seeu.edu.mk

D. H. B. Welsh
University of North Carolina Greensboro, Greensboro, NC, USA
e-mail: dhwelsh@uncg.edu

R. Palalić
Faculty of Business and Administration, International University of Sarajevo, Ilidža, Bosnia and Herzegovina
e-mail: rpalalic@ius.edu.ba

R. Palalić et al. (eds.), *Women's Entrepreneurship in Former Yugoslavia*, Contributions to Management Science,
https://doi.org/10.1007/978-3-030-45253-7_4

sovereign state. Until now there are 102 out of 193 United Nations (UN) member states, 23 out of 28 European Union (EU) member states, 25 out of 29 NATO member states, and 34 out of 57 Organisation of Islamic Cooperation (OIC) member states that have recognized Kosovo.

Although there are continuous attempts of normalizing the relations between Kosovo and Serbia, Serbia still refuses to recognize Kosovo's independence. But, even despite the fact that still not recognized by all countries, Kosovo is a member of many international organizations such as the World Bank, the International Monetary Fund (IMF), the Council of Europe's Development Bank and Venice Commission, the European Bank for Reconstruction and Development (EBRD), the Permanent Court of Arbitration (PCA), the Apostille Convention, the Egmont Group of Financial Intelligence Units, the World Customs Organization (WCO), the International Olympic Committee, and the International Federation of Association Football (FIFA) (United States Department of State 2019).

Kosovo (Exhibit 1) is a small country with an area of 10,905.25 km^2, located in south-eastern Europe, bordering Albania, Macedonia, Montenegro, and Serbia with a total border length of 743.5 km (Kosovo in Figures 2017).

The approximate population in Kosovo is 1.8 million (Kosovo Agency of Statistics 2017). There are many ethnic groups living in Kosovo, although according to the 2011 census, the majority of the population are Albanians with 92.2% followed by Bosnians 1.6%, Serbs 1.5%, Turks 1.1%, Ashkali 0.9%, Egyptians 0.6%, Gorani 0.6%, Romani 0.5%, and others or unspecified with 0.2% (The World Factbook 2018). However, the European Centre for Minority Issues suggests that these figures may under-represent Serbs and Romani minorities due to the boycott of the census from the Serb majority living in Northern Kosovo and a partial boycott by Serbs and Romani living in other parts of Kosovo (ECMI 2018). Even though data of the 2011 census order the Serbs in the third place, the reality is that Serbs are the largest minority living in Kosovo. As far as religion is concerned, Kosovo Albanians are mainly Muslims and a small percentage Catholic, whereas Kosovo Serbs are Orthodox Christians with very strong ties to the Serbian Orthodox Church (OSCE 2010). Similarly, there are also differences in language used with Albanians speaking Albanian while the other ethnicities speak their respective languages.

In the largest city, the capital of Kosovo, Prishtina, more than 15% of the total population lives. Currently, there are 38 municipalities with 1469 settlements organized under the laws of the country. The Kosovo citizens are poorest in Europe, second only to Moldova. The GDP per capita in 2016 (PPP) was only $9600. The unemployment rate in 2017 was 30.5%, whereas the youth unemployment rate, the average of which is age 26, is estimated at 60%. Such high unemployment rate leads to emigration and informal or unreported economy (The World Factbook 2018). Immediately after the 1999 conflict, economic development practically started from zero. Through various development and assistance programs, there were more than 5 billion Euros invested in Kosovo by the year 2005.

Kosovo is an important location for business development. It offers comparative advantages such as a young and well-qualified population, natural resources, favorable climatic conditions, new infrastructure, a fiscal policy with the lowest taxation

Exhibit 1 United Nations (2019). Map of Kosovo. Source: Kosovo Map, No. 4069 Rev. 6 available on https://www.un.org/Depts/Cartographic/map/profile/kosovo.pdf

in the region, and a geographic position with access to the regional CEFTA market and that of the European Union (Ministry of Integration 2019). SMEs in Kosovo represent 99% of all registered companies. They significantly contribute to both employment and gross domestic product (GDP). Based on the Ministry of the Trade and Industry (2013), SMEs' contribution to total employment is 62.24% (MTI 2013), whereas their contribution to GDP is 43.30% (Government of Republic of Kosovo 2012). However, those numbers are considered much higher since the informal economy is 34.4% of the GDP (Government of Republic of Kosovo 2014).

The total number of active companies in Kosovo is 37,518, from which 3804 (10.1%) are female-owned companies, 31,371 (83.6%) are male-owned companies, 271 (5.8%) are jointly male and female-owned companies, and 171 (0.5%) of companies have unreported owner's gender (Kosovo Agency of Statistics 2017). These figures show that there is a considerable difference in the number of companies owned by males and females, and it is clearer that male-owned companies are dominating the private sector. But, according to Hoxha and Krasniqi (2008), there is a higher rate of business registration in women-owned businesses compared to male-owned businesses. This trend was noticed especially after the war of 1998–1999, when many local and international organizations were found to support women entrepreneurs (Ramadani et al. 2015a).

2 Women Entrepreneurship in Kosovo

Women-owned businesses in Kosovo are considered to be still in their infancy (Hoxha and Krasniqi 2008). The number of female entrepreneurs is continuing to grow. Their importance is especially noticeable in transitional economies where the transition process has resulted in thoughtful and dramatic economic, political, and social changes (Aidis et al. 2007; Ramadani and Dana 2013; Ramadani et al. 2015b; Welsh et al. 2017, 2018).

According to Ramadani et al. (2015b), female-owned businesses are of special importance for a variety of reasons. Primarily because they create jobs for themselves and others and because it allows them to take advantage of their experience, skills, and training, as well as helps them to decrease the effect of discrimination against women in the labor market. Secondly, because the private firms are as an alternative to unemployment that gives women the chance to balance their work and family responsibilities, while at the same time helping them improve family welfare and social cohesion. Thirdly, because owning a small business may help in increasing women's autonomy and provides them the opportunity to have a more active and representative role in the country's economic and political life. Fourthly, female-owned businesses can help in fighting the trafficking of women, which is one of the greatest concerns in many transition countries. Fifthly, because women business owners can serve as role models for the next generation, indicating new opportunities for employment. And, finally, because the development of female entrepreneurship results in a more successful and fast transition process for the improvement of innovative capacities and private sector development.

Despite their importance and role in economy, there is a considerable gap between male- and women-owned enterprises in Kosovo. Based on the statistics presented above, the number of registered women-owned companies is only 10% of the total number of businesses. Even though women entrepreneurs represent important contributors to the economy, because many of them run informal businesses, their true impact remains largely unnoticed. Women-owned businesses in Kosovo usually employ non-formal workers and have outdated equipment (Riinvest Institute 2017).

SHE-ERA as Kosovo's first NGO was among the first to undertake the study on the state of female entrepreneurship in Kosovo (SHE-ERA 2006). The lack of analytical data regarding the ownership of women's business in Kosovo served as a base for initiating their research. The primary aim of the study was to provide information about the type, structure, and size of women-owned companies. Additionally, they aimed to identify the key problems and financial constraints in these businesses as well as to make visible the women entrepreneurs' initiatives and successes.

After surveying 1450 female entrepreneurs who run formal and informal businesses from the Albanian, Serbian, Bosnian, and Turkish communities in Kosovo, they found that most of the female entrepreneurs in Kosovo work in the informal sector of the economy and that their contribution is often not appreciated. The results concluded that women entrepreneurs are mainly concentrated in traditional activities such as tailoring, hairdressing, food preparation, and handicrafts. Thirty-five percent of the surveyed companies resulted as informal businesses, 96% of which indicated that economic legislation was not an obstacle, as their business was not registered.

The majority of women entrepreneurs are engaged in trade (food, textiles, cosmetics, bookstores, and miscellaneous goods) and services (hair salon, beauty salon (Exhibit 2), health services, insurance companies, kindergartens, tourist agencies, Internet cafes, and auto schools). A small number was engaged in production (textile—tailoring, handicrafts, dairy products, bakeries, vegetable processing) as well as agriculture (beekeeping, vegetable planting, etc.) (Exhibit 3). It was also found that 56.3% of women entrepreneurs work alone due to the inability to hire additional employees; only 40.3% have less than 5 employees. The interesting fact is that most of the companies were new and founded after the war as a means of survival. Most of the female owners spend more than 8 hours a day at their business on top of the additional family obligations in their homes. According to the conclusions of the study, women entrepreneurs in Kosovo lack the vocational preparedness and competence to successfully manage a business. This was evidenced by their low level of knowledge regarding the legal economic regulations. They have little to no familiarity with existing laws that can protect their business interests. Women reported that they consult with people who are not professionals to provide the advice they need to manage and develop their business. This is evidenced by the fact that 45% of them consult their husbands. One of the biggest problems identified for starting and developing women-owned businesses are credit terms—20% of women reported having difficulty in securing loans from existing banks in Kosovo due to their high interest rates and the short time to repay the loan. Also, banks do not provide startup loans, but loans only to existing businesses.

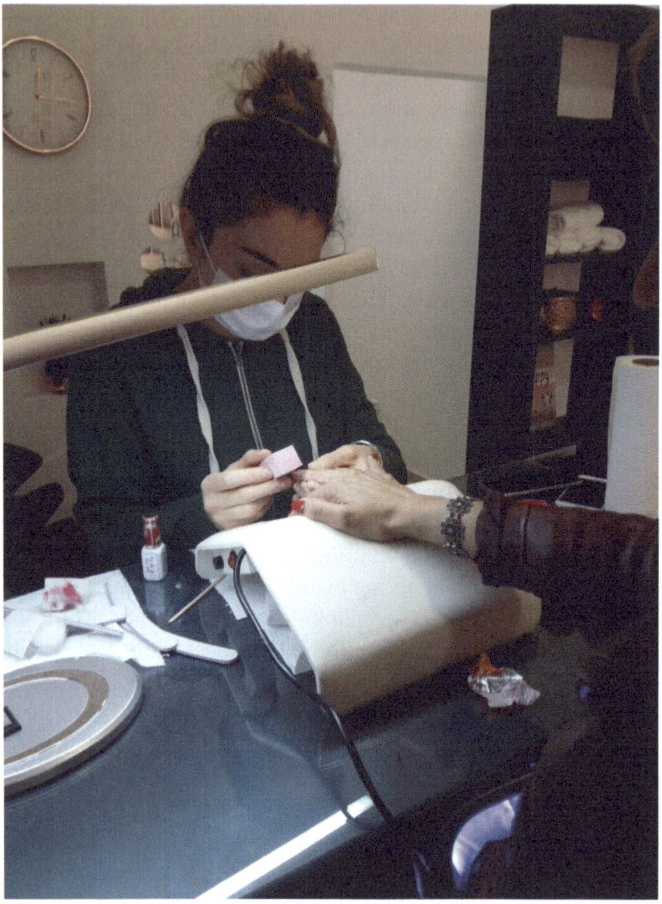

Exhibit 2 Beauty Salon "Italbeauty," Ferizaj Photo © Nora Sadiku-Dushi

Another obstacle in obtaining loans from banks was securing the loan with a mortgage. Most property in Kosovo is registered in the name of a husband, father, or brother, and only in some special cases, women head of households possess real estate. Thirty-two percent of the respondents declared that they have never attended training to improve their managerial capacity, while 68% have participated in different training that was beneficial in running their businesses, whereas 82% admitted that they need professional training to improve their managerial capabilities.

Since the study was conducted, the situation has improved. Interest in Kosovar women's entrepreneurship has started to grow, which has led to more researchers and institutions to study women entrepreneurs in Kosovo. Hoxha and Krasniqi (2008) measured female entrepreneurial activity and female entrepreneurial participation as well as investigating the gender differences of female and male

Exhibit 3 Blerta Haliti's pepper plantation, Krushe e Madhe, Rahovec Photo © Nora Sadiku-Dushi

entrepreneurs across three dimensions: individual, organizational, and environmental. They found that the unfavorable position of women in the Kosovar society that is deeply rooted in traditional norms is also reflected in entrepreneurial developments. They found that female entrepreneurial participation (8.4) and female entrepreneurial activity (3.7) were low, confirming the imbalance between male and female entrepreneurs.

The growing interest in female entrepreneurship in Kosovo was also shown by organization of the First International Conference of Women Entrepreneurs that was held in October 2010 in Kosovo which brought together more than 170 participants from the business community, state agencies, financial institutions, international and national organizations, and prominent businesswomen. Representatives from more than 13 associations of businesswomen from around the world attended. The conference provided a platform for the exchange of experiences and practices for the further advancement of female entrepreneurs' networks in the region. Networks have been found to be integral in women-owned businesses success (Welsh et al. 2019).

Ramadani et al. (2015a, b) focused on conditions and perspectives of female entrepreneurship development and problems that female entrepreneurs in Kosovo are facing. The researchers found that the majority (68%) of surveyed female entrepreneurs in Kosovo run micro-businesses. The major obstacle identified was the balance between family obligations and work commitments. Welsh and Kaciak (2019) confirmed this finding and the role of family interference in women-owned businesses in a recent article. Women cited problems in fulfilling their responsibilities as both wives and mothers. Female entrepreneurs reported not having adequate business experience.

Kosovo SME Promoting Program in their report on SMEs in Kosovo in 2014 (Oberholzner 2014) concluded that women in Kosovo are still hardly active as entrepreneurs—at least in formal terms. According to this report, only 13% of SMEs are owned by women and another 3% are co-owned by women, leaving 84% owned by men. Female entrepreneurship was found to be much higher in personal and business services, where 23% and 35% of enterprises respectively are controlled by women. In the other sectors, the share of women-owned businesses is much lower; in construction, in particular, there are practically no women-owned businesses. Furthermore, businesswomen are mainly active as solo-entrepreneurs. Finally, there are relatively more female entrepreneurs in the Prishtina region (18% women-owned businesses plus 6% co-owned businesses) than in the other regions (10% plus 2% co-ownerships on average). Women-owned companies are on average slightly younger than male-owned businesses, which means that self-employment constitutes a more recent career option for women. Enterprises owned by women usually employ more women than men.

The latest report on women's entrepreneurship issued by Riinvest Institute (2017) provides an in-depth view of women entrepreneurs in Kosovo through the analysis of the data collected from 313 women-owned businesses. The report gives insights on the unique characteristics, current role, and opportunities for the growth of women entrepreneurs in Kosovo. Findings indicate that 94% of the female-owned businesses are micro-businesses, with the majority having less than five employees. The educational background of female entrepreneurs is mostly high school (48%). Women are concentrated more in the service, trade, and production sectors. Most of the services are focused on beauty services, such as hairdressing. About 88% of women founded their business on their own and more than 50% have used their own capital. The main motive to start a business was financial independence, followed by the unwillingness to work for someone else and unemployment. The yearly revenue in female-owned businesses in 70% of the cases is less than 10,000 Euro. Tax rates, small markets, and administrative burdens are ranked as the top three barriers in their business. Regardless of sociocultural issues that women face, the majority claim that they attend business or institutional meetings alone. The majority of women state they have family support for operating their business. Most of the women reported that it is not more difficult for them to close deals, negotiate with institutions, or hire qualified staff comparing to men.

3 Supporting Policies for Women Entrepreneurship Promotion

3.1 *Government Support for Women Entrepreneurs*

Kosovo's government (Exhibit 4) does not seem to be sufficiently engaged in promoting women's entrepreneurship. In the report, "Development Strategy of

Exhibit 4 The Government of Kosovo building, Prishtina. Photo © Nora Sadiku-Dushi

Small and Medium Enterprises in Kosovo 2012–2016," there is a chapter dealing with improving the position of women in business. It states that despite the fact that women constitute more than 50% of the overall population of Kosovo, there is an extremely low participation of women in entrepreneurship which contributes to the unfavorable position of female entrepreneurs. Despite this fact, Kosovo does not still have a long-term vision of sustainable policies that would close the gap between men's and women's participation in entrepreneurial activities (SHE-ERA 2019).

However, there were attempts of the government to increase the involvement of women in entrepreneurship by creating a team which would be responsible to offer a framework for policies with data on female participation in entrepreneurship; training of women for entrepreneurship; improving access to finance for female entrepreneurs; and the creation of business networks and good practices (Ramadani et al. 2015a).

However, these governmental actions are more theoretical than practical. The Government of Kosovo, besides creating "virtual" policies, should focus on improving access to financing as well as preferential interest rates on loans. To this end, it is important to mention that drafting of government policies on this issue requires the implementation of strategies with real action plans, which, up to now, have remained in large part symbolic (Ramadani et al. 2015a).

3.2 *Local Organizations' Support*

While the government is not proactive in this regard, many local organizations have been established to promote and support the women entrepreneurs. Some of these organizations were started with the support of international organizations. As the funding from international organizations has dried up, many of these originations have not continued their support activities. However, there are still a few very active organizations that aim to promote female entrepreneurship in Kosovo, such as SHE-ERA. SHE-ERA was founded in September 1999 as the first local organization that addressed the issue of women's economic empowerment after the war and is still actively involved in female entrepreneurship support. The mission of the organization is to support women's economic empowerment in Kosovo, regardless of age, education, race, ethnicity, and religion, in order to achieve gender balance and all-inclusive economic development and make women an active part of society.

SHE-ERA's main purpose is the economic empowerment of women. Its activities are primarily focused on the following:

- Increasing public access and visibility of the Kosovar budget through transparency
- Increasing participation of women in the labor market
- Developing more partnerships among employers, the state, and NGOs in all cases concerning the economic empowerment of women
- Increasing job opportunities for women with structural transformation of economies particularly waged employment in the services sector, self-employment, and entrepreneurship
- Introducing measures enabling better compatibility of work and family responsibilities
- Delineating the roles and responsibilities of state, trade unions, and employers to work in concerted action to introduce measures for removing obstacles and barriers, such as new codes of conduct, affirmative action, and reevaluation of what is considered "men's and women's" work
- Maximizing opportunities for women to secure and keep jobs

- Developing a set of policies and programs that provide access to training and lifelong learning and are targeted at women according to the different stages of their lives and family situations
- Encouraging self-employment and entrepreneurial skills programs that target women through training, credit schemes, and gender sensitization among bankers and organizations supporting the creation of SMEs
- Ensuring transparency in the appointment process for high-level governmental and other bodies and enlarging the pool of potential women candidates through an active search into existing networks of professional women decision-makers in the relevant areas
- Ensuring the availability and wide dissemination of sex-disaggregated data and gender-related information in order to enable the mobilization and support of all major actors of civil society: NGOs, trade unions, employers, associations, and media in order to gain from their experience and knowledge, as well as to obtain their support, for the promotion of gender equality and benefit from their influence on decision-making bodies
- Ensuring continuity of this involvement through the establishment of frameworks that allow for regular dialogue between governmental and nongovernmental actors, including open and transparent channels of communications.

This organization is also involved in research and analysis, as well as supporting local governmental institutions to gather and apply the political and legal frameworks that promote gender equality and the involvement of Kosovar women in political, social, economic, and cultural areas. The organization has a well-known reputation for its services. Through its services, SHE-ERA offers consulting, business planning, document collection for proposals, marketing strategies and research, and services in human resources and operations management for women-owned businesses in Kosovo. During its existence, SHE-ERA has made numerous partnerships with different organizations dealing with business development in Central, Eastern, and Western Europe, the USA, Canada, and Asia.

Since its founding, SHE-ERA has completed a large number of projects at the local and regional level that have provided training in business, consulting, research, analysis, and mentoring.

> More than 20.000 women and young girls have increased their managerial capacity—through business advisory services at the local/national level. Also 2000 women entrepreneurs in: production, processing, trade, services, handicrafts are active members of SHE-ERA across Kosovo. We have accomplished this through capacity building, collaboration, training and networking with local & international stakeholders. said Mirlinda Kusari, Executive Director of SHE-ERA.

In addition, SHE-ERA has published five analytical reports on women entrepreneurs in Kosovo, the gender budget at the local and central level, woman's position during the privatization process, and a report on the First International Conference on Women Entrepreneurs in Kosovo.

In order to achieve its objectives SHE-ERA has established partnerships with different international and local institutions such as the Agency for Gender Equality,

Exhibit 5 First international conference on women entrepreneurship. Photo © Mirlinda Kusari Purrini (Founder/Executive Director of Women's Business Association SHE-ERA)

Caritas Switzerland, Celim Milano, Center for International Private Enterprise, Swiss Agency for Development and Cooperation, Ministry of Foreign Affairs of Denmark, European Commission, European Training Foundation, the International Alliance for Women, Kosova Women's Network, Embassy of the United States of America in Prishtina, Innovation Center Kosovo, Regional Cooperation Council, Teb Bank, the Ministry of Trade and Industry, Ministry of Agriculture, Forestry and Rural Development, and some of the municipalities.

In 2010, SHE-ERA organized the First International Conference on Women Entrepreneurship. This conference was held in Kosovo and gathered more than 170 participants from the business community, state agencies, financial institutions, international and national organizations, and prominent businesswomen, as well as representatives from 13 national businesswomen associations from around the world (Exhibit 5)

However, SHE-ERA is not the only organization that deals with women in business. Kosova Women for Women-KW4W is also an organization that is established with a mission to support the most marginalized women in Kosovo to earn and save money, improve health and well-being, influence decisions within the family and community, and connect to networks for support. The efforts are focused in five programs:

- Capacity development and professional and personal development of women in Kosovo
- Combating inequalities and raising awareness against discrimination
- Linkages, networking, and advocacy for active women participation
- Employment and Economic Empowerment of women
- Working with men as allies in the process of women's empowerment

Exhibit 6 Practical demonstration of vocational trainings in the field. Photo © Iliriana Gashi

The pillar of employment and economic empowerment of women includes the organization's activities aimed to advance the economic position of women in Kosovo. These activities are implemented through grants, technical and entrepreneurship training, networking, and job mediation, as well as support for branding and marketing of products/services of women entrepreneurs.

Iliriana Gashi, Executive Director of KW4W, named some of the concrete activities that they implemented so far:

- Vocational training in different fields depending on the best opportunities for women to be employed or self-employed, including the service industry (childcare, elder care, maintenance, and retail), handcrafts and sewing, horticulture, bee-keeping, and livestock and poultry.
- Vocational training sessions are always accompanied with experiences (e.g., practical part of the training in the field (Exhibit 6)).
- Combination of vocational trainings with financial incentives such as seed money, inputs based on women's activity, and grants to women individually or to groups Facilitation of link/cooperation between women producers with the potential buyers that can be companies or individuals. Organizing fairs is part of the attempt to create this connection (Exhibit 7).

Exhibit 7 Organization of hand-work fairs before end-year holidays for interested parties and provide space for women's handwork exhibition. Photo © Iliriana Gashi

- Facilitate employment through the Job Placement Office (JPO) for women who are facing difficulties in finding jobs in the areas of the vocational trainings offered by K-W4W.
- Capacity building for businesses owned or co-owned by women through training, technical assistance, professional advice/mentorship, and financial assistance (grants and support to license the products). A dedicated business incubator to house these services will be opened in 2019.

Over the years, Kosova Women 4 Women (KW4W) has created various partnerships with local nongovernmental organizations and relevant stakeholders. Partners include the following: USA Civil Military Support Element (CMSE), Kosovo Job Portal, International Organization for Migration (IOM), and NGO Diakonie. Moreover, KW4W is a member of the CiviKos Platform, Gender Coordination Groups for USAID Programs for Economic Empowerment (EMPOWER), and Property Rights (PRP), as well as a member of the network IRIS established by Center for Legal Aid and Regional Development (CLARD). KW4W is also a member of the Economic Forum of Women organized by the Riinvest Institute.

Another important organization that supports women entrepreneurship is the Kosovo Women's Chamber of Commerce-G7. Lendita Kastrati, Executive Director of G7, explained that the Kosovo Women's Chamber of Commerce-G7 is the outcome of the successful International Women's Summit. The summit featured the former Secretary of State Madeline Albright, Kosovo President Atifete Jahjaga, the Deputy Prime Minister for Economy, as well as the Minister of Industry and Trade. Mimoza Kusari-Lila organized the gathering in September of 2012 in Pristina. The President of Kosovo together with the Minister of Trade and Industry

Exhibit 8 The Kosovo Women's Chamber of Commerce—G7: Photo © Kosovo Women's Chamber of Commerce-G7

appointed seven women to establish an organization that will maximize the participation of women in the economy, serve as a voice for women to be active at all levels in commercial activity, and promote entrepreneurship among women, in general, and young women, in particular (Exhibit 8). This organization was formally registered in June 2013 as nonprofit organization with the statute of public benefit.

The G7's vision is to see women as a major driving force in the economy of Kosovo. It promotes women's participation in all decision- and policymaking from the local to the national level, to include the economy, politics, and all other areas of local development. Whereas their mission is in line with international standards and best practices, G7 works to facilitate, promote, and lobby for the representation of women in Kosovo's economy, politics, and decision-making processes.

Lendita stated that they believe in equal opportunity and economic equity for all women. She said that chamber members maintain the highest level of ethical business practices, commonly and freely sharing knowledge and information through a transparent, democratic process, and not based on the opinion of any one individual or group; provide resources to advance the business, careers, and professional lives of women entrepreneurs and members in Kosovo; and make significant contributions to enhance the lives of women in Kosovo through community support.

MEMBERS—VIBRANT, DIVERSE, UNIQUE (Lendita Kastrati)

She also explained that the organization strives to build a network of interesting and diverse members in the communities in which they live. "*We seek women that own companies or work in industries ranging from accounting to technology, as well as education, government, the arts, nonprofit groups, associations, and other business groups. We will support our members in growing their companies or careers in a vibrant supportive atmosphere and be part of a spirited community of business and professional women unique to G7.*" (Lendita Kastrati)

The Kosovo Women's Chamber of Commerce-G7 is active in the following areas:

- Empowering women entrepreneurs economically and financially
- Supporting the improvement of the business environment for women
- Advocating for the interest of women entrepreneurs by ensuring a fair and equal business environment through an equitable and supportive legal framework and public policies
- Raising awareness, networking, and representing women entrepreneurs and women's businesses
- Promoting women's businesses and improving their growth capacities

G7 cooperates with its partner organizations which include local and international public, not-for-profit, and private organizations. These include the Ministry of Trade and Industry of Government of Kosovo, the Ministry of Innovation and Entrepreneurship, the Ministry of Agriculture, Forestry and Rural Development, the Ministry of Finance, the Ministry of Economic Development, the Parliamentarian Group of Women Caucasus, the Agency for Gender Equality, the Office of the Prime Minister, the United States Agency for International Development, the Kosovo Chamber of Commerce, the American Chamber of Commerce, the South East European Center for Entrepreneurial Learning, and the Business Professional Women Network.

Lendita pointed out that the main areas of intervention are advocacy and lobbying for improving business environment and business for entrepreneurship women, capacity building for women entrepreneurs, networking, promotion, and information.

The main activities of the Kosovo Women's Economic Chamber-G7 are focused on the successful attainment of the first objective, namely advocacy and lobbying for the development of a more favorable environment for doing business with greater participation of women. This works hand in hand with the second and third objective concerning capacity building of women entrepreneurs as well as in improving networking and promotional activities within and outside the country. The importance of promoting the success of women in the economy as well as in every other area of development of society changes perceptions and raises awareness about women's economic and political engagement as an equal part in society.

> To promote and support the women entrepreneurship G7 in cooperation with RTV 21 have started with the joint START UP show dedicated exclusively to women entrepreneurship. From 2015 until now 149 shows have been broadcasted through by addressing various topics related to women entrepreneurship—added Lendita.

On March 10, 2018, through their partnership with Vital Voices, Melita & Partners, and the Business Consultants Council (BCC), with support from the USAID EMPOWER Private Sector and in partnership with SIDA—Styrelsen för

Exhibit 9 Global mentoring walk in Prishtina 2018. Photo © The Global Mentoring Walk Kosova

Internationellt Utvecklingssamarbete, Promoting Private Sector Employment, and Banka Ekonomike, G7 has organized the first Global Mentoring Walk in Prishtina (Exhibit 9) in celebration of International Women's Day. The event is held annually on the same day in over 60 countries throughout the world so that established businesswomen and leaders can mentor and support women aspiring to their roles.

The purpose of this mentoring platform is to strengthen the women entrepreneurship community, to create networking, as well as to create opportunities for sharing experiences, challenges, and successes in the field of entrepreneurship among leading women in business and new entrepreneurs. Fifty women mentors walked with 50 women mentees on Mother Theresas Boulevard in Prishtina, while sharing experiences on professional challenges and opportunities. The theme of the event was Empowering Entrepreneurial Women. The Former Kosovo President Atifete Jahjaga led the walk and spoke during the ceremony at its conclusion. She noted the numerous legal, structural, and cultural barriers that Kosovo women face. The global mentoring walk will be organized every year.

Lately, various organizations have provided support for women's entrepreneurship. FINCA Kosovo (microfinance institution) has launched a training program called "FINCA FemEdu" in March 2019 (Exhibit 10). The training sessions are dedicated exclusively to women entrepreneurs and are held in cooperation with the Women's Economic Chamber of Kosovo-G7. The main goals of these training programs are to empower women in business, decision-making, and society.

Exhibit 10 Training program for empowering women entrepreneurship organized by Finca Kosovo, June 2019. Photo © Arnisa Xharra - FINCA

3.3 International Organization Support

International support was more visible immediately after the war 20 years ago. Now, financial support is considerably lower. However, there are still some organizations which support women entrepreneurs in different ways. One of the biggest supporters is through the United States Agency for International Development (USAID) by focusing on improving access to finance for women-owned companies. The European Bank for Reconstruction and Development has also launched a Women in Business program in Kosovo with a 3 million € loan extended to TEB Bank ("Kosovo Women in Business" 2019). The program combines financing, technical assistance, risk mitigation in the form of the first-loss coverage for local financial institutions, and business advisory services to support women-led SMEs. Technical assistance and advisory services are jointly funded by the EBRD and the governments of Luxembourg and Sweden. The Organization for Security and Cooperation in Europe (OSCE) is also involved in empowering Kosovo's women entrepreneurs. The OSCE Mission in Kosovo organized a series of six training sessions in June of 2017 on project cycle management, marketing and branding, and drafting business plans to help women entrepreneurs improve their management skills and grow their businesses. The mission also organized several trade fairs for women ("Empowering Kosovo's women entrepreneurs | OSCE" 2019). Financial support for female entrepreneurs' projects came from the European Commission through supporting and financing ideas for enterprise development, especially those that are women-owned.

This is done through establishing a "Regional Development Agency" in five major regions of Kosovo. These agencies help by training women entrepreneurs in the preparation of business plans to improve access to the funds offered by these agencies.

4 Toward the Future

Kosovo as a new country still faces different political, social, and economic problems. In the last 20 years, evolutionary progress has been recorded, but there is still much to be done. Data from different studies show that gender inequality exists in Kosovo in all areas of life. This inequality is most notable in business, where the number of women entrepreneurs comprises only about 10% of the total number of entrepreneurs. The low numbers of registered women business owners make the position of women in business difficult as they continue to face unique challenges, especially concerning access to finance and business experience. Given the importance of women's entrepreneurship, the government has taken some small steps to empower women's entrepreneurship, but these efforts have remained largely theoretical rather than practical. Despite some initiatives, women's entrepreneurship in Kosovo has not been one of the main priorities of the government. Greater support for women entrepreneurs has been provided by local and international organizations that, by offering respectable training, grants, and expertise, have consistently improved the state of women in business over the past few years.

Taking into consideration that women play a crucial role in all the segments of life, the government should make more effort to support and empower women entrepreneurship. Assisting and supporting women in business would also produce positive effects in achieving gender equality and the independence of women. This can be achieved if the government would focus on well-defined actions, as well as the implementation of special programs. Overall, the economic impact of successful women in business would lift the country of Kosovo to the next level.

The future steps in advancing and supporting women in business should be focused, but not limited to, the following directions:

- Since there are no accurate data on the number of businesses in Kosovo, and especially there are no data on the number of registered businesses on a gender basis, it is necessary to create a unique database where interested parties can get information on the exact number of businesses run by women.
- In the absence of adequate education and business expertise, it would be valuable to create a unique online platform where women in business can be informed about the business legislation, funding opportunities, offered trainings, access to grants, and other relevant information.
- Since most financial institutions do not offer loans to startups, or even if they do these loans are with high interest rates, an opportunity should be created to support or subsidize women-owned businesses or even to create a guarantee

fund system to enable access to finance for a larger number of women entrepreneurs.

- Based on the fact that the majority of women entrepreneurs are not formally educated in the business field, it is necessary to provide training for all women entrepreneurs in general business training, entrepreneurship training, and specialized fields relevant to their business, so they can be better prepared to compete in the market locally, nationally, and globally.

References

Aidis R, Welter F, Smallbone D, Isakova N (2007) Female entrepreneurship in transition economies: the case of Lithuania and Ukraine. Fem Econ 13(2):157–183

ECMI—European Centre for Minority Issues (2018) Home Ecmi.de. Available at http://www.ecmi.de. Accessed 20 May 2018

FINCA FemEdu (2019) FemEdu. Available at https://www.fincakosovo.org/finca-femedu/. Accessed 20 May 2018

Government of Republic of Kosovo (2012) Strategjia e Zhvillimit të NVM-ve në Kosovë 2012-2016. Republic of Kosovo, Prishtina

Government of Republic of Kosovo (2014) Strategjia Kombëtare e Republikës së Kosovës për Parandalimin dhe Luftimin e Ekonomisë Joformale, Pastrimin e Parave, Financimin e Terrorizmit dhe Krimeve Financiare 2014-2018. Republic of Kosovo, Prishtina

Hoxha D, Krasniqi B (2008) Female entrepreneurship in Kosova: does gender difference hypothesis hold? Int J Bus Manag Sci 1(1):49–61

Independent International Commission on Kosovo (2000) The Kosovo report. Oxford University Press, Oxford

Kosovo Agency of Statistics (2017) Kosovo. Available at http://ask.rksgov.net/. Accessed 28 May 2019

Kosovo in Figures (2017) Kosovo. Accessed http://ask.rks-gov.net/en/kosovo-agency-of-statistics/general-statistics/kosovo-in-figures. Accessed 28 May 2019

Kosovo Women in Business (2019) Retrieved from. https://www.ebrd.com/news/2015/ebrd-supports-women-entrepreneurs-in-kosovo.html

Ministry of Integration (2019) Kosovo's economy. Available at http://www.mei-ks.net/en/kosovo/kosovo146s-economy#sthash.4cqstWlk.dpuf. Accessed 14 May 2019

Ministry of the Trade and Industry (2013) Private sector development strategy 2013–2017. Available at http://www.kryeministri-ks.net/repository/docs/private_sector_development_strategy_2013-2017.pdf. Accessed 23 July 2019

Oberholzner T (2014) Report on SME's in Kosovo. Institute for SME Research in Kosovo. Prishtina: Kosovo

OSCE (2010) Kosovo communities profiles. Available at https://www.osce.org/kosovo/. Accessed 14 May 2019

OSCE (2019) Empowering Kosovo's women entrepreneurs. Available at https://www.osce.org/stories/empowering-kosovo-women-entrepreneurs. Accessed 23 July 2019

Ramadani V, Dana L-P (2013) The state of entrepreneurship in the Balkans: evidence from selected countries. In: Ramadani V, Schneider CR (eds) Entrepreneurship in the Balkans: diversity, support and prospects. Springer, Heidelberg, pp 217–250

Ramadani V, Hisrich RD, Gërguri-Rashiti S (2015a) Female entrepreneurs in transition economies: insights from Albania, Macedonia and Kosovo. World Rev Entrepren Manag Sustain Dev 11 (4):391–413

Ramadani V, Rexhepi G, Abazi-Alili H, Beqiri B, Thaçi A (2015b) A look at female entrepreneurship in Kosovo: an exploratory study. J Enterprising Communities People Places Global Econ 9 (3):277–294

Riinvest Institute (2017) Women's entrepreneurship an analysis on doing business in Kosovo. Riinvest, Prishtine

Rohan A (2018) Kosovo's path to independence. Available at https://www.ecfr.eu/. Accessed 3 July 2019

SHE-ERA (2006) Women entrepreneurs in Kosovo. Prishtine. Available at http://she-era.org/wp-content/uploads/2014/05/grateafariste.pdf. Accessed 3 July 2019

SHE-ERA (2019) National platform for women entrepreneurs in the Republic of Kosovo. Available at http://she-era.org/eng/wp-content/uploads/2013/08/national-platform-for-we-in-rks.pdf. Accessed 23 July 2019

The World Factbook (2018) Kosovo. Available at https://www.cia.gov/library/publications/the-world-factbook/geos/kv.html. Accessed 3 June 2019

United Nations (2019) Kosovo Map, No. 4069 Rev. 6. Retrieved from https://www.un.org/Depts/Cartographic/map/profile/kosovo.pdf. Accessed 28 June 2019

United States Department of State (2019) U.S. Relations with Kosovo. Available at https://www.state.gov/u-s-relations-with-kosovo/. Accessed 3 July 2019

Welsh DHB, Kaciak E (2019) Family enrichment and women entrepreneurial success: the mediating effect of family interference. Int Entrepren Manag J. https://doi.org/10.1007/s11365-019-00587-4

Welsh DHB, Kaciak E, Trimi S, Mainardes EW (2017) Women entrepreneurs and family firm heterogeneity: evidence from an emerging economy. Group Decis Negot 27(3):445–465

Welsh DHB, Kaciak E, Shamah R (2018) Determinants of women entrepreneurs' firm performance in a hostile environment. J Bus Res 88(7):481–491

Welsh DHB, Kaciak E, Koladkiewicz I, Memili E, Iyer L, Ramadani V (2019) The impact of networks on value co-creation for women-owned businesses. Eur J Int Manag. https://doi.org/10.1504/EJIM.2020.10017390

Nora Sadiku-Dushi teaches at Management, Business and Economics Department at the University for Business and Technology in Prishtina, Kosovo, where she teaches statistics and entrepreneurship and innovation courses. She holds a Ph.D. in Business Administration from South East European University, the Republic of North Macedonia. Her research interests include marketing, entrepreneurial marketing, entrepreneurship, small business management, family businesses management, management information systems, etc. She has authored and coauthored research articles in journals such as *Journal of Business Research* (JBR), *Journal of Enterprising Culture* (JEC), *European Journal of Management and Marketing Studies*, *Studia Universitatis Babes-Bolyai*, and *Oeconomica*, as well as has attended several conferences. She acted as a committee member at USAID-Young Entrepreneurs Program/YEP and as a mentor in Global Mentoring Walk Kosova, had lectured marketing in two private universities in Kosovo, and acts as a senior market intelligence analyst at a SIGMA BMC consulting company.

Veland Ramadani is Professor at South East European University, the Republic of North Macedonia, where he teaches both undergraduate and postgraduate courses in entrepreneurship and small business management. His research interests include entrepreneurship, small business management, and family businesses. He authored or coauthored around 120 research articles, 11 textbooks, and 14 edited books. Dr. Ramadani is the Chief Editor of *Journal of Enterprising Communities: People and Places in the Global Economy* (JEC). In 2017, he was appointed as a member of the Supervisory Board of Development Bank of North Macedonia, where for 10 months served as an acting Chief Operating Officer (COO). Dr. Ramadani received the Award for Excellence 2016—Outstanding Paper by Emerald Group Publishing. His last book is *Organizational Mindset of Entrepreneurship*, published by Springer.

Dianne H.B. Welsh is the Hayes Distinguished Professor of Entrepreneurship and Founding Director of the Entrepreneurship Programs at the University of North Carolina Greensboro. She has previously founded two entrepreneurship programs/centers and has held three endowed professorships. In 2015, Dianne was the Fulbright-Hall Distinguished Chair in Entrepreneurship for Central Europe. Dianne is a recognized scholar in family business, international entrepreneurship, women-owned businesses, and franchising and has authored seven books and over 150 publications. Her books include *Creative Cross-Disciplinary Entrepreneurship*, *Global Entrepreneurship*, and *Case Studies in Global Entrepreneurship*. She served as Chair for the Technology and Innovation Management Division of the Academy of Management. Dianne is a Fellow in the Family Firm Institute, U.S. Association for Small Business & Entrepreneurship, Small Business Institute, and the Pan-Pacific Business Association. She was a Presidential Appointee to the USAF Academy. In 2019, she won the North Carolina Board of Governors Teaching Award and the Family Firm Institute's Hollander Award for lifetime achievements.

Ramo Palalić is the Coordinator of Leadership and Entrepreneurship Centre at the IUS. Dr. Palalić's research interests are entrepreneurship, leadership, marketing, and small and family business management. As an Assistant Professor, Dr. Palalić teaches at all three study cycles in the above areas. Apart from this, he is actively involved in business projects in the areas of entrepreneurial leadership and marketing management, in private and public organizations. He has authored and coauthored many articles in reputable international journals, several books, and many book chapters. Additionally, he is serving a few journals as reviewer/editorial board member.

Women's Entrepreneurship in Montenegro

Boban Melovic and Vladimir Djurisic

Abstract This chapter gives an overview of women entrepreneurship in Montenegro. The chapter starts with offering a historical summary of a woman's role in Montenegro, which serves as the basis for further analysis of the development of women entrepreneurship. It further analyzes demographic indicators, as well asobstacles and challenges which are relevant for the development of women entrepreneurship. The analysis shows that women entrepreneurship is a concept that is more used in Montenegrin economic theory, but it is hardly present in everyday life. Besides, there are no precise details on participation of women entrepreneurship in economy. A significant segment of the chapter is analysis of business environment and institutional support in the function of development of women entrepreneurship, with a special overview of the role of the strategy of the development of women entrepreneurship. Entrepreneurial activity brings employment, economic growth, and wealth and represents an essential component of the advanced economy. On the other hand, it is a fact that the participation of women in creating politics in Montenegro is insufficient, i.e., a relatively small number of women are present in the leading positions and positions for decision-making. The chapter finishes with offering recommendations and guidelines for future development of women entrepreneurship in Montenegro. In that sense, a key element for increasing women entrepreneurial activity is multiple support to greater number of women to get involved in the business. Women entrepreneurship in economically less developed countries helps women to avoid the trap of poverty. Additionally, women entrepreneurship breaks entrepreneurial stereotypes which are rooted in society for a long time.

B. Melovic (✉) · V. Djurisic
Faculty of Economics, University of Montenegro, Podgorica, Montenegro
e-mail: bobanm@ucg.ac.me; vladimirdj@ucg.ac.me

R. Palalić et al. (eds.), *Women's Entrepreneurship in Former Yugoslavia*,
Contributions to Management Science,
https://doi.org/10.1007/978-3-030-45253-7_5

1 Introduction

The position of women in the society, business, and politics has been changing rapidly in Montenegro in recent years. Women become more active participants in almost all spheres of activities; however, Montenegro is pretty far away from full equality between men and women, which is the aim they are striving for. New, big challenges on that way are still pending, if we take into account the commitment for integration processes and requests they bring. By reviewing activities that are being realized in Montenegro in the domain of achieving gender equality and economic strengthening of women, we can notice the following (Bojanović 2013): strategic documents are being brought and they treat the issue of women entrepreneurship, organize various seminars, training, and round table, establish organizations which bring business women together, carry out a range of researches in order to determine the current situation of women in business, etc. We can conclude that there are a big number of activities which are being realized in Montenegro for the last few years, but there are more of those that are pending, starting from adjusting the national legislation with the EU heritage, for Chap. 19—*Social policy and employment, activities on eliminating discrimination against women at the labor market*, through the measures for encouraging self-employment, up to decreasing the gap in earnings between men and women. Much of the collaborations in the women entrepreneurship area are still restricted within national boundaries, and there is a need to build research as well as practice networks across transnational borders (Yadav and Unni 2016).

Furthermore, following the restoration of independence and economic reforms implemented in Montenegro, the legal and institutional framework was put in place, and it supports gender equality, development of women's rights, and economic empowerment of women (Despotović et al. 2018). However, up to now, national statistics on women entrepreneurship or entrepreneurial activity of women in Montenegro are not developed at the appropriate level. We can surely highlight the research of the European Commission "*Statistical Data on Women Entrepreneurs in Europe*" published in 2014, which comprised 37 EU countries, including Montenegro (Ministry of Economy and Directorate for Development of Small and Medium Enterprises 2015). It is based on the data concerning the period ending in 2012. However, due to the lack of appropriate data, this research does not offer possibility to deduct necessary comparisons and conclusions related to the development of women entrepreneurship in Montenegro. Furthermore, the research, which also related to women, was carried out during 2012 for the needs of the office of the United Nations Development Programme (UNDP) in Montenegro. It was a research on women in politics, whose results show that Montenegrin society forms deep patriarchal norms. Namely, a great number of people agree with the statements which explicitly express opinions in which women's place is at home, and not in the public and political life (Ipsos Strategic Marketing 2012). It is a very interesting fact that women frequently agree with these opinions, but much more rarely than men. So we can say that both private and public patriarchate, as a combination of attitudes on gender roles and place of men and women in public and private life, are very much expressed and that the generators of such conditions are primarily men, but the women as well (Ministry of Economy and Directorate for Development of Small and Medium Enterprises 2015). In other words, there are numerous peculiarities and limitations of the development of women entrepreneurship in Montenegro, and this chapter discusses about it. On the other hand, the development of women entrepreneurship undoubtedly represents a big chance for development of Montenegrin economy generally and it is certainly an area which should be approached in a strategic way.

2 Historical Framework: Position of Women and Development of Women Entrepreneurship in Montenegro

Montenegrin economy is an economy with a relatively short history of entrepreneurial principle implementation (Despotović et al. 2018), which applies for women entrepreneurship as well. Namely, up to the nineteenth century, women in Montenegro–were mainly in an unprivileged position. We can say that obedience was their main characteristics. That mainly concerned the choice of the spouse who was imposed to them at that time, without respecting their will, and up to the scope of rights and obligations which were predefined. It meant that the Montenegrin girl got married in her early youth, usually between the age of 17 and 20, and her activity was limited to the care of family and household (Bojanović 2013). Most of the responsibility for taking care of the family and household was laid on women (Milić 1994; Blagojević 2002). Furthermore, education was a privilege, so we are talking about a very small number of "privileged" women. When it is about employment, it was definitely reserved only for men. There is an encouraging fact that the period of industrialization offered women from this region a possibility for employment and especially "leaving the house." However, even after the period of social and economic transformation, there is still a traditional understanding of the woman's role in Montenegro and it is connected with the house, i.e., a woman is primarily regarded as a devoted wife, caring mother, and good housewife (Bojanović 2013). Her ambitions and career were often neglected. We can conclude from the abovementioned facts that the traits related to a typical Montenegrin woman are (Vujačić 1980): obedience, loyalty, diligence, altruism, passivity, and patience.

Since forming the former SFRY, equality was a dominant ideology which was promoted until the nineties of the previous century in the area of the whole SFRY, which means in Montenegro as well, and apart from other forms, it included gender equality (Montenegrin Employers Federation and IPSOS Strategic Marketing 2013). Apart from that, patriarchal patterns of relationship are expressed in that period as well. However, although the period of socialism gave a significant step forward to women in emancipation, primarily in the sphere of education and further for winning positions at the labor market, that period meant discontinuity with regard to the development of entrepreneurship. Namely, emerging of socialism stopped the beginning phases of the process of the development of entrepreneurship during the short period of capitalistic industrialization in pre-war Yugoslavia, in the first half of the twentieth century. Socialism model in Montenegro was the model of "a political society." The main socialism trait is strong dominance of ideology in all social spheres (Despotović et al. 2018). After the period of the nineties of the twentieth century, there is finally a phase of restructuring the economy and economic reforms which bring significant development of entrepreneurship, which is still followed by a great number of difficulties and weaknesses.

Further, in the last 20 years, appearance and development of women entrepreneurship are tightly related to the process of gender equality of men's and women's rights, as well as democratization in the whole society. However, even with comprehensive democratization of society, Montenegro is characterized with transitional period in the last 20 years, and it is followed by minor volume of production, accelerated privatization, and transformation of economic organizations (Montenegrin Employers Federation and IPSOS Strategic Marketing 2013). All of the mentioned above are characterized by the growth of unemployment, sudden poverty of certain social layers, and expressed changes of the way of life of women and men. Regardless of the fact that those years of economic stagnation affected both women and men, statistics show that mainly women are more endangered than men, firstly with regard to unemployment, but also in the domain of poverty, especially when we talk about single mothers. Such economic circumstances, unfavorable for women, bring to the understanding of entrepreneurship as an important way for providing earnings by means of self-employment (Wong 1986).

We are witnesses that nowadays a bigger percentage of women acquire higher education. But, despite that fact, the position of women in the labor market is worse compared to male population, which is reflected with managerial positions, especially in the area of self-employment and politics. Still, legislative and strategic documents which Montenegro brought represent a good basis for solving these issues (Ipsos Strategic Marketing 2011). Apart from that, conditions for developing entrepreneurship are less favorable for women than for men, which are the consequence of patriarchal attitude of men, but also women, and they are deeply rooted in the society. Gender inequality is expressed through insufficient political participation of women, economic inequality, inequitable share of family chores, and difference in ownership over the assets which bring women into a very difficult position to start their own business (Protector of Human Rights and Freedom 2017). Hence, women entrepreneurship in Montenegro is now in the early stages and it can be called "entrepreneurship out of necessity" which is characterized by the need to find alternative employment (EESE business).[1]

Although they comprise the majority of the total population, women represent the minority from the aspect of participation in economic and political life. They are significantly less represented in the entrepreneurship compared with men, which is confirmed by data of only 9.6% of women who owned business up to 2017, in which Montenegro lags behind EU countries, but also the countries in the region (Montenegrin Employers Federation and IPSOS Strategic Marketing 2013). This derives from the fact that a large number of women do not experience entrepreneurship as a primary life goal or business objective, but they start the business mainly as necessity, recognizing entrepreneurship as a way to provide existence to their family. In addition, estimates of certain representatives of the private sector show that the abovementioned index of women's business in Montenegro is not a reflection of real situation, but it also contains details of women who are just formally business owners, while the managerial and entrepreneurial activities are being carried out by their male relatives (husband, brother, son) (Montenegrin Employers Federation and IPSOS Strategic Marketing 2013). A higher proportion of women become entrepreneurs in order to balance work and family, while a higher proportion of men seek wealth creation and/or economic advancement (DeMartino and Barbato 2003). When it is about assets, women are owners of only 4% of houses, 8% of land, and 14% of summer houses in Montenegro (Ministry of Human and Minority Rights 2017). Inequality is expressed through insufficient political participation of women, existence of so-called glass ceiling and low level of representation of women in leading and managerial positions, economic inequality, feminization of certain professions, salary differences (for jobs with the same value) and ownership over the assets, and unequal share of family chores (Ministry of Economy and Directorate for Development of Small and Medium Enterprises 2015). For the jobs of the same value, women's incomes make 86% of men's incomes (Montenegrin Employers Federation and IPSOS Strategic Marketing 2013). With regard to the field of education, we can notice that women are often being educated for so-called female professions, and it leads to the existence of gender segregation of professional profiles, although there are positive steps, especially at the tertiary education level. In the part of informal education, there are a significant number of programs of entrepreneurial education for startup and existing business, both of which are especially created for women as a target group, and it is a big step forward compared to the previous period. Support to the entrepreneurship can be realized through both financial and non-financial types of support. However, the Montenegrin banking sector is obviously sustained and inactive when it is about the needs of women entrepreneurs. There is a big problem with women without ownership over the assets, whose chances for self-employment and economic strengthening are limited

[1]EESE business, Women entrepreneurs need further support in Montenegro, available at: http://eese-toolkit.itcilo.org/index.php/en/news/latest-news/236-women-entrepreneurs-need-further-support-in-montenegro.html

to the minimum due to inability to provide guarantee for repaying the credit by means of mortgage. Apart from the abovementioned issues, there is another problem which women face with and it represents adjusting the business and family life, lack of family support, and proactive reaction of the state by means of encouraging them to enter the entrepreneurship business, and it is specially reflected at the local level. Additionally, we should mention the limitations which are reflected in insufficient networking, difficulties in accessing information, business premises, as well as business opportunities.

Apart from all limitations and barriers, the number of women entrepreneurs in Montenegro keeps growing. Until 2017, women were owners of only 6.9% of companies, while today their participation is 24%.[2] This percentage of women entrepreneurs and owners of micro and small and medium enterprises is certainly an index which tells us that economic strengthening of women from the aspect of development of women entrepreneurship is receiving a new trigger and that the new climate is being created.[3] Although in almost all countries the participation of women in entrepreneurial activities is less than that of men, Montenegro belongs to the group of countries where women have less participation than average. On the other hand, according to the data from the *Report of the Global Gender Gap of the World Economic Forum* (2018), Montenegro is at number 69 on the list of 149 countries.[4] Based on this report, Picture 1 shows relative differences between men and women in the field of health, education, economy and politics.

In traditional economies such as Montenegro, challenges of the development of women entrepreneurship are possible to regard from two sides (Montenegrin Employers Federation and IPSOS Strategic Marketing 2013). Above all, it is necessary to legally define and strengthen the basis for economic activities for companies owned by women within the formal economy, so that they can strengthen and widen their business. Then, it is necessary that educated and qualified women get familiar with entrepreneurship and business opportunities which are characterized with the high growth potential, so that their companies can be strong immediately after they are established and have the potential for growth and opening new workplaces. Namely, women should be provided with access to a range of key financial and non-financial resources, both for doing business which excludes gender-based institutional, cultural, regulatory, and legal barriers which limit potential and total level of their business activities. Current data for Montenegro are not quite encouraging.

[2]The number of women entrepreneurs in Montenegro is almost tripled (2018), available at: https://www.bankar.me/2018/10/15/broj-preduzetnica-u-crnoj-gori-skoro-utrostrucen/

[3]Ibid.

[4]Global Gender Gap Index measures one important aspect of gender equality—relative difference between men and women within four key areas: health, education, economy, and politics. Report of the Global Gender Gap 2018 for Montenegro is available at: http://www3.weforum.org/docs/WEF_GGGR_2018.pdf

COUNTRY SCORE CARD

	rank	score	avg	female	male	f/m
Economic participation and opportunity	**57**	**0.696**	**0.586**			
Labour force participation	74	0.812	0.669	52.3	64.4	0.81
Wage equality for similar work (survey)	41	0.702	0.645			0.70
Estimated earned income (PPP, US$)	36	0.692	0.510	15,386	22,236	0.69
Legislators, senior officials and managers	106	0.284	0.329	22.1	77.9	0.28
Professional and technical workers	1	1.000	0.753	58.3	41.7	1.40
Educational attainment	**71**	**0.992**	**0.949**			
Literacy rate	76	0.981	0.882	97.5	99.4	0.98
Enrolment in primary education	94	0.992	0.978	95.5	96.2	0.99
Enrolment in secondary education	107	0.997	0.967	89.2	89.5	1.00
Enrolment in tertiary education	1	1.000	0.939	65.6	51.4	1.28
Health and survival	**42**	**0.979**	**0.955**			
Sex ratio at birth	114	0.943	0.921			0.94
Healthy life expectancy	1	1.060	1.034	70.1	66.1	1.06
Political empowerment	**83**	**0.157**	**0.223**			
Women in parliament	63	0.306	0.284	23.5	76.5	0.31
Women in ministerial positions	68	0.250	0.208	20.0	80.0	0.25
Years with female head of state (last 50)	71	0.000	0.189	0.0	50.0	0.00

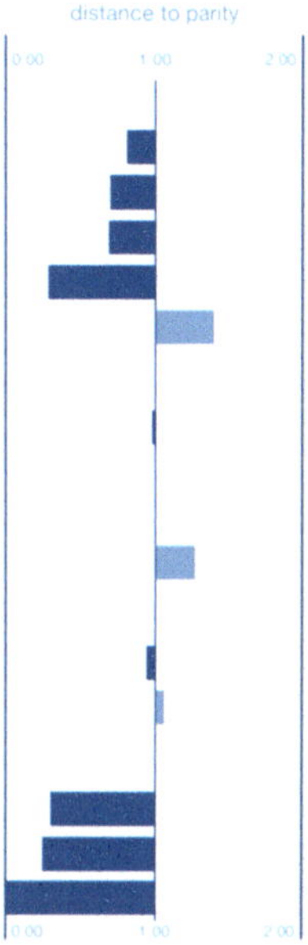

Picture 1 Global Gender Gap Index for Montenegro: relative differences between men and women in the field of health, education, economy and politics. Source: Report of the Global Gender Gap of the World Forum (2018), available at: http://www.weforum.org/docs/WEF_GGGR_2018.pdf

3 Analysis of Demographic Indexes Relevant for the Development of Women Entrepreneurship

Since twenties of the last century, when 311,341 inhabitants have lived in the territory of Montenegro, by the last conducted census 2011 (620.029) the number of inhabitants is almost doubled.[5] This increase can partly be attributed to the relatively high natural increase, but also migrations have had a large impact on demographic change.

Changes in the gender structure are generally moving in the direction of increasing the share of female population, which is shown in Table 1.

By analyzing the previous table, we can conclude that the lowest masculinity rate in the last 50 years was recorded in 2003 when it was 969 males per 1000 women.

Furthermore, due to the increase in life expectancy in Montenegro and decreasing of birth rate, the participation of older population is growing. Also, according to the 2011 census, the aging index moves in the direction of the constant decrease of youth

[5]This section is based on the Statistical Office of Montenegro, Ministry for Human and Minority Rights of Montenegro (2018) Men and Women in Montenegro, Podgorica.

Table 1 Population indicators by gender, Montenegro 1921–2011 Censuses

Year of census	Total	Women	Men	Women	Growth rate 1921 = 100		Coefficient of masculinity	Coefficient of feminity
1921	311,341	156,040	155,301	50.12	100.00	100.00	995.26	1004.76
1931	360,044	180,279	179,765	50.07	115.53	115.75	997.15	1002.86
1948	377,189	199,111	178,078	52.79	127.60	114.67	894.37	1118.11
1953	419,873	218,155	201,718	51.96	139.81	129.89	924.65	1081.49
1961	471,894	242,620	229,274	51.41	155.49	147.63	944.99	1058.21
1971	529,604	270,395	259,209	51.06	173.29	166.91	958.63	1043.15
1981	584,310	294,571	289,739	50.41	188.78	186.57	983.60	1016.68
1991	615,035	309,104	305,931	50.26	198.09	196.99	989.73	1010.37
2003	620,145	314,920	305,225	50.78	201.82	196.54	969.21	1031.76
2011	620,029	313,793	306,236	50.60	201.09	197.18	975.92	1024.68

Source: Statistical Office of Montenegro, Ministry for Human and Minority Rights of Montenegro (2018). *Men and Women in Montenegro*. Ministry for Human and Minority Rights of Montenegro, Podgorica

participation, while simultaneously increases in old people participation. This trend is particularly expressed in the female population. Besides, the average age of men is constantly lower than the average age of women. The average age of women and men increases and in 2011 it is 38.4 for women and 36 for men (Statistical Office of Montenegro and Ministry of Human and Minority Rights 2018).

Also, according to the 2011 census, greater participation of women was reported in a population with no education (81%). Within the population who finished one of the high level of education by new system women are majority related to men.

Thus, in 2017 there were 3048 graduates, on basic studies, showing a decrease of 2% compared to the previous year. Of the total number of graduates on basic studies, 57.6% were women, and 42.4% men (Statistical Office of Montenegro and Ministry of Human and Minority Rights 2018). By analyzing educational structure, the latest available data show that in 2017 in total 163 students finished master's studies, which is 14.2% less than in the previous year. 56.4% female students finished master's studies, and 43.6% male students (Statistical office of Montenegro and Ministry of Human and Minority Rights 2018). On the other hand, 8 women and 10 men acquired the title of Ph.D. in 2017, whereas 19 women and 9 men acquired the same title in 2016 (Statistical office of Montenegro and Ministry of Human and Minority Rights 2018).

Women make the majority of employees in education. Although women represent the majority of employees in education, they are in absolute minority in positions which take part in decision-making process, except for preschool education.

The gender structure shows that the same number of women and men are computer literate. However, if we consider only women older than 15 years, 34 percent are computer literate, 16 percent are partially skilled, and 50 percent cannot work on the computer (Statistical office of Montenegro and Ministry of Human and Minority Rights 2018).

Taking into account what is mentioned above, the following picture gives an overview of employees according to sectors, activities and gender (Table 2).

We can notice from the picture that in the transport, storage, and communications sector men are significant majority (9.4 thousand) related to women (2.8 thousand), while in the education sector women are majority (10.6 thousand) related to men (3.7 thousand).

On the other hand, if we talk about unemployment, data show that in the total number of unemployed (51.262) in 2017, women take up 58.6 percent (30.035), and men 41.4 percent (21.227). Compared with the same month last year (2016), the share of unemployed women increased by 16.2 percent and 10.2 percent decreased for men (Employment office of Montenegro).

Significantly less representation of women compared to men is present when we talk about politics. Pictures 2 and 3 show the structure of the government and composition of the Parliament of Montenegro in 2017, where exactly we can notice less participation of women compared to men.

For analysis of the development of women entrepreneurship, apart from the abovementioned data, we need other data as well. Namely, although there are

Table 2 Employees according to sectors of activity and gender, Montenegro (2017)

		In 1000	
	Total	Men	Women
1. Agriculture	(18.2)	(11.2)	(7.0)
2. Mining	1.6	1.4	–
3. Manufacturing	12.7	((9.3))	–
4. Electricity, gas, steam, and air conditioning	2.5	2.0	–
5. Water supply, wastewater management	5.0	3.9	–
6. Construction	17.4	(15.3)	(2.1)
7. Wholesale, retail; certain repair	46.3	20.1	26.1
8. Transport, storage, and communications	12.1	9.4	2.8
9. Accommodation and food services	19.9	12.5	((7.4))
10. Information and communications	(5.4)	(2.9)	((2.5))
11. Financial and insurance activities	4.0	(2.0)	(2.0)
12. Real estate, leasing, and business activities	–	–	–
13. Professional, scientific, and technical activities	10.9	–	–
14. Administrative and support service activities	12.4	((9.0))	–
15. Public administ. And defense	20.5	(11.2)	–
16. Education	14.3	((3.7))	10.6
17. Health and social work	12.8	((3.7))	(9.0)
18. Arts, entertainment, and recreation	4.9	2.6	–
19. Other social and personal services	7.7	(3.3)	(4.3)
Total	229.3	128.5	100.8

Source: Statistical Office of Montenegro, Ministry for Human and Minority Rights of Montenegro (2018). *Men and Women in Montenegro*. Ministry for Human and Minority Rights of Montenegro, Podgorica

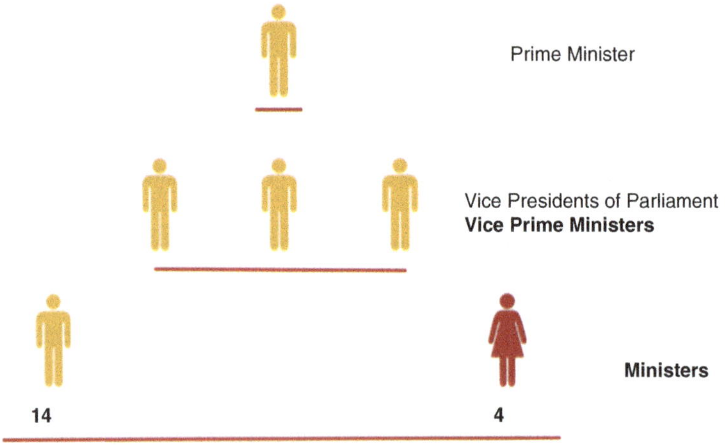

Picture 2 Structure of the government. Source: General Secretariat of the Government

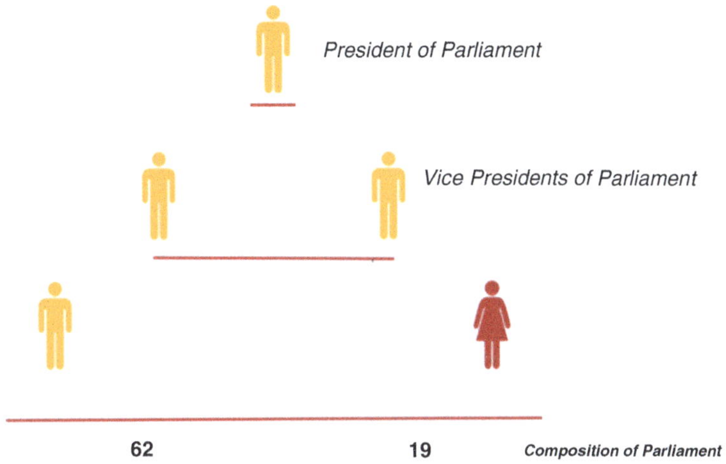

Picture 3 Composition of the Parliament of Montenegro. Source: Parliament of Montenegro and Committee on Gender Equality

some positive steps toward statistical evidence of data on ownership structure of business premises (according to gender), this should be significantly improved in the following period (Montenegrin Employers Federation and IPSOS Strategic Marketing 2013). If we want to strengthen gender equality, we need to make appropriate statistical data available and they should be distributed according to the gender. In Montenegro, women entrepreneurs showed to be responsible in business, accurate, persistent, systematic, and rational (Montenegrin Employers Federation and IPSOS Strategic Marketing 2013). By dedicated and efficient management, responsible approach to fulfilling obligations, as well as making good quality decisions, they managed to win the economic crisis and maintain business in difficult conditions, characterized by problems of collecting receivables, reduced liquidity, and lack of financial resources.

4 Obstacles and Challenges for the Development of Women Entrepreneurship in Montenegro

Women, owners of small and medium enterprises, are often perceived as unequal players in the economic "arena." In comparison with men entrepreneurs, women often have unequal status and credibility, they have more obstacles while establishing the company, and they need more time to become accepted in the business community. It is usually typical for women that while establishing and developing their business, they do not have the same attitudes related to social, educational, and technological challenges, as well as access to economic and financial resources. If we add the lack of development of gender-sensitive politics, economic sectors in which men are dominating and then family obligations whose burden is usually carried by these women, it is unquestionable that women entrepreneurship is followed by numerous factors which significantly limit or slow down its development.

As a candidate for the EU membership, Montenegro is preparing for taking part at the unique EU market by building its capacities within the guidelines of the development of the European Union until 2020: *smart growth, sustainable growth, and inclusive growth* (Bujković 2015). For small countries like Montenegro, guidelines of the smart and inclusive growth have important meaning–in that context, the activities which contribute the activation of all human resources, regardless of the gender, geographical distribution, or age, have priority meaning (Ministry of Economy and Directorate for Development of Small and Medium Enterprises 2015). Gender equality represents one of the basic EU principles. In 2007, Montenegro provided regulation on that field by passing the *law on gender equality,* which prescribes the way of obtaining and realizing the right based on gender equality, as well as measures for eliminating discrimination based on the gender.[6] State body which deals with the issue of gender equality is *Office for gender equality*, established in 2003 (Bojanović 2013). The fact that is emphasized in this area is related to the achievement of economic independence of women, equaling incomes of men and women, adequate representation of women in the managerial and decision-making positions, sanctioning gender violence, etc. Special accent was put on encouraging women entrepreneurship because women represent a big opportunity for the economy of Montenegro, since they are the majority population—50.7%,[7] according to the census from 2011. On the other hand, we point out as a special disadvantage the fact that Montenegro still does not have the *law on social entrepreneurship*, which would help a great number of women, members of certain vulnerable groups, for example persons with disability, women victims of violence, women victims of transition, and harder employable categories of women to provide higher level of inclusion into society and in that way to contribute both personal affirmation and economic growth.

Women entrepreneurship has an important potential for the development of global economy, i.e., women entrepreneurship influences the reduction of unemployment, setting up business in new spheres, application of new technologies, and developing entrepreneurship (Vukmirović 2005). There are numerous obstacles on the way toward entrepreneurship, both for women and men, and some of them have objective character and relate to both genders, whereas some of them are exclusive for women only. Female entrepreneurs have faced more challenges in startups than men. Women face systemic social and financial challenges while starting a business

[6]Law on gender equality ("Official Gazette of the Republic of Montenegro," no. 46/07 from 31.07.2007 and "Official Gazette of Montenegro", no. 73/10 from 10.12.2010, 40/11 from 08.08.2011, 35/15 from 07.07.2015).

[7]Statistical Office of Montenegro, MONSTAT, census of population, households, and flats in 2011, available at: https://www.monstat.org/cg/page.php?id=322&pageid=322

(Gutierrez 2017). Namely, potential barriers can be *economic, educational, and cultural.*[8] Montenegro, as well as the majority of countries, is characterized by a female paradox—women represent a majority in the population, but minority in accessing chances, looked through setting up business opportunities, employment, taking part in the ownership over business subjects, and managerial functions in companies and in political engagement (Ministry of Economy and Directorate for Development of Small and Medium Enterprises 2015). Furthermore, the paradox is reflected in the fact that in the population group with the university degree, academy, and master of Ph.D. title, women make 44.9%; however, out of total number of unemployed with a university degree, 66.4% are women (Chamber of Commerce 2018). More than 90% of women's enterprises in Montenegro are micro size and they are directed toward the local market.[9]

There is a significant gap between the intensity of entrepreneurial activity of men and women, observed through the number of newly established enterprises, measured with *TEA index*—index of total entrepreneurial activity (Amoros and Bosma 2014), as well as significant underrepresentation of women in ownership and managerial structure of existing enterprises, which is the result of long-term presence of various obstacles (Ministry of economy and Directorate for Development of Small and Medium Enterprises 2015). The previous researches carried out on women entrepreneurship in Montenegro identified the following obstacles (Strategy of the development of women entrepreneurship in Montenegro 2015–2020):

- *Structural obstacles* are the hardest, they derive from traditional view of the women's role in society, and they are based on the values which are a result of cultural heritage and they have the following as a consequence:
  - Lack of adequate support for making life easier for women with two jobs—family and profession (places in kindergartens, day care for schoolchildren, care of senior family members, etc.)
  - Existence of stereotypes in choosing educational profiles and professions and lack of adequate education which reduces the possibilities for women to start the business in technologically intensive areas
  - Insufficient efficacy for implementation of political-regulatory framework on which the strengthening of gender equality depends.
- *Economic obstacles* contribute to the discrimination of women in accessing business chances, from the aspect of developing a new business, then improving and growth of the existing ones, primarily in possibilities of obtaining missing resources. Women are in less favorable position for getting bank loans because the majority of women are not owners of real estate, and lack of alternative ways of financing business in Montenegro (business angels, funds of risky capital, etc.)

---

[8]Chamber of Commerce of Montenegro (2018). Status and conditions for the development of women entrepreneurship, available at: http://www.privrednakomora.me/announcements/stanje-i-uslovi-razvoja-zenskog-preduzetnistva

[9]Ibid.

narrows the access to financial resources. Key economic obstacles which have negative consequences for the development of women entrepreneurship are as follows:

- Lack of funds for the startup and development of the business, as well as unfavorable and complex access to the financial resources
- Inappropriate level of networking which hardens the access to human resources necessary for the development of business
- Presence of informal economy which distorts the labor market and the level of competition

• *Infrastructural obstacles* result from insufficiently developed institutional infrastructure and lack of range of services which make skills stronger, knowledge, and self-confidence of potential women entrepreneurs. Lack of appropriate training and educational programs is a very strong obstacle, which together with lack of advisory and mentoring services does not allow that the women's aspirations for setting up a business venture turn into an entrepreneurship activity. It is important to mention insufficiently developed institutional capacities which should realize various types of services and training. Also, it is obvious that there is unequal regional availability of advisory services, mentoring, and training for setting up business ventures with women. Entrepreneurship centers (within local self-governments), employers' associations (national, local, industrial), development agencies, and universities should cooperate and support the development of such services and in that way to directly help women networking and spreading the examples of good practice. Underdevelopment of appropriate institutional infrastructure and creating non-financial support has the following as a consequence:

  - Uncoordinated institutions and lack of long-term development programs of support
  - Lack of mentoring, counseling, networking, and business contacts
  - Administrative obstacles and perception on complexity of registering a business
  - Lack of aspiration to get out of the local/national market
  - Lack of innovativeness in creating a product or services, as well as the entrance into the market
  - Lack of role models and creating the perception of lack of self-confidence and capacities for risk-taking

Interconnection of the abovementioned obstacles hardens solving the challenges with which the creators of politics of the development in women entrepreneurship are facing, especially because they require compatibility and at the same time acting through various politics and measures of resource responsible public politics holders (Ministry of Economy and Directorate for Development of Small and Medium Enterprises 2015).

Namely, as key *challenges* which the creators of politics and development of women entrepreneurship are facing with in Montenegro, we can single out the following (Strategy of the development of women entrepreneurship in Montenegro 2015–2020):

- Significantly less representation of women in entrepreneurial activities
- Lower percentage of employment for women compared with men
- Lower level of salaries of women compared with men
- Significantly less representation of women in managerial structures
- Significantly less representation of women in ownership company structures
- Insufficient availability and development of gender-distributed statistical data and underdevelopment of mechanisms for evaluation of implementation of certain activities of support to the development of women entrepreneurship

Based on the abovementioned obstacles, we can conclude that the reasons for the small number of women entrepreneurs in Montenegro are mainly rooted in the traditional understanding of a woman as a mother and a housewife, where the space for doing business is limited to its minimum. However, what we can notice in the recent period is that the stereotypes become weaker by time and that the starting position of doing business with women is much different compared with men. This is primarily with regard to women entering the business with much bigger burden of family obligations. Furthermore, she is expected more, because if she tries and fails, she usually faces with bigger judgment and belittling than it is the case with men (Bojanović 2013). From the abovementioned reasons, a woman approaches business with great attention and very cautiously, she does not go into excessive risk, and she directs herself toward familiar business activities, such as trade and service sector. In other words, women start the business modestly and they hire very small number of employees. Basic motive for entering the business usually relates with satisfying needs of the household, and, more rarely, women who do it are led by ambition and self-affirmation (Bojanović 2013). Current literature reveals that, while there are many similarities between female and male entrepreneurs, a number of differences—particularly with regard to career preference and motivators—exist (Brush 1992; Moore and Buttner 1997; Fischer et al. 1993).

5 Analysis of Business Environment and Institutional Support to the Development of Women Entrepreneurship

When we talk about the business environment of women entrepreneurship in Montenegro, we can conclude that it has significantly improved recently. Its contribution reflects in adopting various strategic documents, as well as in passing a set of laws adjusted with EU standards, institutional reforms carried out in the fiscal system, financial sector, payment transactions, and other key areas.

A special segment in the analysis of women entrepreneurship relates to the unavailability of the source of financing due to inability to provide mortgage, because as we pointed out, women are usually not the owners of real estates. However, we have noticed a step forward toward the issue of providing more convenient conditions for financing women in the business world. As the most significant financial institution which provides support to the development of women entrepreneurship, we can single out *Investment and Development Fund of Montenegro (IDF MN).* In cooperation with the Directorate for Development of Small and Medium Enterprises and Employment Agency of Montenegro, IRF offers non-financial and financial support for the sake of better conditions for employment and development of entrepreneurship.[10] From the abovementioned reasons, *Investment and Development Fund of Montenegro* has, within the direct financing of investment projects, introduced the lines with regard to financing projects whose holders are women, whose aim is to additionally encourage women to start their own business with special credit conditions.[11] Loans are intended for women who plan to start their business, thus as a support and development of startups where a woman has to be majority or 100% owner and executive manager of a company.[12]

Fund can finance up to 75% of the value of the total investment; applicants for the loan can provide their own participation up to 25% value of the total investment within 1 year from the date of concluding the loan agreement, while the loan amount aimed at investing in the working capital can be up to 30% of the total loan amount.[13] The loan terms are as follows[14]:

- Maximum amount up to €50,000.00 (for women entrepreneurs up to €30,000.00)
- Interest rate 0%
- Repayment period up to 12 years (including the grace period)
- Grace period up to 4 years

Credits of the *Investment Development Fund* are intended for investments in fixed assets (material assets, where construction objects, equipment, devices, basic herds, long-term plantings, etc. are considered, as well as intangible assets related to the development of products or services, patents, licenses, concessions, copyrights, franchises, etc.) and *working capital.*

When we talk about institutional support, issues of women entrepreneurship in Montenegro are being dealt by the state administration bodies, nongovernment

[10]Chamber of commerce of Montenegro (2016). Women entrepreneurs need favorable finances, available at: http://www.privrednakomora.me/saopstenja/preduzetnicama-potrebne-povoljne-finansije

[11]In this way they can manage to achieve goals defined by the Strategy of development of women entrepreneurship 2015-2020.

[12]Vukčević, Z. Program of support for women in business - Start-up, Investment and Development Fund of Montenegro, available at: https://www.irfcg.me/me/2015-01-13-12-14-58/program-podrske-zenama-u-biznisu-start-up

[13]Ibid.

[14]Ibid.

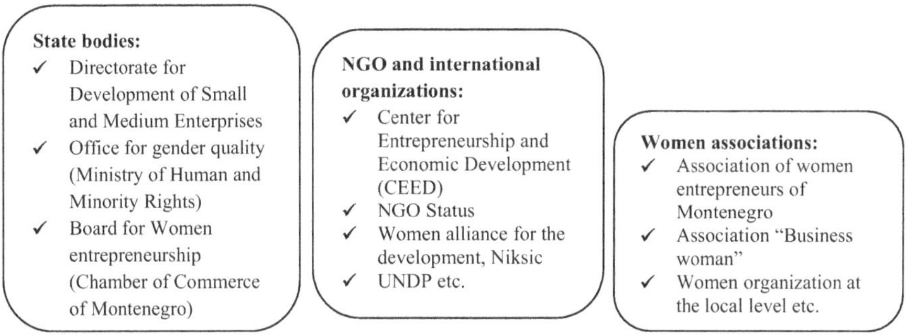

Picture 4 Organizations/institutions which deal with issues of women entrepreneurship in Montenegro. Source: Bojanović, V. (2013). *Women entrepreneurship in Montenegro.* Institute for Entrepreneurship and Economic Growth, Podgorica

organizations—NGOs, business associations, international organizations, etc. A review of the abovementioned institutions is given below (Picture 4).

Organizations or institutions which are mentioned in the previous picture are mainly active in the field of regulation, encouragement, promotion, and other aspects of women entrepreneurship. Apart from that, there have been activities recently which are directed toward showing support to the development of women entrepreneurship in Montenegro, and which relate to researching the status of the women who live in rural areas, in gray economy, in business, etc. through training, crediting up to networking. There were intensive activities in recent years on eliminating gray economy; however, it is still significantly represented in the Montenegrin economy. Thus, the female part of the population do not skip this business zone and offer their products and services at the informal market; most often these are hairdressers' and cosmeticians' services, but also selling products like clothes, jewelry, cosmetics, and such, and the results of a research *Challenges that women entrepreneurs in Montenegro are facing with*[15] carried out in 2012 can witness this (Bojanović 2013). Graph 1 shows the activities done by women and they are related to the gray economy.

In order to review the situation in the business in gray economy more realistically, it is necessary to take into account basic business characteristics which are related to small businesses, with regard to the level of monthly incomes which are generated, and which hardly exceed an average monthly income, as well as a small number of people they hire. Thus, we are not surprised by the women's attitude that taxes and duties are high, as well as costs for registering and regular business are main factors why women do business at the raw market—simply because their modest scope of business cannot afford the abovementioned costs (Regional Developmental Agency Bjelasica, Komovi, and Prokletije 2014a, b).

[15]Research was realized by the Center for Entrepreneurship and Economic Development (CEED) on the sample of 100 women who do business in the gray economy in 9 Montenegrin municipalities (Podgorica, Nikšić, Cetinje, Bijelo Polje, Pljevlja, Rožaje, Bar, Ulcinj, and Kotor).

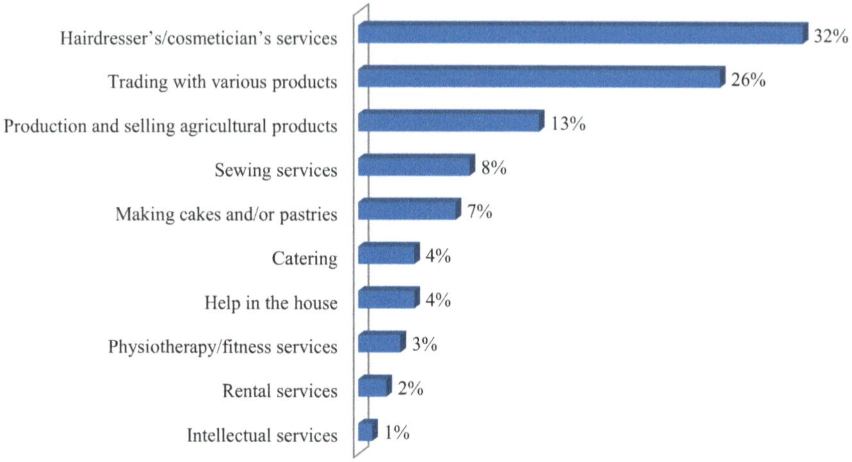

Graph 1 Activities done by women in the gray economy (%). Source: adapted from Bojanović, V. (2013). *Women entrepreneurship in Montenegro*. Institute for entrepreneurship and economic growth, Podgorica

There are efforts toward improving women entrepreneurship and position of women at the labor market. In the first half of 2018, there are a bigger number of women entrepreneurs for 1.5% (Government of Montenegro 2018). Within the project IPA-2014 "*Support to the antidiscriminatory and gender equality politics*,"[16] carried out by the Ministry of Human and Minority Rights and UNDP office in Montenegro, with financial support of the EU in the area of economic growth, there is a training program for women who are business beginners and who wish to continue the development of their business (Ministry of Human and Minority Rights 2019).

6 Role of the Strategy of the Development of Women Entrepreneurship in Montenegro: Analysis of Achieved Objectives

Achieving gender equality in all areas of social life was defined by the European Union as one of their priorities until 2020. Starting from 2006, through strategic document, EU defines principles and framework within which member countries are expected to adjust their strategic directions, regulatory frameworks, and institutional capacities for achieving gender equality. Actual strategic framework for encouraging women entrepreneurship in the EU until 2020 was represented in the following

[16]Abovementioned project was realized through the Institute for Entrepreneurship and Economic Growth.

documents (Ministry of Economy and Directorate for Development of Small and Medium Enterprises 2015):

- Europe 2020[17]—an umbrella strategic framework of economic growth for the period 2014–2020.
- Small business Act[18]—a strategic EU document which creates the framework and principles for encouraging the development of entrepreneurship. A special dimension was devoted to encouraging women entrepreneurship.
- European Pact for Gender Equality for the period 2011–2020[19]—strategic framework within which they follow the achievement of gender balance in all aspects of the social life.
- Women's charter[20]—EU is obliged to strengthen gender equality through implementation of all their policies.
- Women active in the ICT sector[21]—better involvement of women in the area of information communication technologies.

When we talk about Montenegro, there is a special document *Strategy of the development of women entrepreneurship in Montenegro* 2015–*2020* which represents umbrella document, which is complementary with other relevant policies and strategic development documents in Montenegro. *Strategy of the development of women entrepreneurship in Montenegro* 2015–*2020* should be regarded as a continuation of the started process, but also as a support to various initiatives and institutions whose activities significantly offer contribution to economic strengthening of women and gender equality, reducing risk of poverty and increasing the welfare.

Unlike men, Montenegrin women do not have the same chances and possibilities to achieve their rights, to give a full contribution, and to collect appropriate profits from modern socioeconomic development. By creating and implementation of the *Strategy of the development of women entrepreneurship*, one strives toward creating necessary preconditions and basics upon which women will be able to show equally their entrepreneurial potential and to improve their position in society at all levels.

According to the report on realization of the action plan for implementing the Strategy of the development of women entrepreneurship in Montenegro during 2018, a total amount of €1,601,022.00 was spent for realization of activities anticipated by the action plan, majority of funds of €1,405,000.00 were spent on financial support to women entrepreneurship (Ministry of Economy 2019). Also, a big number of activities were realized during 2018 and they contribute to successful realization of strategic objectives.

[17]Europe 2020: A strategy for smart, sustainable and inclusive growth, EC, 2010.

[18]Small Business Act, EC, 2010.

[19]European Pact for Gender Equality for the period 2011–2020, EP, 2011.

[20]Women's Charter, EC, 2010.

[21]Women active in the ICT sector, EC, 2013.

Within the Strategic objective 1. *Improving favorable business environment for the development of the women entrepreneurship*, counseling, and mentoring services have been improved, agreements with 11 municipalities were achieved, and they granted €144,000 for women entrepreneurship in the Budgets for 2019 (Herceg Novi, Tivat, Pljevlja, Mojkovac, Rožaje, Bijelo Polje, Ulcinj, Podgorica, Bar, and Danilograd) (Ministry of Economy 2019).

Within the Strategic objective 2. *Improving financial support*, during 2018 IDF MN, based on 3 credit lines (Program of support for women in business—UNDP/ Program of support for women in business/Program of support for women in business—startup) supported 39 projects, valued at € 1.2 mil. In 2018, the Employment Agency of Montenegro approved 36 credits for women in the amount of €205,000.00 (Ministry of Economy 2019).

Strategic objective 3. *Providing necessary knowledge and skills*—Within this strategic objective, a great number of educations intended for women entrepreneurs were realized. More than 300 women passed through various training programs designed for existing and potential women entrepreneurs. As an additional value of the training, more than 20 women got business plans with elaborated business idea for starting the business (Ministry of Economy 2019).

Strategic objective 4. *Promotion, networking, and advocacy of women entrepreneurs' interests*—by participating in a large number of international and local conferences, round tables, and promotional events of representatives of institutions/organizations from Montenegro awareness of the importance of women entrepreneurship was raised. Also, they improved the business cooperation at the local, regional, and international plan (Ministry of Economy 2019).

Strategy of the development of women entrepreneurship in Montenegro, thus, aims at encouraging faster and easier economic strengthening of women through creating favorable business environment and offering support to the development of their entrepreneurial potentials, which will at the same time contribute to the development of existing and creating new enterprises, creation of new job positions and employment growth, and in that way total development of the SME sector and entrepreneurship (Ministry of Economy and Directorate for Development of Small and Medium Enterprises 2015).

In the report of realization of the action plan and implementing *Strategy of the development of women entrepreneurship in Montenegro* 2015–*2020,* there are special recommendations for realization of the following measures (Ministry of Economy 2019):

- To start the initiative for questioning the possibility of reducing tax costs in the first years of doing business for women entrepreneurs
- To improve access to finances, especially taking into account the forming of Guarantee fund which is especially important for women in business
- To start the initiative toward commercial banks for opening special credit lines for women entrepreneurs

- To improve support services for business and business counseling through forming and strengthening business infrastructure (business centers and incubators)
- To improve non-financial support to the business beginners (information, counseling, training, consulting, mentoring, etc.)

Apart from the abovementioned measures, there are also important recommendations of the *Small Business Act*—SBA according to which it is necessary to (Ministry of Economy 2019):

- Encourage ecosystem for women entrepreneurship. Form a working group of several stakeholders in charge of annual monitoring of the strategy of women entrepreneurship, which should set up a formal cooperation with all relevant and government and nongovernment organizations. This would enable the government to have a full image on women entrepreneurship and to financially support implementation of strategy for women entrepreneurship.
- Strengthen monitoring and evaluation of initiatives for supporting women entrepreneurship. One should pay more attention to create gender-sensitive statistical data as well as carry out a national report on evaluation of women entrepreneurship in Montenegro, which will be useful for further promotion of women entrepreneurship.

Related to the abovementioned recommendations, the final results that are necessary to achieve at the mid-term period in implementing the support to the development of women entrepreneurship in Montenegro are as follows (Ministry of Economy and Directorate for Development of Small and Medium Enterprises 2015):

- To increase the women entrepreneurial activity at the level of EU average from 2013 (*measured with the TEA women index and TEA men index*)
- To motivate women to become entrepreneurs and start their own business (*measured with increased number of established enterprises by women*)
- To increase self-confidence with women who run their business successfully (*measured with increased number of existing startup enterprises which are run by women; measured by the increased number of women—owners of growing enterprises*)
- To encourage connecting/networking women entrepreneurs and managers at the local, national, and international level (*measured through the number of members in relevant national and international associations; measured through the number of women entrepreneurs who take part in national and international clusters and chains of value*).
- To strengthen the role of women in managerial structures (*measured with increased number of women at managerial positions in companies*)

Taking into account all of the mentioned above, Diagram 1 shows the structure of the politics of women entrepreneurship and key measures for its achievement in the period until 2020.

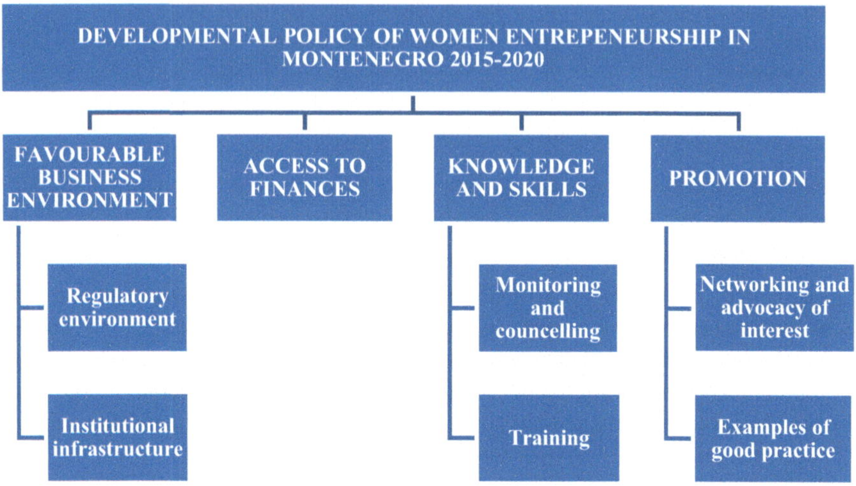

Diagram 1 Overview of the structure of politics of women entrepreneurship and key measures for its achievement. Source: Ministry of Economy, Directorate for Development of Small and Medium Enterprises (2015). *Report from the public debate on the draft of the Strategy for lifelong entrepreneurial learning 2015–2020*. Ministry of Economy, Directorate for Development of Small and Medium Enterprises Podgorica, p. 26

In order to achieve the abovementioned objectives, it is necessary that the state, government, and institutions in charge, in good spirit of tripartite social dialogue and in full cooperation with the private and civil sector, implement economic and social policies that support measures and affirmative actions aimed at improving and developing women entrepreneurship at the local and national level, in response to identified key challenges that they face with in Montenegro.

7 Examples of Good Practice: Association of Women Entrepreneurs of Montenegro

The Association of Women Entrepreneurs of Montenegro (AWEM) was founded in 2009 with the aim to strengthen women's entrepreneurship by providing opportunities for interconnection of women entrepreneurs and providing expert advice on starting and developing business and financial information and educational opportunities.[22] Association of Women Entrepreneurs is the first national women entrepreneurs' organization with that purpose, founded as NGO by 10 successful women entrepreneurs, supported by voluntary donations and sponsorships. The Association of Women Entrepreneurs of Montenegro has 150 members, all active in various

[22]This section is based on internal data by AWEM.

activities and branch areas (Dautović 2019). The association brings together entrepreneurs from all over Montenegro and it acts organized and continuously to improve the business environment, the removal of business barriers, and strengthening business connections at the international level. The organization, together with its members, is functioning on a voluntary basis. Association promotes women entrepreneurship by organizing various sociocultural activities, capacity building, awareness of gender equality, promotion of women in business, support to women startups, lobbying through different institutions, etc. The Association of Women Entrepreneurs of Montenegro encourages all women in Montenegro to find personal motivation and to get engaged in entrepreneurial activities.

Key tasks which derive from their mission are as follows (Dautović 2019):

- Protection of rights and advocacy for interest of women entrepreneurs with business partners, public, and other institutions
- Encouragement of community and entrepreneur's image, enabling environment for gender equality at work capacity building for women
- Enhancement of networking among women in business and crafts
- Information of members of the association on measures of state and local bodies in charge, relating to their interests
- Support in scientific research and specialized scientific journals
- Public information on current issues related to women entrepreneurship
- Negotiation in women interests before Unions
- Consulting and coaching of members in terms of business operations (procurement, HR, promotion and sales, networking, export-import)

In the association, there are great inspirational models in practice, which play an important role in encouraging women to become entrepreneurs. Projects which they implement support women startups directly through legal, institutional, expert, and financial support (trainings, coaching, grants, promotion, etc.). They are mostly recognized for having high rate of women working in gray zone enter legal flows in terms of their own contractual conditions with an employer or their own income generating activities (crafts, trade, manufacture, food processing, etc.).

The association took part in a great number of projects, among which the following stand out (Dautović 2019):

1. Project "WEST BALKAN" financed by the Ministry of Finance of the Federal Republic of Germany and SEQA organization partners with middle classed bureau of Balkan network for exchange of information and experience of Southeast Europe, Balkan association of women's trade, and other 9 countries. The project aims at strengthening of capacities of partner organizations, affirmation of young entrepreneurs with 20% at the end of the project, and environmental protection (energy efficiency, green surfaces, corporate social responsibilities). The role in the project has been to represent our organization of Balkan women in trades and to increase the capacity of our partner organizations for 10%, and to reduce the unemployment rate of young people and women. They have educated

women for certain activities such as optician, hairdresser, beautician, a jeweler, and cook.
2. Organizers of International Conference "Women Power" 2013, 2014, 2015, 2016, 2017, and 2018 where business meetings B2B were held and supported by Enterprise Europe Network (EEN) Montenegro. The conference is international in character and in the framework of the conference will take place Fair of women's entrepreneurship.
3. Organizers: "Fair of SMEs and women's entrepreneurship" Budva 2014 and 2015; "The company that supports families in the countries of Southeast Europe" in 2013, 2014, 2015, and 2016 and "Freja Forum" 2013, 2014, 2015, 2016, 2017.
4. Project partners "Woman driver of the company" (2015–2016). The overall goal of the project is education and affirmation that women entrepreneurship belongs to different professional profiles in secondary schools and colleges.
5. Project partners "Willing and capable" (2014). Overall objective: Improving inter-ethnic understanding through the exchange of ideas and mutual interaction for common ideas and strengthening of inter-ethnic trust
6. Partners on the project "Affirmation of tradition through workshops in the North of Montenegro" (2016). The overall goal of the project is education and affirmations that women entrepreneurship belongs to different professional profiles in secondary schools and colleges.

With regard to international activities, the association is a member in the Middle classed Biro of Balkan network for the exchange of information and experience of Southeast Europe, the Balkan Association of Women in Crafts. Montenegro chaired Balkan Association of Women in Crafts by 2017, which included nine Southeast European countries. The association is one of the founders of the NGO "Balkan association of women in the trades," which gathers ten member states of the Balkans. This alliance of 2009 is implementing a project of affirmation of craft and entrepreneurship of women in the region of the Western Balkans.

The following part will show an example of a successful woman entrepreneur in Montenegro, Edita Dautovic.

Edita Dautović: Modern Age Entrepreneur

Ms. Edita Dautovic is the owner of a real estate agency "Millennium" in Podgorica, and she is a president of the Association of Women Entrepreneurs of Montenegro. She is one of the founders of the Balkan association of women in crafts, member of the board of "Middle class bureau Balkan," international network for exchanging information and experience of south eastern Europe, a coordinator of the "Freja forum"—platform which gathers countries of the Western Balkan and Turkey, and coordinator for Montenegro of "Business Forum Prizren." In 2018, Edita joined the establishing the Balkan women network "I love Balkans," a unique network which gathers women of various professions from the Balkan region and which encourages development of economy and culture, with special accent on preserving Balkan tradition.

Edita is particularly proud to have obtained a master's degree in entrepreneurship and management and to have begun her involvement in entrepreneurship when it was at a nascent stage in Montenegro, particularly for women. She emphasizes the supportive role of her family while pursuing her endeavors. While she sees herself remaining in the private sector, she is also open to becoming involved in the public sector if it allows her to continue to support and promote women entrepreneurship. In addition to being a successful entrepreneur and advocate for women entrepreneurship in the Balkans, Edita enjoys writing poetry and has authored two books (Novicevic et al. 2017).

Edita won prestigious awards twice—"The best woman of the XXI century 2015" in the area of real estate for the home country and the region and "The best woman of the XXI century 2016" in the area of promoting innovative-social entrepreneurship. She defended her master's thesis "Women entrepreneurship in Montenegro" and published a few scientific works, such as *Challenges of women entrepreneurship in Montenegro, Good quality informing on women mentoring and business angels in Montenegro, Analysis of women entrepreneurship in Montenegro, Entrepreneurship in tourism on the example of ethno villages*, etc. In her free time, Edita writes prose and poetry. She published the books: *Senses*, *Ophelia's tears*, and *Good deeds outlive the time* (Saga of Pava and Ahmet) where she gave her personal stamp to her ancestors. Her poetry has been translated into three languages: English, Bulgarian, and Turkish. Her ability to have a clear entrepreneurial vision which is followed by a great number of women in Montenegro is recognized outside the boundaries of our country.

8 Conclusion

Distorted perception of value, credibility, ability, responsibility, and knowledge which a woman has or can have, and for which the term *minorization* is a common name, represents *invisible obstacle* and it is the biggest stumbling block to the development of women entrepreneurship (Vrbanac 2018). Deeply rooted patriarchal attitudes of men, but women in Montenegro as well, still represent a significant barrier for the development of women entrepreneurship (Popović 2013). Namely, gender equality is expressed through a low level of representation of women in the leading and decision-making positions, insufficient political participation of women, as well as economic inequality, feminization of certain professions, segregation of education profiles, difference in salaries, although it is about the jobs of the same value, and ownership over assets, and unequal share of family chores. In practice, there is a problem of insufficient use of legal solutions, but it is necessary to overcome certain stereotypes in society. We are witnesses that strict patriarchal understanding of a women and her role in the Montenegrin family and society slowly enters the history, but, when it is about business, limiting patterns of behavior are still present.

In the previous period, national statistics on entrepreneurial activities of women in Montenegro have not been developed at the appropriate level, and thus there are no appropriate analyses based on which we could generate necessary conclusions.

Future researches need to comprise the data related to the phase of the company life cycle, starting up and growth of a company, regional schedule and activity, added value, international trade performances, leaving the business activity, etc.

By analyzing the current state, as well as ecosystem for the development of women entrepreneurship in Montenegro, we can mention the following four basic limitations:

- *Adjusting business and family obligations*—Frequently discouraged, insufficiently self-confident, and without the support of the relatives, women in Montenegro do not start their business plan further than the idea level, primarily because of fear that they would not be able to adjust the requirements of their two roles: successful businesswoman on one side and a good mother, wife, and housewife on the other side.
- *Insecurity in the knowledge for doing the business they wish to do*—With lack of self-confidence to appropriately valorize what they can do, and readiness to work on the missing skills, women often give up their ideas.
- *Providing the source of financing*—Average Montenegrin woman does not possess a real estate on her name, so she is faced with a problem of providing the source of financing, so it is difficult for her to provide the mortgage for a loan by herself.
- *Doing business in the gray economy*—At the beginning, women are aware that the income most likely will not be enough to satisfy fixed costs of the business. Under the pressure of negative expectations, majority of them decide to do business in the gray economy, at least until the "business grows"; however, that "temporary solution" lasts for a longer period of time.

Based on abovementioned limitations, it is possible to determine the proposal of measures for overcoming these obstacles (Bojanović 2013):

1. Fear of being unable to adjust the roles of a businesswoman, mother, wife, and housewife
    - Promoting examples of successful women entrepreneurs through *storytelling*
    - Motivational workshops
    - Collective childcare
2. Lack of necessary knowledge and self-confidence for doing business
    - Training
    - Mentoring concept
3. Difficult access to finances
    - Reviving the idea of a guarantee fund for women entrepreneurs
4. Choosing gray economy
    - Starting business incubators for women entrepreneurs
    - Tax incentives for women entrepreneurs

Finally, we can conclude that the period ahead of us in terms of affirmation of women in business will be very demanding and challenging, but it is encouraging that Montenegro has made basic steps in this area and that by implementing the *Strategy for the development of women entrepreneurship* will realize actions aimed at empowering women in business. Since Montenegrin women often make for more than a half of the population and in that way they represent a significant potential for the economic growth, encouraging women entrepreneurship is one of the ways to valorize that potential.

References

Amoros JE, Bosma N (2014) GEM 2013 global report. Global Entrepreneurship Research Association, p 12

Blagojević M (2002) Men and women in Serbia 1990-2000: gendering the price of chaos. Institute for sociological researches, Belgrade, pp 283–314

Bojanović V (2013) Women entrepreneurship in Montenegro. Institute for entrepreneurship and economic growth, Podgorica

Brush CD (1992) Research on women business owners: past trends, a new perspective, and future directions. Entrep Theory Pract 16(4):5–30

Bujković R (2015) EXPOBUDVA info – Official Newsletter of the Adriatic Fair. no. 107, Montenegro, p. 2

Chamber of Commerce Montenegro (2018) Gazette – no. 4. Chamber of Commerce Montenegro, Podgorica

Chamber of Commerce of Montenegro (2016) Women entrepreneurs need favourable finances. http://www.privrednakomora.me/saopstenja/preduzetnicama-potrebne-povoljne-finansije

Chamber of Commerce of Montenegro (2018) Status and conditions for the development of women entrepreneurship. http://www.privrednakomora.me/announcements/stanje-i-uslovi-razvoja-zenskog-preduzetnistva

Dautović E (2019) Internal documents of the Association of Women Entrepreneurs of Montenegro, Podgorica

DeMartino R, Barbato R (2003) Differences between women and men MBA entrepreneurs: exploring family flexibility and wealth creation as career motivators. J Bus Ventur 18 (6):815–832

Despotović A, Joksimović M, Jovanović M, Maletić R (2018) Female entrepreneurship in Montenegro: motives and barriers. Agric For 64(4):195–218

EESE business, Women entrepreneurs need further support in Montenegro. http://eese-toolkit.itcilo.org/index.php/en/news/latest-news/236-women-entrepreneurs-need-further-support-in-montenegro.html

Fischer E, Reuben RA, Dyke LS (1993) A theoretical overview and extension of research on sex, gender, and entrepreneurship. J Bus Ventur 8(2):151–168

Government of Montenegro (2018) Report on realization of middle-term working program of the government of Montenegro 2018-2020 for the period February-July 2018. Government of Montenegro, Podgorica

Gutierrez C (2017) Women entrepreneurs are driving economic growth. Huffpost. https://www.huffpost.com/entry/women-entrepreneurs-are-driving-economic-growth_b_59f7c3dce4b04494283378f3

Ipsos Strategic Marketing (2011) Women entrepreneurship in Montenegro. Delegation of the European Union in Montenegro, Ministry for Human and Minority Rights and UNDP

Ipsos Strategic Marketing (2012) Women in politics. Delegation of the European Union in Montenegro, Ministry of Justice and UNDP
Law on gender equality ("Official gazette of Republic of Montenegro", no. 46/07 from 31.07.2007 and "Official gazette of Montenegro", no. 73/10 from 10.12.2010, 40/11 from 08.08.2011, 35/15 from 07.07.2015)
Milić A (1994) Women, politics, family. Institute of political studies, Belgrade
Ministry for Human and Minority Rights (2017) Plan of activity for achieving gender equality 2017-2021 with the program of carrying out for the period 2017-2018. Ministry for Human and Minority Rights, Podgorica
Ministry for Human and Minority Rights (2019) IPA 2014 project "support for antidiscriminatory and gender equality politics". Ministry for Human and Minority Rights, Podgorica
Ministry of Economy (2019) Report on realization of the action plan for implementing the strategy of women entrepreneurship in Montenegro 2015-2020 for the year 2018. Ministry of Economy, Podgorica
Ministry of Economy, Directorate for Development of Small and Medium Enterprises (2015) Report from the public debate on the draft of the Strategy for lifelong entrepreneurial learning 2015-2020. Ministry of Economy, Directorate for Development of Small and Medium Enterprises, Podgorica
Montenegrin Employers Federation and IPSOS Strategic Marketing (2013) Assessment of the environment for women entrepreneurship in Montenegro. Montenegrin Employers Federation Montenegro, Podgorica
Moore D, Buttner H (1997) Women entrepreneurs: moving beyond the glass ceiling. Sage, Thousand Oaks, CA
Novicevic R, Hayek C, Hayek M (2017) Women entrepreneurs in a country in transition – the perspective of edita dautovic, a woman entrepreneur and social leader. J Appl Manag Entrep 22 (1):101–108
Number of women entrepreneurs in Montenegro is almost tripled (2018). https://www.bankar.me/2018/10/15/broj-preduzetnica-u-crnoj-gori-skoro-utrostrucen/
Popović M (2013) Gender dimension of the development of entrepreneurship in post-socialist Montenegro. Sociological sparkle, Faculty of Philosophy, Nikšić, pp 40–43
Protector of Human Rights and Freedom (2017) Report on the work for 2016. Protector of human rights and freedom, Podgorica
Regional Developmental Agency Bjelasica, Komovi & Prokletije (2014a) Manual for women entrepreneurs: step by step in developing business. Regional Developmental Agency Bjelasica, Komovi & Prokletije Podgorica, p 3
Regional Developmental Agency Bjelasica, Komovi & Prokletije (2014b) Recommendations for improving the environment for women entrepreneurship in Montenegro, CEEED consulting. http://www.bjelasica-komovi.me/wp-content/uploads/Brosure/Preporuke%20zensko%20preduzetnistvo%20MNE.pdf
Report of the Global Gender Gap 2018 for Montenegro. http://www3.weforum.org/docs/WEF_GGGR_2018.pdf
Statistical Office of Montenegro, Ministry for Human and Minority Rights of Montenegro (2018) Men and Women in Montenegro. Ministry for Human and Minority Rights of Montenegro, Podgorica
Statistical Office of Montenegro, MONSTAT, Census of population, households and flats in 2011. https://www.monstat.org/cg/page.php?id=322&pageid=322
Strategy of the development of women entrepreneurship in Montenegro 2015-2020. https://ec.europa.eu/epale/sites/epale/files/strategija-razvoja-zenskog-preduzetnistva-2015-2020.pdf
Vrbanac M (2018) Barriers and drivers for women entrepreneurship in Serbia. University Union – Nikola Tesla, Belgrade, p 45
Vujačić V (1980) Ethnos of a Montenegrin woman. Titograd

Vukčević Z. Program of support for women in business - start-up, Investment and Development fund of Montenegro. https://www.irfcg.me/me/2015-01-13-12-14-58/program-podrske-zenama-u-biznisu-start-up
Vukmirović N (2005) Models of support for the development of women entrepreneurship. Industry 4:2
Wong Y-c (1986) Entrepreneurship, marriage, and earnings. Rev Econ Stat 68(4):693–699
Yadav V, Unni J (2016) Women entrepreneurship: research review and future directions. J Glob Entrep Res 6:12

Boban Melovic is Associate Professor at the Faculty of Economics, University of Montenegro, Vice Dean for International Cooperation. He holds a Ph.D. in brand management. Professor Boban Melović teaches Strategic marketing, Business, Entrepreneurship, Management in tourism, Management theory, Marketing management for small business, and Brand management. He is the author of the books *Principles of Modern Management*, *Strategic Marketing*, and *International Benchmarking* and of over 80 scientific research papers published in national and international journals and conferences. Also, he participated in a number of national and international projects.

Vladimir Djurisic is teaching assistant at the Faculty of Economics, University of Montenegro. He is engaged in several subjects such as: Marketing, Strategic management, Consumer behavior, Strategic marketing, Business, Entrepreneurship. He received his master's degree in 2013 and started his doctoral studies at the Faculty of Economics in the same year. He is currrently working on his doctoral dissertation. He has participated in several projects and conferences of national and international character.

Women's Entrepreneurship in North Macedonia

Veland Ramadani, Esra Memili, Léo-Paul Dana, and Visar Ramadani

Abstract This chapter provides insights into women entrepreneurship in the Republic of North Macedonia. The chapter begins with an overview of North Macedonia and then presents an evidence-based current state of women entrepreneurship. The chapter continues with government and other policies, initiatives, and activities for facilitating women entrepreneurship. In the end, an outlook toward the development of women entrepreneurship in the future is presented.

1 Introduction

Located in the Balkan region, the Republic of North Macedonia is a small country which gained its independence on September 8, 1991, after the dissolution of the Yugoslav Federation. A political contest with Greece about the name of the country led to admission in the United Nations in 1993 under the name "Former Yugoslav Republic of Macedonia" (FYROM). It has a territory of 25,713 km^2 and borders with Albania, Kosovo, Serbia, Bulgaria, and Greece (Exhibit 1).

Skopje, the capital and the city of Mother Teresa, is the largest city of the country and inhabited by 30% of the total population. The Republic of North Macedonia is a landlocked country, but enriched with many gorgeous mountains, valleys, lakes, and rivers. Most of the tourists would have seen the Macedonian landmarks, such as Sharr Mountains and Ohrid Lake, or for sure they have tasted the delicious coffee on

V. Ramadani (✉)
South-East European University, Tetovo, North Macedonia
e-mail: v.ramadani@seeu.edu.mk

E. Memili
University of North Carolina at Greensboro, Greensboro, NC, USA

L.-P. Dana
Dalhousie University, Halifax, NS, Canada

V. Ramadani
International Balkan University, Skopje, North Macedonia

R. Palalić et al. (eds.), *Women's Entrepreneurship in Former Yugoslavia*,
Contributions to Management Science,
https://doi.org/10.1007/978-3-030-45253-7_6

Exhibit 1 Map of North Macedonia. Source: https://nl.m.wikipedia.org/wiki/Bestand:Macedonia_Map.png

the edge of the Vardar River. The Skopje's Old Bazaar, from the twelfth century, with its landmarks Kale Fortress (Exhibit 2), Bezisten, Stone Bridge, Çifte Hamam, Clock Tower, Daut Pasha Hamam, Kurşumli Han, Mustafa Pasha Mosque, and Church of the Holy Salvation, recently became a popular tourist attraction (Ramadani et al. 2018).

According to the State Statistical Office of the Republic of North Macedonia (2016), in this country, there are 2,072,490 inhabitants, which is 2.46% more than the census taken in 2002, and 79.7% more comparing with the census of 1948. The 2002 Census envisioned the following figures based on the ethnicity of the citizens of North Macedonia: Macedonians, 1,297,981 (64.2%); Albanians, 509,083 (25.2%); Turks, 77,959 (3.9%); Romani, 53,879 (2.7%); Serbs, 35,939 (1.8%); Bosnians/Muslims, 19,571 (0.9%); and others (30,688 (1.4%). The GDP of North Macedonia in 2017 was 616,600 million denars (around 10 billion Euros). In nominal terms, it increased by 3.7% in comparison with 2016, while the real GDP growth rate in 2017, compared to 2016, was 0.2% (State Statistical Office of Republic of North Macedonia 2019a).

In many countries, especially in transition economies, data on women entrepreneurship are very rare or incomplete (Ramadani et al. 2013). The OECD (2004, p. 13) noted that "the scarce availability of reliable and valid data continues to be one of the key obstacles to understanding the challenges specific to women's

Exhibit 2 Kale Fortress in Skopje. Photo © Veland Ramadani

entrepreneurship. Sex-disaggregated statistics and sex-based policy analyses have become more widespread in recent years." Researchers (e.g., Brush 2006; Brush and Cooper 2012; Hughes et al. 2012; Jennings and Brush 2013) point out that the population of women entrepreneurs across countries is still under-researched although women constitute one of the fastest growing entrepreneur groups by substantially contributing to economies around the world through job creation and innovations. Brush (2006) also suggests that this issue stems from the newness of women's entrepreneurship phenomenon, assumptions that there may not be gender differences among entrepreneurs, and relatively less legitimacy, institutional support, and funding for research on women entrepreneurs largely due to stereotypes on women's entrepreneurial qualifications and capabilities and the reward system geared toward studies on corporations rather than women-owned firms that are often service-based SMEs. These issues also apply to the Republic of North Macedonia. Official information regarding women entrepreneurs, business types in ownership and management by women, their input in employment and GPA, etc. is almost absent although women represent almost half of the population of the Republic of North Macedonia (1,027,868 out of 2,072,490 total population). Moreover, in the total workforce which counts 940,000, women represent 44.7% (Ramadani et al. 2015).

According to the State Statistical Office (2019b), the share of women in the total number of employees in the country is lower than the share of men. In numbers, women represented 37.7% in urban, and 30.5% in rural areas. A very similar situation applies for the countries of the region with respect to the participation of women in the total workforce. Namely, women represent 41% of the total employees in Serbia; 45% in Croatia; 45% in Montenegro; 46% in Slovenia; 36% in Albania;

47% in Bulgaria; 46% in Romania, 30% in Kosovo; and 34% in Bosnia and Herzegovina (Hontz and Rotanu 2010).

In this chapter, findings about the entrepreneurship of women in the Republic of North Macedonia are presented. A summary of findings and results of a survey conducted by Ramadani et al. (2015) is provided as well. The survey addressed topics such as conditions, perspectives, and main problems of women entrepreneurs in the Republic of North Macedonia. The key purpose of this chapter and research is to find out the difficulties that women entrepreneurs face in their engagement, as well as the reasons that stimulate them to build up an entrepreneurial career.

2 Women Entrepreneurship in North Macedonia

Due to the fact that official data regarding women entrepreneurs are lacking, gender-based analysis will rely on data provided by surveys implemented by local or international organizations (Anggadwita et al. 2017; Fang et al. 2019; Welsh et al. 2017). It is the Global Entrepreneurship Monitor (GEM) that brings a very relevant database on women entrepreneurs from various countries. With respect to this, Sarfaraz and Faghih (2011, p. 52) state that "GEM's contribution to providing consistent cross-country information and measurement of women's entrepreneurial activity are useful tools to identify entrepreneurial dimensions and rank different countries in this field as well." The lack of official information about women entrepreneurs represents an important obstacle to trustworthy research, since a "base set of measures cannot be shown to decision-makers" (Hontz and Rotanu 2010, p. 8).

Referring to the data of the reports of GEM and according to Total Entrepreneurial Activity (TEA) index for women, women from Montenegro, Croatia, Serbia, Bosnia and Herzegovina, and Greece are keener to build up or manage personal business (Exhibit 3). The TEA index for Turkey, Slovenia, Romania, and Macedonia is around 3%. Unfortunately, data for Bulgaria and Albania are not found in these reports (Kelley et al. 2011; Allen et al. 2008). However, studies on entrepreneurship in Albania (Ramadani and Dana 2013; Dana 1996, 2010) and Bulgaria (Ramadani and Dana 2013; Dana 1999, 2010) are published.

2.1 *Characteristics of Women Entrepreneurs*

The majority of women entrepreneurs in the Republic of North Macedonia who were subject in the conducted survey are owners and managers of micro enterprises (1–9 employees). Our research through the survey showed that 39% of women deal with micro business, 28% of them have small businesses, 19% medium-sized businesses, and only 14% of them engage in larger enterprises with more than 250 employees.

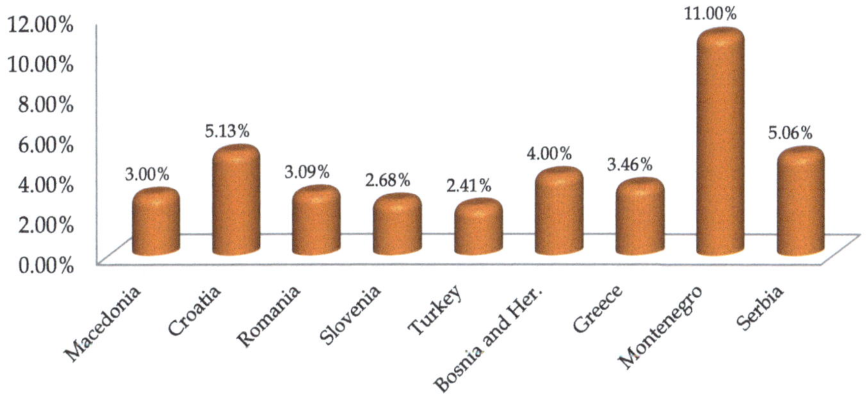

Exhibit 3 TEA index for women entrepreneurs in the Balkans' countries. Source: Based on Ramadani et al. (2015)

This research took the family status of women entrepreneurs into consideration as well. We noted that 78% of the surveyed women were married or engaged, and 84% of them had one or more children. The rest of 22% declared that they are not married or engaged, whereas 16% responded to have no children. Regarding their experience in business, 36% of them were active 3–6 years, 24% of them 7–10 years, and 17% of women entrepreneurs had 10–15 years of experience. 23% of the respondents were active in business more than 15 years, and none of the respondents had less than 2 years of experience. With regard to revenue generation, 34% generate revenues below 10,000 € and 34% generate revenues above 25,000 €. Revenues between 10,000 € and 15,000 € are generated by 18%, 15,000 € to 20,000 € are generated by 11%, and 20,000 € to 25,000 € by 3% of the respondents interviewed in the survey.

Figures from the analysis of the age when women entrepreneurs have started their businesses show that over 70% of women have gone into business before the age of 35, according to the survey of Eurochambres (2004). 15% of them have started business at the age of 36–40, whereas 14.4% of them after the age of 40. According to data we obtained, women in the Republic of North Macedonia established their own businesses at the age between 25 and 35 years. 42% of the respondents answered that they began their own business at age between 25 and 30 years, i.e., 31 and 35 years, whereas 8% thereof answered that they started their business below the age of 25, i.e., over 35 years.

The largest portion of women entrepreneurs earn a higher education degree, namely they graduate from a university, whereas 20% of women entrepreneurs complete a master's or doctoral degree, according to the research of Taylor and Newcomer (2005). Out of the total number of women entrepreneurs included in the survey, 20% of them have finished their secondary school; 35% have graduated from a university; 10% have completed 2-year university studies; 25% hold a master's degree; and 10% of respondents hold a doctoral degree in various fields, mostly in business and economics. As for the Republic of North Macedonia, 72% of

Exhibit 4 Level of education

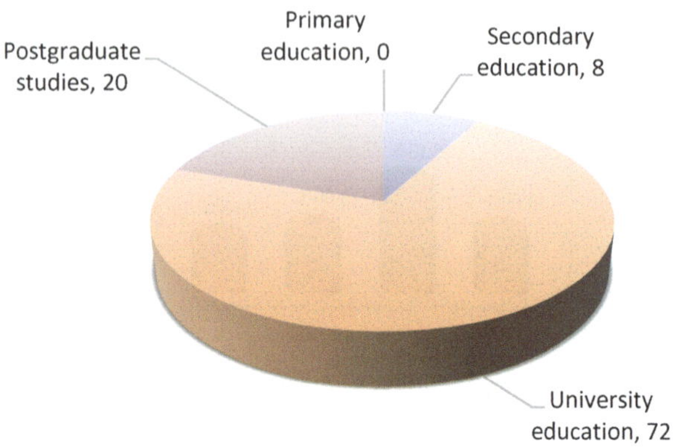

Table 1 Motives to be self-employed

Focus	Motives
The self	High need for achievement Innovativeness Ability to take calculated risks
The ethnocultural milieu	Culture Thrift Frugality Asceticism Ethnic resources
The host society	Stratification Social blockage Government assistance Occupational clustering

Source: Dana (1997, p. 54)

interviewed women entrepreneurs have graduated from a university; 20% of them have completed their master's studies; 8% have finished secondary education. None of them declared to have completed primary education only (Exhibit 4).

The motives of women to run a business are diverse. Table 1 addresses the main reasons of women entrepreneurs why they decide to enter the business world. Dana (1997) provides a broader interpretation of these motives.

No variation has been noticed in the research on the general motives to start a business in various countries or between men and women (Carter and Marlow 2007; Bennett and Dann 2000; Hisrich and Ozturk 1999). Walker and Brown (2004) underline several financial and non-financial factors as motives for women entrepreneurs to start a business. Financial factors are profit and wealth. The non-financial factors are the following: the tendency to be their own boss, ability to spare time for personal activities, the compliance of the business structure, the women entrepreneur's own values and goals, etc.

Our survey findings show that 64% of women entrepreneurs find freedom and control in the decision-making as their motive to go into business; 62% of them state it is the profit; 50% of are bound to their ambition for success; 38% of them note the

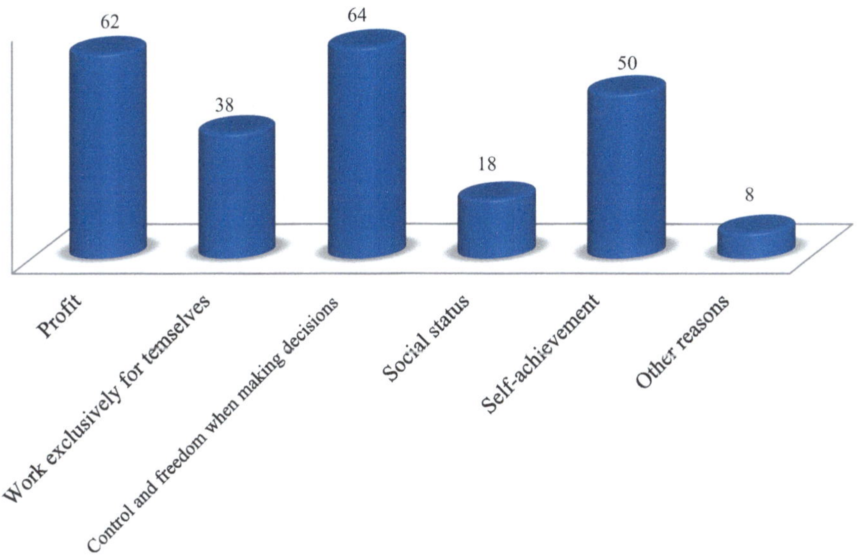

Exhibit 5 Motives for starting own business

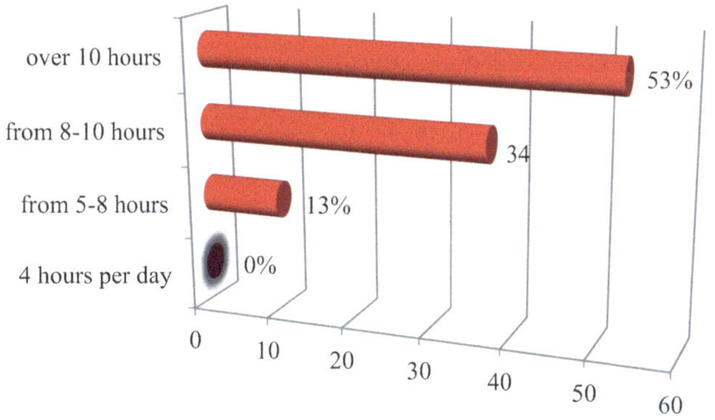

Exhibit 6 Hours dedicated to business

flexibility to be their own boss and work for themselves as the key motive to start an entrepreneurial career. Only 18% pay attention to the social status as their motive for business, while 8% of respondents declare other reasons as main motives for their business (Exhibit 5).

Lifestyle and professional commitment play an important role in the entrepreneurial world. Women entrepreneurs dedicate a substantial amount of time to their work and business. Our findings show that 53% of women entrepreneurs in North Macedonia spend 10 h a day at work; 34% of them work 8–10 h a day; 13% work 5–8 h a day. None of the respondents stated that they spend less than 4 h a day in their business (Exhibit 6).

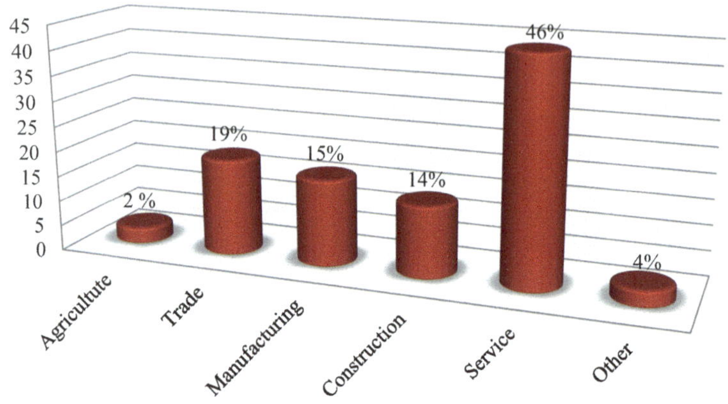

Exhibit 7 Preferred sectors

In modern times, women entrepreneurs are significantly contributing to the creation of workforce, with particular focus on new businesses (Brush 2006). The general perception on the types of businesses they set up ranges from innovative businesses such as private post offices to traditionally masculine ones like production of oil, water installation, etc. Moreover, they are also active in the services sector, such as fashion stores, travel agencies, etc. Studies reveal that women entrepreneurs mainly prefer retail, consulting, educational services, and public relations as fields for business (Franco and Winqvist 2002; Ramadani et al. 2017).

Women entrepreneurs prove to have the managerial abilities and skills to correctly evaluate the market needs through their innovative approach in providing new services or updating and upgrading the existing ones. Around 90% of businesses run by women entrepreneurs operate in the services sector; 7% of them deal with production and the rest of 3% is in finance (Hisrich and Brush 1986). Carter and Marlow (2007) noted an important increase in the number of women entrepreneurs who are dealing with traditional masculine businesses such as construction, manufacturing, and high-tech sectors. Exhibit 7 illustrates the sectors in which women entrepreneurs operate their businesses in North Macedonia. Accordingly, 46% of women entrepreneurs who were surveyed are involved in the sector of services, 19% in trade, 15% in manufacturing, 14% in construction, 2% in agriculture, and 4% in other sectors.

2.2 *Barriers and Problems*

Practical examples, followed by studies, confirm that the constant increase of self-employed women is a social and economic phenomenon. The conservative preconception on the role of women entrepreneurs should be revised and adjusted in accordance with these new circumstances (Ahl 2006; Hisrich and Ramadani 2017;

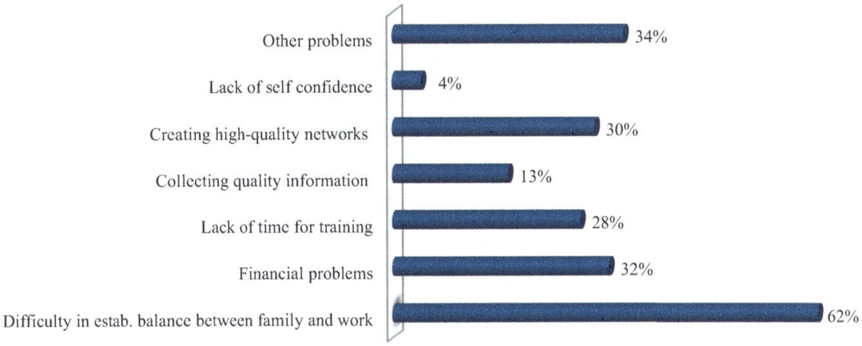

Exhibit 8 Main problems faced by women entrepreneurs

Hughes et al. 2012). In this direction, we also address the barriers for women entrepreneurs while setting up their businesses after terminating their previous professional engagement. Our research displays several barriers faced by women entrepreneurs while establishing their businesses.

The hardship in achieving balance between work and family appears to be the first barrier for women entrepreneurs in North Macedonia. 62% of the women have stated this problem as their main challenge. This finding is consistent with findings in other developing economies such as Lebanon (Jamali 2006) where patriarchal culture ascribes household and family caregiver responsibilities mainly to women, whereas in the US context women entrepreneurs tend to attain family-to-business enrichment and work–family synergies (Powell and Eddleston, 2013). In North Macedonia, 32% consider finances as their main problem, and 28% consider lack of time for improving their skills by attending seminars and trainings. The difficulties in networking with highly qualified individuals which would help the growth of their business represents a barrier for around 30% of women entrepreneurs. While 4% declared their insufficient self-confidence as a problem, 13% of them insisted that lack of valid and eligible information is their main problem. 34% noted problems different from the ones listed in the questionnaire (Exhibit 8).

2.3 Success Factors

The success of women entrepreneurs is driven by various factors. Box et al. (1995) list four factors correlated with the success of women entrepreneurs: past experience in entrepreneurial management, number of previous startups, entrepreneur's age, and scanning intensity. Hisrich et al. (1997) consider the level of education, years of experience, business skills, personal goals, and strategy for performance assessment as key factors in the success of women entrepreneurs. Fielden and Davidson (2005) evaluate the success of women entrepreneurs through two groups of factors. The first group includes "push" factors such as lack of control, lack of challenge, lack of good

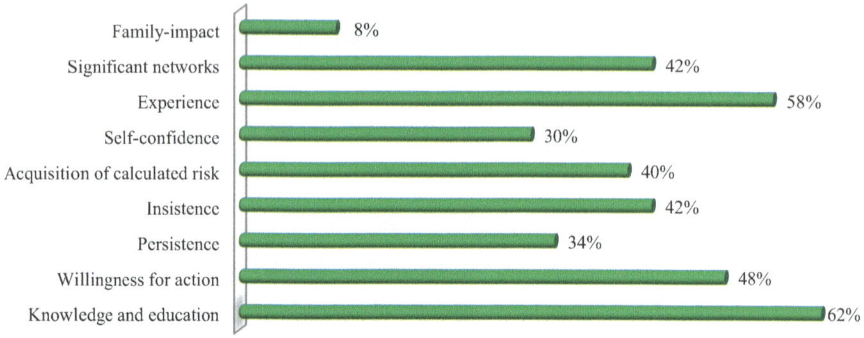

Exhibit 9 Success factors of women entrepreneurs and their businesses

example, family influence, lack of opportunities, limited education, etc. The second group includes "pull" factors such as control flexibility, independence, being an owner, financial independence, realization of personal ambitions, need of dominance, etc. While "push factors" have an influence in women's decision about their type of business, "pull" factors are related with motivators to start up a personal business (Baughn et al. 2006; Hughes 2003).

In the Republic of North Macedonia, 80% of women entrepreneurs declared that they have the ability to build quality relationships with their clients. 44% of them believe in their abilities to define goals, policies, and plans, as well as their implementation. 42% of them state that they are able to manage their finances and develop and execute ideas, 26% are able to deal with marketing, and 18% are able to manage inventory and execute specific business strategies.

Management skills and approaches have been frequent issues in women's entrepreneurial endeavors (Buttner 2001; Gardiner and Tiggemann 1999; Palalić et al. 2017). Before they actually start up the business, women entrepreneurs should carefully assess their managerial skills which have important influence on the success or failure of the business. Namely, the ability to manage is related to factors which substantially affect the success of the business of women entrepreneurs.

Among women entrepreneurs who were part of our survey, 62% of them consider their knowledge and education as the key factor in reaching successful business. The second most frequent factor noted by 58% of women entrepreneurs is the experience in the business world. Women entrepreneurs also indicate willingness to engage in specific activities with the aim to manage business more efficiently (48%), insistence and networking of contacts (42%), acquisition of calculated risk (40%), persistence (34%), self-confidence (30%), and family impact (8%) as success factors in their business (Exhibit 9).

2.4 Portraits of Successful Women Entrepreneurs

Gëzime Fejzi (Exhibit 10) was born in Gostivar, North Macedonia. She is the director and owner of "Caseificio Cesarina—Fejzi." In the 1990s, she emigrated with her family to Italy, where in 1996 they established her own business. She was awarded for successful business in Rome. Her company is operating in the dairy industry and holds an Italian license for production of cheese and mozzarella. For many years, along with her husband Nagip, she worked in Italy where they acquired the necessary knowledge, experience, and skills in the field. They decided to bring their know-how to their birthplace, Gostivar. In 2003, they opened the second manufacturing company in their hometown, Gostivar. She managed the business in Gostivar, while her husband continued working in Rome. In 2013, they closed the business in Rome and focused all forces on the business in Gostivar.

Her accomplishments as a successful woman entrepreneur are acknowledged by various institutions and organizations, such as US Embassy in Macedonia Plaque for Successful Businesswoman (2006); MCA-USAID Plaque for Successful Achievement (2006); National Council for Business and Concurrency Plaque for Successful Achievement (2006); Wine and Cheese Festival in Ohrid, North Macedonia—1st Place (2005); Ministry of Economy of North Macedonia "Zlatno Sonce" Festival—1st Place (2005); Wine and Cheese Festival in Ohrid, North Macedonia—1st Place (2004); Municipality of Gostivar Plaque for Best Company (2004); and "Em mozam, em umeam" Festival—1st Place (2004). In 2015, Gezime Fejzi established

Exhibit 10 Gezime Fejzi with her husband Nagip at "Caseificio Cesarina—Fejzi". Photo © Gezime Fejzi

Exhibit 11 Receiving an award for strengthening the cooperation between Hungary and North Macedonia women entrepreneurs. Photo © Merita Ramadani-Alimi

the Business Women Group (GGA) within the Economic Chamber of North-West Macedonia.

Valentina Taseva is a co-owner and CEO of SEMOS Education, ClearView, and Certiadria—all ICT training and certification companies. She holds a master's degree in management and a certificate in management consultancy. After more than two decades, since she has been the managing director, today SEMOS Education has an annual growth of 20%, a market share of 50%, and a very sustainable strategy for the future developments (Tašaminova 2012). During this period, she succeeded in making SEMOS Education a reputed brand in the sector of IT education in North Macedonia and border. Besides North Macedonia, SEMOS is today operating in Albania, Kosovo, Norway, Denmark, Sweden, Hungary, Italy, Estonia, Bulgaria, Romania, Croatia, and Serbia. In 2011, at the Annual Assembly and Business Forum of the European Bank for Reconstruction and Development (EBRD) held in Aspana, Kazakhstan, Valentina Taseva was awarded the first place for "Woman in Business—Excellence in the Industry." An added value to the award was the fact that she got this prize during the panel entitled "Women in Business—Meeting the Challenges," another certification of her success as a woman entrepreneur (Ramadani et al., 2015). In 2016, she received the "20 years jubilee in business—Women manager in Republic of Macedonia" award.

Merita Ramadani-Alimi (Exhibit 11) was born in Skopje, in 1980. She comes from a family with a tradition in business. After finishing her undergraduate studies at the University of "St. Cyril and Methodius" in Skopje, Merita joined

ARKOMPANI, her father's private company which dealt with agricultural goods and served as a general distributor of several goods in Macedonia, Kosovo, and Albania. In 2008, she took over the company by becoming a general manager. She is currently a CEO of DOGAN Air Conditioning Solutions, a renowned Turkish company that has been active in the market for over 30 years, specializing in designing, construction, and maintenance of all types of cooling heating systems. She is also a partner in Vardar Resources, a company that explores minerals and mining—copper and gold.

Merita has received numerous recognitions for her work: The Municipality of Çair (Skopje) awarded her with certificate of "Successful Woman" (2010). Her profile was included in a publication in Albania together with 58 other profiles of successful businesswomen (2014); received recognition as a "Successful Business-woman" from the Municipality of Gjakova/Djakovica in Kosovo (2015); became Vice President of the Women's Branch at the Economic Chamber of North-Western Macedonia; and elected by U.S. International Visitor Leadership Program (IVLP) to attend the International Women Entrepreneurship Exchange Program in the USA (2018). She provided a great contribution in creation of networks between women entrepreneurs from Macedonia, Kosovo, Albania, Serbia, and other countries.

3 Supporting Policies and Organizations for Women Entrepreneurship Promotion

A few activities oriented toward raising awareness about the role of women in the economic, political, and social life are noticed in the Republic of North Macedonia. For example, the Association of Women Organizations in Macedonia and some other nongovernmental organizations take effective actions designed to engage women in public life. In this direction, the enforcement and support of the government are crucial for the strong development of women entrepreneurship. The Republic of North Macedonia is still distant to these arrangements. Findings show that the perception of women practicing the right to work through their ideas and personal commitment makes progress day by day. The governmental assistance and initiatives provided to women are facilitating their active participation in the economy of the Republic of North Macedonia (Ramadani et al. 2015; Tašaminova 2012).

3.1 Strategy for Development of Women Entrepreneurship

In October 2018, the Government of Republic of North Macedonia (Exhibit 12) presented the Strategy for Development of Women Entrepreneurship in the Republic of North Macedonia, for the period of 2019–2023. This strategy is designed for the needs of the Ministry of Economy with the financial and technical support from GTF

Exhibit 12 The Government of the R. of North Macedonia. Photo ©Veland Ramadani

(Gender Task Force)—Sustainable Growth Initiative and in cooperation with Association of Business Women of North Macedonia.

In this regard, the Minister of Economy Mr. Kreshnik Bekteshi stated that Following the European policies for economic growth, the Ministry of Economy prepared the Strategy for Women Entrepreneurship 2019–2023 with an Action Plan. In order to implement the measures and activities foreseen in the Action Plan, the Ministry established an inter-ministerial working group composed of representatives of governmental institutions and representatives of the nongovernmental sector. Further, in accordance with the Competitiveness, Innovation and Entrepreneurship Program for 2019, the measure for Financial Support for Women Entrepreneurship was realized, where 2,500,000 denars were provided. Following the call for proposals, 38 applications were received. 60% of cost for equipment/office spaces/ introducing software solutions were subsidized for 21 companies owned and managed by women. For 2020, there is a plan for financial support for women entrepreneurship for purchasing equipment, tools and arrangement of office space (4,000,000 denars); and co-financing projects of civil society organizations for development and support of women entrepreneurship (3,000,000 denars)."

The strategy (Exhibit 13) aims at economic empowerment of women in North Macedonia by creating a favorable business environment and providing support for the development of women's entrepreneurial potential, developing existing and opening new businesses, creating new jobs, and strengthening the overall economy. The long-term goal of this strategy is to build an entrepreneurial ecosystem for the continuous development, promotion, networking, and advocacy of women entrepreneurship in the country, while the medium-term goals include improvement of business environment, opportunities, and conditions for the development of women entrepreneurship; active involvement of all concerned stakeholders in the

Exhibit 13 Structure of priorities of the Strategy 2019–2023. Source: Ministry of Economy (2019)

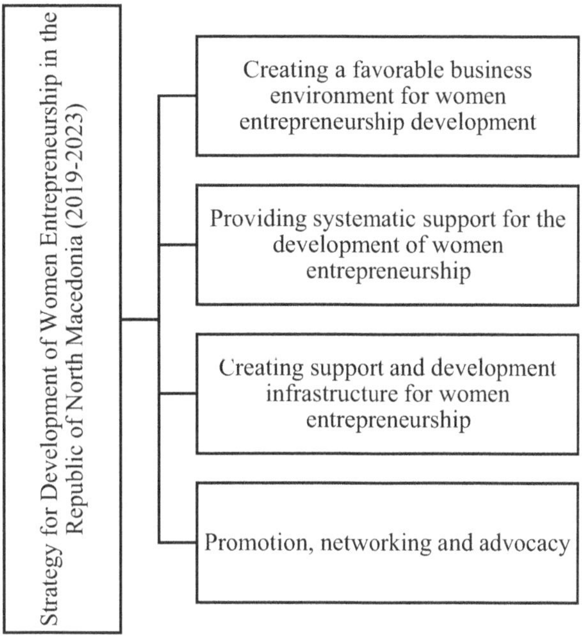

implementation of the women entrepreneurship development strategy; increase the number of women who start their own businesses; elevate the number of employees in companies established by women entrepreneurs; and raise the women employment rate in North Macedonia (Ministry of Economy 2019).

3.2 *National Council for Women Entrepreneurship*

The National Council for Women Entrepreneurship (NCWE) is the first council for women entrepreneurship and the only institution that operates at the national level in North Macedonia. This council consists of representatives from the civil sector, policy makers, and other institutions engaged in the development of women entrepreneurship.

Council activities include creating a favorable business environment for women entrepreneurs, improving the quality of the permanent networking between women entrepreneurs and civil and business organizations, increasing the availability of opportunities for adequate education of women entrepreneurs, etc.

It was created as a result of "Enhancing contribution and efficiency of women's entrepreneurship CSOs related to the EU integration reforms in the area of economic policy—WE Contribute" project (https://wecontribute.mk).

3.3 *Association of Business Women of North Macedonia*

Association of Business Women of North Macedonia (http://abw.mk/) functions as a chain for connecting women entrepreneurs at the local, regional, national, and international levels. This association has a leading role in organizing dialogue and cooperation, in order to provide support and promotion of women entrepreneurs in North Macedonia. It provides information on training, financing, and networking opportunities for women entrepreneurs in North Macedonia and region.

Valentina Disoska (Exhibit 14), the President of the Association, noted that "Women entrepreneurship is important because it opens new jobs, new perspectives in entrepreneurship and doing business and in all its forms ensures the improvement of the society. Women entrepreneurs very often achieve sustainable growth, not only by generating profits, but also by raising the quality of life for their families, employees, and the community. Women entrepreneurs with their abilities are indispensable drivers of society and should be supported with equal opportunities to participate in economic life in line with their abilities."

3.4 *Business Women Group (GGA)*

Business Women Group (GGA) was created in 2015 within the Economic Chamber of North-West Macedonia in order to promote and develop entrepreneurship among women from this part of the country. The GGA's main objective is strengthening the position of women in society, encouraging and promoting women entrepreneur

Exhibit 14 Valentina Disoska, the President of Association of Business Women of North Macedonia. Photo © Valentina Disoska

Exhibit 15 GGA's members participating in a conference on women entrepreneurship at South-East European University, Skopje North Macedonia. Photo © Gezime Fejzi

activities, sharing experiences, and networking (https://oemvp.org/category/grupacionet/grupacioni-i-grave-afarise/). This group have organized several meetings and events in cooperation with other groups and associations within the region, especially from Kosovo and Albania (Exhibit 15).

4 Toward the Future

Despite limited access to data and qualitative information on women entrepreneurs, research leads to the conclusion that women are rising to become a relevant factor for the economy across countries (e.g., Brush 2006; Brush and Cooper 2012; Brush and Greene 2015). They usually reach to the managerial positions earlier than their 30s and remain active in their businesses for about 10–15 years. The potential for profit, willingness to work for themselves, and aspiration for personal accomplishment and successful careers appear to be their main motives to engage in business. These results are consistent with those in the US context where the primary entrepreneurial motives among women are self-realization, financial success, status, and autonomy within the domain of expectancy theory (Manolova et al. 2008). Moreover, North Macedonian women entrepreneurs are very committed to their businesses, as the survey shows that they work more than 10 h a day.

The primary managerial qualities among the women entrepreneurs in North Macedonia are their capacity to establish stable communication with individuals, develop ideas, and define goals, plans, and policies, followed by their successful execution. Lastly, when addressing the problems in the business, women entrepreneurs in North Macedonia consider lack of sufficient finances, challenges in work–family balance, time limitations in improving their qualifications and skills by participating in trainings and programs, etc. as their main difficulties in entrepreneurial endeavors. Our findings demonstrate that women need a qualitative education and a compatible degree, knowledge and skills, and the courage in order to be proactively (not only reactively) involved in business activities. In other words, experience, persistence, perseverance, and self-confidence are necessary features which can play a significant role in the success of new ventures, including those of women entrepreneurs.

Every economic and social development is related to entrepreneurship as the foundation. Thus, we target the development of entrepreneurship and recommend related public policy and initiatives. In this direction, we consider that women entrepreneurs play a crucial rule in the business world and represent an initial resource.

Women entrepreneurs require support in their efforts to start up and grow businesses, respectively. In this direction, we consider that the recommendations given below will lead to the further development and progress of women entrepreneurs in the Republic of North Macedonia (which may also be applicable to the other developing economies around the world):

- *Providing access to quality financing sources.* Lack of finances is the main difficulty faced by women entrepreneurs. Due to the concern for risk, there is a hesitation by investors or banks to support startups of women entrepreneurs. Inevitably, gender-related under-capitalization can result in long-term underperformances in new ventures (Jamali 2006). Even in developed economies such as in the USA, research draws attention to the gendered aspect of entrepreneurial financing and gender biases that prevent women from equal opportunity for being funded and rewarded for their businesses' viability and their commitment, and where lenders charge female sole proprietorships higher than male sole proprietorships although women have made progress in gaining access to bank financing like men and gender-based differential treatment of business borrowers has been illegal for a long time (Eddleston et al. 2016; Wu and Chua 2012). Therefore, the implementation of programs that are directly oriented toward advancing the financial environment and offering financial instruments that will help women in building up their businesses is a must.
- *Providing useful training and educational programs.* One of the key incentives should be to encourage women entrepreneurs to build their business careers, as entrepreneurship creates the foundations for competitiveness and innovation in a country. They should get a competent education and should be motivated to engage in their own business and develop their careers in entrepreneurship. European Network of Mentors for Women Entrepreneurs is implementing a project in this context, particularly focusing on the support for women entrepreneurship. The goal of this program is creating a network of mentors for women entrepreneurs at the national level and providing support and help to women in

meeting their challenges at the startup phase of their businesses. Additionally, the project intends to improve the development of women entrepreneurship in North Macedonia by taking into consideration the particular characteristics of businesses women who are involved in.

- *Supporting micro-initiatives*. Around 40% of the business entrepreneurs included in the survey are engaged in micro businesses. The limitations in the business size and availability of finances have caused difficulties for their businesses. As also stated above, it is a crucial challenge to have access to the fundamental finances to establish a new business. Another challenge is their struggle to follow the recent trends and novelties on the new ICT and implement it in their business. As a result, it is decisively important that women entrepreneurs get the relevant assistance and support through diverse financial instruments, fewer bureaucratic procedures, and more networking opportunities in order to overcome their challenges.
- *Creating databases and policies for women entrepreneurship*. The creation of a database of businesses run by women entrepreneurs is a precondition for the development of effective support policies and strategies for promotion of women entrepreneurship as well as facilitation of their networking. In this regard, gender-based policies oriented toward advancing the economic status of women and formulation of special educational programs and training for women entrepreneurs are very much needed.

References

Ahl H (2006) Why research on women entrepreneurs needs new directions. Entrep Theory Pract 30 (5):595–621

Allen EI, Elam A, Langowitz N, Dean M (2008) 2007 report on women entrepreneurship. Babson College, Wellesley, MA

Anggadwita G, Ramadani V, Alamanda DT, Ratten V, Hashani M (2017) Entrepreneurial intentions from an Islamic perspective: a study of Muslim entrepreneurs in Indonesia. Int J Entrep Small Bus 31(2):165–179

Baughn C, Chua BL, Neupert K (2006) The normative context for women's participation in entrepreneurship: a multi-country study. Entrep Theory Pract 30(5):687–708

Bennett R, Dann S (2000) The changing experience of Australian female entrepreneurs. Gend Work Organ 7(2):75–83

Box TW, Beisel JL, Watts LR (1995) Thai entrepreneurs: an empirical investigation of individual differences, background and scanning behaviour. Acad Entrep J 1(1):18–25

Brush CG (2006) Women entrepreneurs: a research overview. In: The Oxford handbook of entrepreneurship. Oxford University Press, Oxford

Brush CG, Cooper SY (2012) Female entrepreneurship and economic development: an international perspective. Entrep Reg Dev 24(1–2):1–6

Brush CG, Greene PG (2015) Women's entrepreneurship. In: Wiley Encyclopedia of management. Wiley, Boca Raton, NJ, pp 1–5

Buttner EH (2001) Examining female entrepreneurs' management style: an application of a relational frame. J Bus Ethics 29(3):253–269

Carter S, Marlow S (2007) Female entrepreneurship: theoretical perspectives and empirical evidence. In: Carter MN, Henry C, O'Cinneide B, Johnston K (eds) Female entrepreneurship: implications for education, training and policy. Routledge, Abington
Dana L-P (1996) Albania in the twilight zone: the Perseritje model and its impact on small business. J Small Bus Manag 34(1):64–70
Dana L-P (1997) The origins of self-employment in ethnocultural communities: distinguishing between orthodox entrepreneurship and reactionary enterprise. Can J Adm Sci 14(1):52–68
Dana L-P (1999) Bulgaria at the crossroads of entrepreneurship. J Euromarketing 8(4):27–50
Dana L-P (2010) When economies change hands: a survey of entrepreneurship in the emerging Markets of Europe from the Balkans to the Baltic States. Routledge, New York
Eddleston KA, Ladge JJ, Mitteness C, Balachandra L (2016) Do you see what I see? Signaling effects of gender and firm characteristics on financing entrepreneurial ventures. Entrep Theory Pract 40(3):489–514
Eurochambres (2004) Women in business and in decision-making: a survey on women entrepreneurs. Eurochambres, Brussels
Fang HC, Memili E, Buttner EH (2019) Women family members in family business: performance implications. Acad Manag Proc 2019(1):11841
Fielden SL, Davidson JM (2005) The way forward for women small business owners. In: Fielden SL, Davidson JM (eds) International handbook of women and small business entrepreneurship. Edward Elgar, Cheltenham
Franco A, Winqvist K (2002) The entrepreneurial gap between women and men. Eurostat, Brussels
Gardiner M, Tiggemann M (1999) Gender differences in leadership style, job stress and mental health in male- and female-dominated industries. J Occup Org Psychol 72(3):301–315
Hisrich RD, Brush GC (1986) The woman entrepreneur: starting, financing and managing a successful new business. Lexington Books, Lexington, MA
Hisrich RD, Ozturk S (1999) Women entrepreneurs in a developing economy. J Manag Dev 18 (2):114–124
Hisrich RD, Ramadani V (2017) Effective entrepreneurial management. Springer, Cham
Hisrich RD, Brush CG, Good D, DeSouza G (1997) Performance in entrepreneurial ventures: does gender matter? Frontiers of entrepreneurship research. Babson College, Wellesley, MA
Hontz E, Rotanu C (2010) Women's business associations from around the world: central and Eastern Europe. Center for International Private Enterprise, Washington, DC
Hughes KD (2003) Pushed or pulled: women's entry into self-employment and small business ownership. Gend Work Organ 10(4):433–454
Hughes KD, Jennings JE, Brush C, Carter S, Welter F (2012) Extending women's entrepreneurship research in new directions. Entrep Theory Pract 36(3):429–442
Jamali D (2006) Constraints and opportunities facing woman entrepreneurs in developing countries: a relational perspective. Gend Manag Int J 24(4):232–251
Jennings JE, Brush CG (2013) Research on women entrepreneurs: challenges to (and from) the broader entrepreneurship literature? Acad Manag Ann 7(1):663–715
Kelley JD, Brush DG, Greene GP, Litovsky Y (2011) 2010 report: women entrepreneurs worldwide. Babson College, Wellesley, MA
Manolova TS, Brush CG, Edelman LF (2008) What do women entrepreneurs want? Strateg Chang 17:69–82
Ministry of Economy (2019) Strategy for development of women entrepreneurship in the Republic of North Macedonia 2019–2023. Government of North Macedonia, Skopje
OECD (2004) Women's entrepreneurship: issues and policies. OECD Publishing, Paris
Palalić R, Ramadani V, Dana LP, Ratten V (2017) Gender entrepreneurial leadership in family businesses: a case study from Bosnia and Herzegovina. In: Ratten V et al (eds) Women entrepreneurship in family business. Routledge, London, pp 208–226
Powell GN, Eddleston KA (2013) Linking family-to-business enrichment and support to entrepreneurial success: do female and male entrepreneurs experience different outcomes? J Bus Ventur 28(2):261–280

Ramadani V, Dana L-P (2013) The state of entrepreneurship in the Balkans: evidence from selected countries (in English). In: Ramadani V, Schneider CR (eds) Entrepreneurship in the Balkans: diversity, support and prospects. Springer, Heidelberg, pp 217–250

Ramadani V, Dana L-P, Gërguri S, Tašaminova T (2013) Women entrepreneurs in the Republic of Macedonia: waiting for directions. Int J Entrep Small Bus 19(1):95–121

Ramadani V, Dana L-P, Gërguri-Rashiti S, Abazi-Alili T (2015) The profile of female entrepreneurs in the Republic of Macedonia. In: Ramadani V, Gërguri-Rashiti S, Fayolle A (eds) Female entrepreneurship in transition economies: trends and challenges. Palgrave Macmillan, London, pp 159–180

Ramadani V, Dana L-P, Sadiku-Dushi N, Ratten V, Welsh DHB (2017) Decision-making challenges of women entrepreneurs in the family business succession process. J Enterp Cult 24 (4):411–439

Ramadani V, Rexhepi G, Dana L-P, Gerguri-Rashiti S, Ratten V (2018) Entrepreneurship in Macedonia. In: Palalić R, Dana L-P, Ramadani V (eds) Entrepreneurship in former Yugoslavia: diversity, institutional constraints and prospects. Springer, Cham

Sarfaraz L, Faghih N (2011) Women's entrepreneurship in Iran: a GEM based data evidence. J Glob Entrep Res 1(1):45–57

State Statistical Office of Republic of North Macedonia (2019a) Macedonia in figures. Government of Republic of Macedonia, Skopje

State Statistical Office of Republic of North Macedonia (2019b) Women and men in North Macedonia. State Statistical Office, Skopje, North Macedonia

State Statistical Office of the Republic of North Macedonia (2016) Structural business statistics, press release 6.1.16.17. Government of Republic of Macedonia, Skopje

Tašaminova T (2012) Women entrepreneurs in Macedonia: situation, problems and perspectives. Master Thesis, South-East European University, Tetovo

Taylor RS, Newcomer DJ (2005) Characteristics of women small business owners. In: Fielden SL, Davidson JM (eds) International handbook of women and small business entrepreneurship. Edward Elgar Publishing Limited, Cheltenham

Walker E, Brown A (2004) What success factors are important to small business owners? Int Small Bus J 22(6):577–594

Welsh DHB, Kaciak E, Memili E, Zhou Q (2017) Work-family balance and marketing capabilities as determinants of Chinese women entrepreneurs' firm performance. J Glob Mark 30 (3):174–191

Wu Z, Chua JH (2012) Second–order gender effects: the case of US small business borrowing cost. Entrep Theory Pract 36(3):443–463

Veland Ramadani is Professor at South East European University, the Republic of North Macedonia, where he teaches both undergraduate and postgraduate courses in entrepreneurship and small business management. His research interests include entrepreneurship, small business management, and family businesses. He authored or coauthored around 120 research articles, 11 textbooks, and 14 edited books. Dr. Ramadani is a Chief Editor of *Journal of Enterprising Communities: People and Places in the Global Economy* (JEC). In 2017, he was appointed as a member of the Supervisory Board of Development Bank of North Macedonia, where for 10 months served as an acting Chief Operating Officer (COO). Dr. Ramadani received the Award for Excellence 2016—Outstanding Paper by Emerald Group Publishing. His last book is *Organizational Mindset of Entrepreneurship*, published by Springer.

Esra Memili is an Associate Professor of Entrepreneurship and Dean's Notable Scholar at the Bryan School of Business and Economics, University of North Carolina-Greensboro. She has accepted and/or published manuscripts in *Entrepreneurship Theory and Practice*, *Global Strategy Journal*, *Long Range Planning*, *Family Business Review*, *Journal of Small Business Management*, *Journal of Family Business Strategy*, and *Small Business Economics*. She is an Associate Editor of *Journal of Family Business Strategy* and an ERB member of *Journal of Management Studies*, *Family Business Review*, *Journal of Leadership and Organizational Studies*, and other business journals.

Léo-Paul Dana is Professor at Dalhousie University in Canada. A graduate of McGill University and HEC-Montreal, he has served as Professor and President of the Scientific Council at Montpellier Business School and was formerly Marie Curie Fellow at Princeton University and Visiting Professor at INSEAD. He has published extensively in a variety of journals including *Entrepreneurship & Regional Development, Entrepreneurship: Theory & Practice, International Business Review, International Small Business Journal, Journal of Business Research, Journal of Small Business Management, Journal of World Business, Small Business Economics,* and *Technological Forecasting & Social Change.*

Visar Ramadani is Secretary General of International Balkan University, North Macedonia. He is LL.M. candidate in the field of international law and international relations. He has participated in several national and international conferences, workshops, and seminars. Ramadani has attended study visits in the UK, France, Turkey, Slovakia, and Romania. His areas of interest are international relations, educational legislation, European affairs, labor policies, etc.

Women's Entrepreneurship in Serbia

Maja Ivanović-Đukić and Saša Petković

Abstract The position of women in Serbia on the labor market is very unfavorable, so they represent a traditionally discriminated social group. One way to improve the position of women in society in Serbia is to encourage self-employment and the development of women entrepreneurship. Many measures have been implemented in order to develop women entrepreneurship in Serbia. This has led to the development of women entrepreneurship in Serbia, but it is developing very slowly, due to the influence of several factors. The subject of this chapter was to explain the genesis of the development of women entrepreneurship in Serbia and to analyze the limiting and incentive influencing factors of the development of women entrepreneurship in Serbia. Our research has shown that motives that have a significant impact on women in Serbia to start their own business are the need for higher earnings, necessity (unemployment), need for independence in work and autonomy, childcare, and need to provide a better future for the children. The key restrictions on women entrepreneurship in Serbia are lack of one's own capital, lack of managerial knowledge and experience, lack of knowledge of the nature of business, childcare, and responsibilities in the home and the family.

1 Introduction

Entrepreneurial activity is becoming one of the key driving forces of the economic development of the Republic of Serbia (Petković and Ivanović Đukić 2018). At the same time, small and medium-sized enterprises and entrepreneurs (SMEs), as forms of individual entrepreneurial activity manifestation, play an increasingly important

M. Ivanović-Đukić (✉)
Faculty of Economics, University of Niš, Niš, Serbia
e-mail: maja.djukic@eknfak.ni.ac.rs

S. Petković
Faculty of Economics, University of Banja Luka, Banja Luka, Bosnia and Herzegovina
e-mail: sasa.petkovic@ef.unibl.org

R. Palalić et al. (eds.), *Women's Entrepreneurship in Former Yugoslavia*,
Contributions to Management Science,
https://doi.org/10.1007/978-3-030-45253-7_7

role in its economic flows. Particularly important role is played by small women-owned enterprises. These enterprises, in addition to contributing to job creation and economic growth, play an important role in solving social problems and eliminating gender inequalities. Establishing women-owned enterprises encourages the social inclusion of women in economic flows, leads to the breakdown of established cultural clichés that allow discrimination against women, and generally contributes to the increase of gender equality (Carter 2000). At the same time, their presence leads to an increase in the diversity of entrepreneurship as an economic process (Verheul et al. 2006). Women and men entrepreneurs differ significantly on the basis of their personal and business profile that affects the choice of the sector in which they start and develop their businesses, characteristics of products and services they provide, as well as business goals and organizational structure they build in order to achieve these goals. Diversity of products, processes, and ways of organizing their businesses provide more choices for consumers, leading to higher quality of entrepreneurship (Zwan et al. 2012). For these reasons, Serbia, like most other countries in the world, encourages the development of women entrepreneurship and contributes to the improvement of the competitiveness of women-owned small enterprises through various forms of support (Popović-Pantić 2014).

The implementation of the abovementioned measures had led to the fact that the number of small enterprises and entrepreneurial businesses owned by women in Serbia has been increasing gradually since 2007 (Babović 2012). However, their share in total economic activity is still significantly lower compared to the share of SMEs owned by men. Also, the development of women entrepreneurship in Serbia is much slower compared to the EU average (Popović-Pantić 2014).

The slow development of women entrepreneurship in Serbia is influenced by a large number of factors. A certain group of factors, such as the high level of unemployment of women, the need for flexible working hours, the need for self-realization and personal development, and the like, stimulates and encourages women in Serbia to start their own businesses. But, on the other hand, there are a large number of factors (problems in securing the initial capital, a large number of family obligations, lack of freedom and self-confidence, etc.) which discourage women from self-employment and entrepreneurship (Babović 2012). In order to propose measures that can lead to faster development of women entrepreneurship in Serbia, it is necessary to identify incentive factors that have the greatest positive impact on the decision of women in Serbia to start their own businesses and the factors that have the most discouraging influence. The subject of this chapter is to explain the genesis of the development of women entrepreneurship in Serbia and to analyze the limiting and incentive influencing factors of the development of women entrepreneurship in Serbia. The goal of the research is to identify the factors that have the greatest positive and negative impact on the development of women entrepreneurship in Serbia and to propose measures whose implementation can influence the faster development of women entrepreneurship in Serbia in the future.

In this chapter, we will first explain the position of women in the labor market in Serbia through history and show the development of women entrepreneurship in Serbia. Then we will analyze the factors that act as incentive and limiting to the development of women entrepreneurship in Serbia. In the last part of the chapter, we will examine the influence of these factors on the women's preference for entrepreneurship, based on primarily conducted empirical research. In conclusion, on the basis of the obtained results, we will provide recommendations for economic policy makers and potential women entrepreneurs in Serbia.

2 Position of Women in Society in Serbia Throughout History

Women in Serbia are traditionally discriminated social group, which is largely the result of a long-standing belief about the position and role of women in the family and society and the prevailing concept of hegemonic masculinity and gender inequality (Hugson 2018). Ever since the founding of the Serbian state, the organization of work was such that the role of a husband and father who provides livelihood and creates a reputation in the social community was reserved for the man, and the role of a woman is to organize a household, take care of children, and contribute to the reputation by her appearance and behavior (Zlatkov Cvetković 2015).

The family was also organized according to the model of the father—provider and mother—housewife. In relations between the genders, almost nothing has changed during the Middle Ages. The man remained the "head of the family," who works for an employer or in his company and provides the means of living, and the wife is a parent and housewife. This gender role and division of tasks was supported by religion, thanks to which it passed from one generation to another. This would not be so bad, if the work of women was not neglected. They performed a large amount of work in the family, which was not paid, so their work was not visible; it was not presented in the form of money; it was implicit in itself. Even when they worked with employers for money, women were paid less for the same job than men. During the eighteenth and nineteenth century with industrial revolution women began to work in factories but were paid less than their male counterparts (Blagojević 2006). The explanation for this was the weaker physical strength of women, because at the lower level of technological development there was a large share of manual labor.

> However, for jobs that did not require great physical strength, women were paid less. Lower wages for the same jobs in all branches were justified by the thesis that women were intellectually inferior, overly emotional, irrational, unstable and unpredictable, and that they were more interested in maternity and family than in work. All this speaks about the great discrimination of women in Serbia that has been present for centuries (Gudac-Dodić 2010).

With the increase of industrialization in Serbia, in the early twentieth century, there is a transition of the population from the village to the cities. Following their husbands, women and their families came to towns and began to work as hired laborers or to offer their own services (most often in the domain of traditionally "women's tasks" such as laundry, tailoring and sewing, etc.) (Vučetić 2007). However, even in that period the position and role of women did not change significantly. Women, apart from neglecting their work and role in the family, did not have the right to vote, and very few of them had the opportunity for any kind of education (a large percentage of women was illiterate) (Aritonović 2009).

After the Second World War, the position of women in Serbia has been formally equalized with the position of men. The Constitution of FPRY[1] guaranteed equality for women. As a result, women received the right to vote, older women began learning how to write and read, and the position of girls in education was equalized with the position of boys.[2] What additionally contributed to this were scientific and technological achievements that enabled women to plan the time they devoted to their careers and maternity, which primarily affected the level of education they had achieved, as well as the expectations related to business and public life. The achieved victory, however, did not ensure real gender equality, which has not been realized to date (Gudac-Dodić 2006).

The acquisition of the right to employment and equal participation in social life has not liberated women in Serbia from their previous responsibilities so far, so they obtained the right to employment and equal obligations with men at work, but they retained all other responsibilities in the home and the family. According to the results of the empirical research carried out in 1997 (Blagojević 1997), women perform most of the household work: they prepare food in 78.2% of cases, wash dishes in 80.8% of cases, go to grocery on a daily basis in 47.5% of cases, do the laundry and ironing in 93.6% of cases, care for sick family members in 38.9% of cases, and care for parents in 27% of cases.

This situation in Serbia has not changed significantly until today. The fact is that even today the largest number of house chores are performed by women, regardless of whether they are employed or not. In theory, this phenomenon is called the "double burden" of employed women. The housework is also considered a marginal form of work in the modern world: women—housewives do not enjoy some rights and privileges of employees even today; the adverse impact of such status on their employment prospects, economic independence, and civil rights is ignored; the work they perform is called "work from love," and is actually a combination of everyday housework, a complex "emotional work" with children, and care of the elderly (Gudac-Dodić 2010).

---

[1]FPRY – Federal People's Republic of Yugoslavia. After the Second World War, the Federal People's Republic of Yugoslavia (FPRY) was declared of which Slovenia (as well as Serbia, author's comment) was a constituent part. In 1963, the FPRY was renamed the Socialist Federal Republic of Yugoslavia (SFRY) (Source: http://www.slovenia.si/slovenia/history/the-federal-yugo slavia/,retrieved on May 1, 2019.

[2]Constitution of the Federal People's Republic of Yugoslavia. Chap. 5. Rights and duties of citizens. Article 24. Belgrade: Official Gazette FPRY, 1946.

> Although women continue to have a high participation in performing tasks such as: cooking and preparing food, house cleaning, washing and maintaining clothes, the share of the answer "equally" is growing. Especially encouraging is a large share of the answers "together", referring to the performing of tasks such as: purchasing food and other household items, paying home bills, but also taking care of elderly parents and ill and dependent household members. Car maintenance and home repairs remain the domain of male activities, while garden and courtyard tasks are shared equally (Hugson 2018, p. 57).

"In this division, women remain in the sphere of private, and men in the sphere of public life. The perception of a woman shaped by her role in the private sphere continually marginalizes a woman when it comes to acquiring and exercising her civil rights" (Gudac-Dodić 2010). Adding to this the fact that employers in Serbia prefer to opt for men when they are able to choose between a woman and a man due to their responsibilities to children (because they expect a woman to use sick leave or leave a job due to the birth of children or their illness, while a man, if he has the family and is expecting a child, will not leave the job at any cost in order to support the family), while retaining traditional beliefs that women are intellectually inferior, overly emotional, irrational, unstable, and unpredictable, it can be concluded that the position of women in Serbia in the labor market is still less favorable compared to men (Babović 2008). This is confirmed by the data of the Statistical Office of the Republic of Serbia (2017). They show that the rate of employed women in Serbia is 16% lower than employed men (42% of women, 58% of men), and the rate of self-employed women is twice lower than the rate of self-employed men (aged 15–64 years 29% of men and 14% of women). Women in Serbia are much less likely to appear in the position of the holder of the holding than men. At the level of entire Serbia, they are represented by only 17.3% among the holders of the holdings, although they perform a far greater percentage of agricultural activities on the holding. Due to the large number of responsibilities toward children and house tasks, women most often work in areas with more flexible working hours, such as education, health care, social work, etc. On the other hand, women more rarely work at workplaces with a changeable beginning and end of working hours, because it is harder for them to coordinate their work at the workplace with household responsibilities and family care.

On average, women work more than 4 h a day on unpaid housework, while on weekends women spend more time on unpaid tasks than men do throughout the entire week. In addition to the official data included in the statistics, there are even more worrying facts that point to the discrimination of women in Serbia in the field of employment and work.

> When applying for the job and during employment, women experience numerous sexual harassments, blackmail and abuse; they are the first on the layoff list and the last on the list of candidates for promotion. Women are more often denied job offers on the grounds that it is a "man's job" or because of their age, and it is not uncommon for women to get fired after using maternity leave. Particularly exposed to discrimination are women in reproductive age, women with underage children, elderly women, young women, Roma women, women with disabilities, women of other nationalities (Zlatkov Cvetković 2015).

> The problems of employed women are reflected in discrimination in the performance of managerial and the most paid jobs. Women in Serbia occupy only a quarter, i.e. 25.8% of the highest decision-making positions in companies. Existence of the so-called "glass ceiling", segregation of occupations to "male", more paid and more prestigious, and "female", less paid and less prestigious, massive female work "off the books", high concentration of female workforce in lower paid jobs, sexual harassment and the like are additional facts that point to the difficult position of women in the Serbian labor market. Unemployment, low pay and job insecurity affect their unfavorable negotiating positions, as well as delaying the founding of a family and birth, which adversely affects the population development of Serbia (Stojanović-Jovanović and Jovanović 2015).

Therefore, all indicators of activity, employment, and unemployment of women in Serbia are much more unfavorable compared to men, and the position of women on the labor market is very difficult. One way to improve the position of women in society is to encourage self-employment and the development of women entrepreneurship.

3 Development of Women Entrepreneurship in Serbia

There are different views among authors and a large number of different definitions in the literature about what is considered as entrepreneurship. The classic approach to entrepreneurship refers to the application of innovative solutions for the establishment of new enterprises (individual entrepreneurship) or the innovation of the business of existing enterprises (corporate entrepreneurship) (Ivanović-Đukić and Radosavljević 2018). In this sense, entrepreneurs imply individuals who introduce radical innovations that include the introduction of brand-new products, the use of new raw materials, the use of new forms of organization in newly founded or existing enterprises, and new ways of market appearance (Schumpeter 1947). On the other hand, there is a concept implying that entrepreneurship is every form of starting a new business (Gartner 1989a). In this chapter, the second concept will be adopted, according to which the women entrepreneurship and women entrepreneurs will be defined. Below we will present a wide range of definitions of women entrepreneurship.

The term women entrepreneurship indicates that a set of activities related to the establishment of an enterprise, the acquisition of ownership or part of the ownership of the enterprise, and the management of the established enterprise are performed by women (Aidis 2002). Women entrepreneurs include women who have founded a company to achieve profit and growth, including women owners of small businesses who have also launched their business for achieving personal ambitions, where the business is the main source of income (Bennett and Dann 2000). Women entrepreneurs are women who own more than 50% of the ownership of the company (regardless of the way in which they acquired the ownership), who are actively involved in the company's operations as managers, and who create employment for themselves and for others (Popović-Pantić 2014).

Women entrepreneurship does not significantly differ from other forms of entrepreneurial activity, nor from entrepreneurial activity of men. This concept has been introduced and it has been promoted and supported in various ways, in order to increase the participation of women in overall entrepreneurial activity, to ensure gender equality, and to improve the position of women in society (Stefanović et al. 2015).

Women entrepreneurship in the territory of Serbia, as well as other countries of the former Yugoslavia, started to be more significantly addressed several years after the breakup of Yugoslavia and the end of war. By signing various documents and contracts with international and European institutions, taking over the obligations under the Stabilization and Association Agreement with the European Union, activities on harmonization of legislation and institutional restructuring of public administration have been intensified. By implementing various projects by international organizations, which have respect for human rights and freedoms and gender equality in the focus of their action, projects of economic empowerment of women have also emerged. These projects, inter alia, influenced the launching of women's businesses by awarding grants, the establishment of nongovernmental organizations that bring women together, the regional integration of women entrepreneurs, the cooperation of individual regions to use the pre-accession funds of the European Union, and the like. However, due to the lack of coordinated action, more serious effects did not occur. So, the development of women entrepreneurship in Serbia has begun only since 2007 (Babović 2012) (Exhibit 1).

Exhibit 1 Founder and owners of Aleksic Winery: Maja Aleksić-Ilić, Dragana Janjić, Marija Aleksić, photo © 2017 Maja Aleksić-Ilić

The development of women entrepreneurship in Serbia in this period was contributed by the improvement of the institutional framework for the development of entrepreneurship and the adoption of numerous documents with the aim to increase gender equality. First of all, certain institutions that provide different forms of support to SMEs have been developed (SIEPA, Agency for the Development of SMEs, etc.). Also, various forms of incentives for entrepreneurship development and self-employment have been provided (grants from the National Employment Service, startup loans from the Development Fund, education, training, etc.).

In addition, a number of strategic documents have been adopted. At the beginning of 2009, the National Strategy for Improving the Position of Women and Promoting Gender Equality was adopted in the Republic of Serbia. In December 2009, the Law on Gender Equality was adopted that stipulates that everyone is obliged to respect the equal participation of women and men in all areas of the public and private sectors, in accordance with generally accepted rules of international law, ratified by international agreements, the Constitution of the Republic of Serbia and laws (Nikolić-Ristanović et al. 2012).

> In 2016, a new National Strategy for Gender Equality for the period from 2016 to 2020 was adopted. The goals of the strategy are: changed gender patterns and improved gender equality culture, increased equality of women and men by applying equal opportunities policies, systemic introduction of gender perspective in the adoption, implementation and monitoring of public policies. (Vrbanac 2018)

However, none of the listed strategic documents, as well as undertaken initiatives, have been accompanied by sufficient integration of the elements of the gender perspective and specific needs of women entrepreneurs and the problems they encounter when establishing and developing the business. As a result, we have a very slow development of women entrepreneurship in Serbia. According to Babović (2012), the share of companies and shops owned by women was only 26%, while the share of men in entrepreneurial activity amounts to almost three-quarters. On the other hand, the percentage of closed enterprises is higher among women than among men, especially during the first 5 years of the startup—47% of those owned and managed by women as opposed to 38% of those owned and managed by men (Popović-Pantić 2014).

Gender differences in the characteristics of entrepreneurship are also reflected in the sectoral structure, the way of starting a business, the age of women entrepreneurs and enterprises, etc.

First of all, what is characteristic for women entrepreneurship is that it is much more concentrated in the service sector (80.4% of shops and companies of women entrepreneurs are in the service sector), while the share of men entrepreneurs in this sector is smaller (shops and SMEs owned by men participate with 19.6% in the service sector) (Babović 2012, p. 8). Within the service sector itself, most women's enterprises are in the field of personal services (beauty salons: cosmetic and hairdressing, health services, education, intellectual services, retail, mediation, tailoring, laundry, hygiene, food preparation, and the like) (Popović-Pantić 2014) Also, women in the Republic of Serbia start to get involved in entrepreneurship much later than men, they have less entrepreneurial experience, they more often choose simpler legal forms (mostly entrepreneurial shops, rather than companies), and they work independently (in the form of a proprietorship) (Babović 2012, p. 8).

4 Factors That Encourage and Limit the Entrepreneurial Activity of Women in Serbia

The development of entrepreneurial activities of women can be influenced by a large number of incentive and limiting factors. In the following lines, we will classify and explain the influence of the most important incentive and limiting factors for the development of women entrepreneurship in Serbia.

4.1 Incentives for the Development of Women Entrepreneurship in Serbia

Previous research shows that key drivers of entrepreneurial activity are providing income, increasing capital, acquiring different material values (Poggesi et al. 2015), the need for success (self-realization), the need for independence and autonomy (to be their own boss), control over their own destiny, gaining status in society, etc. (Sloka et al. 2014). In some of the abovementioned incentives for entrepreneurial activity, there are no significant gender differences, while for certain factors, the gender significantly determines the dominant motivation factor for entrepreneurship. For example, research shows that autonomy and independence (e.g., the ability to independently make business decisions, personal freedom, and security) (Leszczyński 2014) and the need to gain wealth (increase revenue and profits, provide a more comfortable life, increase earnings, maximize business growth rates) (Lewis 2013; Sloka et al. 2014) are equally important motivating factors for both sexes to become entrepreneurs, and especially in national cultures dominated by individualism.

In contrast, gaining status in society and prestige (to gain public recognition, to prove oneself in the profession) are motivational factors that are more pronounced in men than in women (Lebakeng 2008; Verheul et al. 2009; Tomski 2014; Fielden and Davidson 2005). On the other hand, the need for self-realization and personal development (the development of one's own career, personal growth) are more pronounced in women who start an entrepreneurial venture. (Hughes 2006; Lewis 2013) (Exhibit 2).

Also, Mallon and Kohen (2001) prove that the family is one of the most important factors affecting women to embark on entrepreneurship. Research shows that, when it comes to family motivation factors (family care, family commitment, securing a better future for children, obtaining funds for pensions), there are significant

Exhibit 2 Awarding woman entrepreneurs of the Summit of Entrepreneurs in Dubrovnik, photo © 2017 Maja Aleksić-Ilić

statistical differences among genders; that is, women are more motivated than men due to these factors (Kirkwood 2009; Dawson and Henley 2012; Lebakeng 2008; Ismail et al. 2012; Yukongdi 2018). Also, the need for flexible working hours is a factor that has a major impact on the motivation of women to start their own business (Heilman and Chen 2003; Lebakeng 2008).

In addition to the abovementioned factors, dissatisfaction with the current job can be the incentive to start a business among women in Serbia, as explained in the previous section. Also, necessity (unemployment, lack of secure income) can lead women to start thinking about their own business. Taking into account the large number of studies that analyzed women's entrepreneurial motives in the world, as well as the analysis of studies conducted in Serbia (Stefanović et al. 2015), the following factors distinguish as the most important drivers of entrepreneurial activity of women in Serbia: (1) dissatisfaction with the current job, (2) presence of business opportunity, (3) the desire to be "their own boss," (4) freedom and flexibility, (5) the need to earn more money, (6) independence, (7) realization of ambitions, (8) the tendency to make better use of knowledge, (9) personal challenges, and (10) the desire for achievement.

Studies carried out in Serbia on the motives of women to start their own business have identified very different factors that acted encouragingly on women in the previous period. According to the extensive research conducted by Babović (2012), the following motives had the greatest influence over the majority of women entrepreneurs in Serbia (68%) for starting their own business: the need to provide a source of income for the family, the need for flexible working time, and the necessity (loss of work). Based on the analysis, Stefanović et al. (2015, p. 127) conclude that the decisions of women to become entrepreneurs are motivated, on the one hand, by their psychological needs for personal achievement and achievement of ambitions, as well as by the response to business opportunities and challenges (psychological motives), and on the other hand, by their objective needs arising from dissatisfaction with the current position, the need to earn more money, use of their knowledge and experience, and better balance between family and business obligations (existential motives). According to a study conducted by Popović-Pantić (2014), women in Serbia most often decide to establish their own company out of necessity (mostly only when they are out of work, when they are declared redundant in the company where they were employed, or when they get fired due to restructuring), many women decide to do so in order to provide additional income, and a part of women in Serbia decides to enter entrepreneurship because of independence and autonomy (to independently work and manage, express creativity, have freedom of decision-making, personal selection of associates, one's own organization of working time, good earnings, and a dynamic job) (Popović-Pantić 2013). Recent research in Serbia shows that the need for achieving additional income is the strongest motivational factor for entrepreneurship among women in Serbia (Vrbanac 2018).

> Due to the fact that there are low salaries in companies and businesses in Serbia, many women choose to start their own business precisely because of this. Unemployment is the second factor according to the ranking of women respondents in this research (necessity). It is interesting that "stress at work" falls within the group of the most common motivational factors among the women respondents in this research, which speaks about the difficulties encountered by women employed by other owners and their direct and indirect experience. The desire to avoid situations in which women are exposed to stress during work motivates them to start their own business, although by doing so they will also encounter tasks that bring stressful situations. (Vrbanac 2018)

Unfortunately, all previous research on the incentives of women entrepreneurship in Serbia was done using the measures of descriptive statistics, so it was not examined which of these factors had a statistically significant impact on the development of women entrepreneurship in Serbia.

4.2 Restrictions on the Development of Women Entrepreneurship in Serbia

Contrary to the incentives, there are many factors that have a disincentive effect on the decision of women to enter entrepreneurship, as well as on the inferior position of women entrepreneurs. All factors that discourage the development of women entrepreneurship can be divided into internal (factors related to the personality of women and their entrepreneurial preferences) and external factors (environmental factors).

As is well known, many authors in the past studied the characteristics of successful entrepreneurs. Some of the characteristics that are most commonly mentioned as the characteristics of successful entrepreneurs are pronounced need for success (McClelland 1961), a high degree of self-confidence (Gartner 1989b), tendency to risk-taking and great tolerance of uncertainty (Schere 1982), presence of initiative (Mishra 1996), internal control locus (Rotter 1966), and innovativeness

(Schumpeter 1934). Traditional concepts were that women lack many of these characteristics, so their involvement in entrepreneurship was significantly lower in comparison with men. Earlier studies proved these claims, arguing that women are characterized by low self-esteem, fear of failure, passive orientation, tendency to avoiding risk, and dominance of women's values (Henning and Jardim 1977; Jianakoplos and Bernasek 2007). However, the latest studies prove the opposite. For example, a study conducted by Sanchez and Licciardello (2012) shows that gender differences are not statistically significant in important entrepreneurial characteristics such as control locus, tendency to risk and proactivity, and the only dimension where a significant difference in favor of men has been identified is entrepreneurial self-efficacy associated with self-confidence (Holienka et al. 2016). Caliendo et al. (2014) demonstrate that women entrepreneurs on average have the same characteristics as men, excluding the issue of risk. Based on this it can be concluded that internal factors are not the dominant limiting factors for women entrepreneurship (Lockyer and George 2012).

When it comes to Serbia, there are no serious empirical studies that examine the characteristics of women entrepreneurs, but several studies have analyzed external constraints of the development of women entrepreneurship. Some of the common factors identified in these studies are (Babović 2012; Popović-Pantić 2014):

- Remnants of traditional patriarchal customs that affect the acquisition of the necessary funds to start a business.
- Free time for education and commitment to the development of one's own business.
- Cultural clichés, etc.

The problem of financing is considered one of the most serious problems in the development of entrepreneurship in Serbia, which is especially characteristic for women (Stefanović et al. 2013). Since loans for startups offered by banks in Serbia are too expensive for small businesses, women are often forced to rely on some form of self-financing, or to use sources of financing such as personal savings, family or friends' loans, or the most unfavorable, microcredits. However, women in Serbia face additional restrictions in securing their own capital. In many, especially underdeveloped and traditional, patriarchal communities, it is a common practice that when inheriting immovable property (land, house, buildings) women are expected to give their share of inheritance to a brother or a male member of the family. Also, when entering into marriage, as a rule, ownership is transferred to a man, even in cases of joint construction or purchase of a house or apartment (Babović 2008). In this way, women remain deprived of the right to dispose of their own property, especially if it is necessary to take a mortgage loan (it is very difficult for them to provide guarantees), if we add the fact that women on average earn less because they perform less paid jobs in order to complete all unpaid family responsibilities, and the low standard of living in Serbia, we can assume that it is very difficult for women in Serbia to provide startup capital for the start of business and that this represents a very serious restriction on the development of women entrepreneurship in Serbia.

As far as informal financial networks are concerned, there are women in a rather inferior position compared to men. Women in Serbia often lack information about potential investors, as well as support and understanding for their business ideas both in society and in the family. On the other hand, the decision on who will be granted favorable funding is very often made by men in managerial positions. In addition to generally accepted prejudices, men in managerial positions often misjudge the value of business that can be achieved by the venture created by women, as they have no insights into specific problems for which women offer solutions within their enterprises. For example, a man can hardly assess the potential of a business idea related to the day care of children, catering, or household maintenance, because he does not deal with it in his everyday life or does not share information about it in his informal and private contacts.

Lack of entrepreneurial and managerial experience and underdevelopment of sales and marketing skills are also serious problems faced by women in Serbia. Lack of entrepreneurial and managerial experience is the problem of most potential entrepreneurs in Serbia (Popović-Pantić 2014). But it much more affects women because a much smaller number of women have been able to make decisions independently, because in Serbia there is little participation of women in managerial positions. Also, traditional "women" occupations are less profitable; as a rule they are predominantly intended for state and public institutions, which can rarely be used as a source of knowledge and experience that can be used for private business. Often businesses fail because women cannot find ways to effectively prepare and respond to changed market conditions, for example, the decline in demand and increased competition. On the other hand, women who leave large systems in order to enter entrepreneurship, either by their own choice or because they have no other options, on average leave from lower managerial positions than men in the same situation. This affects not only the self-confidence of women and their business ambitions, but also the business contacts that they had the opportunity to make in their previous career (Vrbanac 2018).

Traditional education of women in Serbia represents the next barrier to entrepreneurship. In order to decide to engage in entrepreneurship, women need to overcome the prejudices and stereotypes that prevail in society, which often makes them lack self-esteem and awareness of their own abilities. Additionally, women in Serbia carry much heavier burden of responsibilities related to children and family, because they expect of themselves, as well as the social community expects of them, to put the care of their offspring and family life in the first place and employment and career in the second place (Vukmirović 2011). As explained above, in Serbia, the obligations of women in family life are extensive, as the model of housewife's behavior is deeply ingrained in consciousness. Women are expected to cook, clean the house, prepare children for school, and control how they perform school and out-of-school duties (Hugson 2018). Whether employed as hired employees, managers, or independent entrepreneurs, family responsibilities do not cease to exist for them. Organizing home and family life is also an area in which a woman and mother is expected to organize and implement a range of activities. The family's social life, family gatherings and celebrations, and contacts with relatives and friends are also an area in which not much happens without the engagement of a woman. A woman is still a housewife "who carries the house," who should solve the everyday problems. Too many obligations in the family leave women with little time to devote themselves to developing their own careers, personal improvement, which leads to the lack of knowledge and skills necessary for successful development of work. Also, awareness of the large number of responsibilities in the house limits many women to get involved in starting the business in the first place, which implies great dedication and engagement, especially in the early period (Babović 2012).

We should add to this traditional marital relations in Serbia which imply that women should be less successful in business than men and that they have no right to devote some of their free time to their work, especially when they need to spend several extraordinary, sometimes even evening hours at business meetings, trips, or dinners with clients. In entrepreneurship, such situations are more frequent than when working for the company, so it can be assumed that many women in Serbia do not decide to start their own business for these reasons as well (Babović 2012).

The above arguments from the literature review indeed justify the "separation" of women entrepreneurship as a special type of entrepreneurship, although we face the lack of understanding in the very academic community in transition countries and frequent questioning of justification of the specific treatment of women entrepreneurship.

5 Research of Factors That Influence the Development of Women Entrepreneurship in the Republic of Serbia

5.1 Research Methodology

In order to check which factors influence the development of women entrepreneurship in Serbia, primary research was conducted. The attitudes of women entrepreneurs in Serbia were examined whether they would again decide to start their own business or they would rather seek a job in a company, which factors influenced their decision to start their own business, and what problems they were facing (what discouraged them). During 2018 data collection was carried out using a questionnaire by interviewing women entrepreneurs in the Republic of Serbia. 117 women entrepreneurs in the Republic of Serbia were interviewed. Out of 117 distributed questionnaires, 95 returned questionnaires were useful, while 12 questionnaires were rejected due to defects and incomplete responses. The questionnaire consisted of two parts.

In order to examine which of the above factors had a statistically significant impact on women entrepreneurship in Serbia, a logistic regression was made. In order to determine the dependent variable, we took into account the response of women respondents whether they would start their own business again (it has the character of the binomial variable 1) or they would seek employment in the existing company (it has the character of the binomial variable 0). The performance of the model was verified through the *Omnibus Tests of Model Coefficients*, which are a kind of *goodness of fit* test. Another confirmation of the validity of the model is *Hosmer and Lemeshow test*, after which a logistic regression was made. The results of applying the Wald test are given in the Wald column, and in the Sig column there are values indicating which variables significantly contribute to the predictive possibilities of the model.

5.2 Research Limitations

The basic limitation of this research is a relatively small sample of respondents. However, this does not diminish the results of the research in view of the complexity of the statistical methods by which we tested the variables and created the assumptions for the predictability of the model.

5.3 Research Results

The first part of the questionnaire consisted of questions related to general information about respondents and their businesses: age of a woman entrepreneur, level of education of a woman entrepreneur, position in the enterprise, age of the enterprise, size of the enterprise, and activity of the enterprise. The second part of the questionnaire included issues related to factors that acted encouraging/discouraging to the decision to start a business.

When it comes to the age structure of the women respondents, the situation is as follows: women respondents aged up to 25 made up 18.7% of the sample, women respondents aged between 26 and 35 made up 23.6%, women respondents aged between 36 and 45 made up 31%, and women respondents older than 45 made up 26.7% of the sample. Regarding the educational structure, 44% of the women respondents have a secondary school, 38% have a higher education degree, and 15% have a university degree, while 3% of them have Ph.D. degrees. Out of the total number, 19% of women respondents responded that they were in the managerial position (they manage the company and make the most important decisions), 77% of women respondents responded that they were in the managerial position, but they were also involved in executive affairs, 2% of the women respondents were involved in executive affairs, but they did not make strategically important decisions, and 2% of the women respondents stated other.

As for the characteristics of enterprises, they were as follows: 63% of the enterprises that were founded by the surveyed women entrepreneurs were micro enterprises (entrepreneurial shops), 28% were small enterprises, 8% were medium-sized enterprises, and 1% were large enterprises. By age, 18% were enterprises aged up to 12 months, 68% of enterprises were aged between 42 and 120 months, and

14% of enterprises were older than 10 years. Service enterprises had the largest share of 46%, followed by trading enterprises of 32%, manufacturing enterprises of 18%, and enterprises from other branches of 4%.

Women entrepreneurs were first asked the question "If they could decide again would they choose to start their own business or find an employment?" 82.1% (78) of the respondents would start their own business again, while 17.9% (17) would rather decide to find an employment. The results are shown in Fig. 1.

In order to identify the factors that acted encouraging on women entrepreneurs when starting their business, they were offered ten factors that were selected as the most influential (sources) based on the literature review (Hughes 2006; Ismail et al. 2012; Yukongdi 2018). They were asked to mark the factors that motivated them to start their own business (it was possible to select several factors). The list of factors as well as the number of women entrepreneurs who selected them is shown in Table 1 (Fig. 2).

Fig. 1 Attitudes of women entrepreneurs in Serbia toward entrepreneurship as a repeated option for self-employment. Source: Authors' calculation

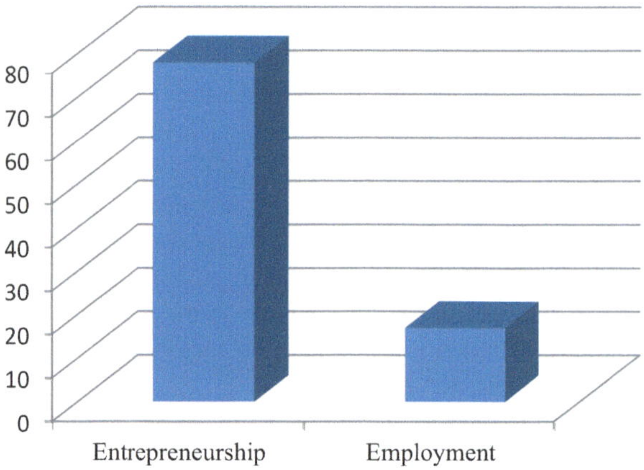

Table 1 Factors that encourage women in Serbia to start their own business

	Variable	Number of women entrepreneurs
1	Opportunity (identified chance)	21
2	Necessity (unemployment)	47
3	Dissatisfaction with current job	34
4	Need for independence and autonomy	68
5	Need for flexible working hours	42
6	Higher earnings	75
7	Better future for children and family	27
8	Need for personal development	31
9	Better use of knowledge and experience	9
10	Other	5

Source: Authors' calculation

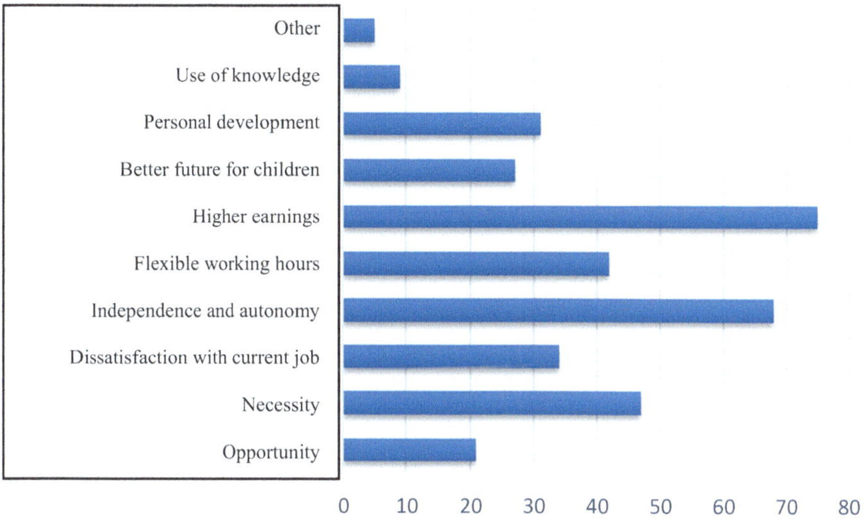

Fig. 2 Factors that stimulate women in Serbia to start their own business. Source: Authors' calculation

As can be seen, a much larger number of women entrepreneurs in Serbia started a business out of necessity (47) than on the basis of recognized opportunities on the market (21), and also dissatisfaction with current job was a motive in almost one-third of women from the sample.

The most significant incentives for women in Serbia that encourage them to entrepreneurship are the possibility of making higher earnings, independence in work, and flexible working hours. Women in Serbia give a somewhat smaller significance to personal development and the use of knowledge.

In order to identify factors that discourage women in Serbia from starting their own business, women entrepreneurs were also offered ten factors that were identified as the most influential ones, based on previous studies in Serbia and reviewed literature (Babović 2012; Popović-Pantić 2014). They were asked to mark the factors that were the biggest barriers when making a decision on entrepreneurship and starting and developing a business (it was possible to select several factors). The list of factors as well as the number of women entrepreneurs who selected them is shown in Table 2.

As can be seen, the most serious restrictions on the development of entrepreneurship among women in Serbia are the lack of one's own capital (78) and the lack of managerial experience and fear of independent decision-making and accountability (56), followed by a heavy burden of home responsibilities and care for children.

In order to examine which of the above factors had a statistically significant impact on women entrepreneurship in Serbia, a logistic regression was made. In order to determine the dependent variable, we took into account the response of women respondents whether they would start their own business again (it has the character of the binomial variable 1) or they would seek employment in the existing

Table 2 Restrictions on women entrepreneurship in Serbia

	Variable	Number of women entrepreneurs
1	Lack of one's own capital	78
2	Problems in obtaining favorable sources of financing	34
3	Lack of information on investors and possible sources of financing	12
4	Lack of managerial experience and independence in decision-making	56
5	Lack of business-related knowledge and experience	41
6	Heavy burden of home responsibilities	45
7	Caring for children and family	38
8	Fear of failure	35
9	Lack of family support	29
10	Other	15

Source: Authors' calculation

company (it has the character of the binomial variable 0). First, the performance of the model was verified through the *Omnibus Tests of Model Coefficients*, which are a kind of *goodness of fit* test. The statistical significance is less than 0.05, so accordingly the model is acceptable. Another confirmation of the validity of the model is *Hosmer and Lemeshow test*. Then, logistic regression was made. The results are shown in Table 3.

The results of applying the Wald test are given in the Wald column, and in the Sig column there are values indicating which variables significantly contribute to the predictive possibilities of the model. In the case of preference for women and men in Serbia in terms of whether they would prefer to work for the employer or start their own business, and based on the data from Table 3, we find that the main factors dictating this determination in women are possibility of securing the initial capital (access to sources of financing), tendency to risk, age, level of education, and managerial experience, while the influence of other factors is not statistically significant.

In men, we find that entrepreneurship tendencies are influenced by the possibility of securing financial resources to start a business, tendency to risk, occupation, managerial experience, and entrepreneurial orientation of parents.

As can be seen in Table 3, the strongest and statistically significant incentives for women in Serbia to start their own business are the need for higher earnings (3.25) and necessity (2.42). The data of descriptive statistics also showed that the need for higher earnings was reported by most women as an incentive for entrepreneurship, which coincided with the results of previous research (Popović-Pantić 2014; Vrbanac 2018). This can be explained by the fact that the standard of living in Serbia is extremely low, and, as explained above, the income of women who work in lower paid jobs is especially low. Women are aware of the fact that their own business, i.e., independent control of finance, is one of the few ways to provide relatively high income in Serbia (in domestic and foreign companies salaries are determined in accordance with the average of the branch, and women who are rarely

Table 3 Influence of different factors on women entrepreneurship in Serbia

Factors	*B*	Sig.
Incentives		
Opportunity (identified chance)	1.337	0.026
Necessity (unemployment)	2.242	0.001
Dissatisfaction with current job	3.223	0.998
Need for independence and autonomy	1.682	0.019
Need for flexible working hours	2.118	0.511
Higher earnings	3.251	0.001
Better future for children and family	0.465	0.008
Need for personal development	2.465	0.342
Better use of knowledge and experience	−0.465	0.876
Other	2.465	0.531
Restrictions		
Lack of one's own capital	−4.223	0.041
Obtaining favorable sources of financing	−1.477	0.999
Information on sources of financing	1.477	0.071
Managerial experience	−1.120	0.024
Knowledge of business	−1.185	0.006
Heavy burden of house responsibilities	−0.966	0.047
Care for children and family	−1.036	0.012
Fear of failure	−0,356	0.053
Lack of family support	0.672	0.311
Other	−2.324	0.102
N	95	
R	0.345	
R^2	0.231	

Source: Authors' calculation

in managerial positions cannot expect any additional bonuses and incentives other than salaries). Another very influential incentive is a necessity, which is also shown by previous studies conducted in Serbia (Babović 2012; Global Entrepreneurship Monitoring 2009). This is logical because the unemployment rate is extremely high[3] in Serbia and the position of women on the labor market is very unfavorable.

The next motive reported by the women in Serbia is the need for independence in work and autonomy (1.68), which is also confirmed by previous studies (Popović-Pantić 2013). This can be explained by the fact that women in Serbia are very often in a subordinate position in the family and at work and that they are dependent on men, even when it is not realistic; therefore, they have a pronounced need for independence and autonomy.

[3]Unemployment rate in Serbia in the fourth quarter 2018 was 12.9% (Source: Statistical Office of the Republic of Serbia, 2019). Statistic by Theme. Labor Market. Retrieved May 4, 2019, from http://www.stat.gov.rs/en-US/oblasti/trziste-rada

Identified opportunities (1.33) are in the fourth place by influence. Identified opportunities as a motive were not identified in previous studies. Also, Global Entrepeneurship Monitoring (2009) shows that relatively few women entrepreneurs in Serbia decide to start a business based on opportunities. Considering that all previous research and studies were done 5–7 years ago, and Global Entrepeneurship Monitoring contains data for Serbia only for years 2007, 2008, and 2009, it can be assumed that the situation in the field of women entrepreneurship is moving in a positive direction. Identified chances from the market are becoming the motive of an increasing number of women, which promises the development of women entrepreneurship in Serbia and a greater contribution to economic growth. Previous research shows that entrepreneurship based on opportunities has a much greater contribution to economic growth compared to necessity-based entrepreneurship (Ivanović-Đukić et al. 2018).

Somewhat smaller (0.46) but a statistically significant impact on the decision of women to enter entrepreneurship is care for children and the need to provide a better future for children. This motive was also identified as a key one in the Popović-Pantić study (Popović-Pantić 2013). This can be explained by the fact that most families in Serbia try to leave material resources as inheritance and secure employment for their heirs. Since women in Serbia are mostly responsible for children, it is logical to expect that they care the most about their children's future. By starting their own business, they expect to provide adequate income to children in the current period, as well as possible employment and sources of income for them in the future through the development of a family business.

Dissatisfaction with the existing job, the need for personal development, and the need for flexible working hours had the greatest influence on the surveyed women entrepreneurs to start their own business, but this influence was not significant so that it cannot be generalized to the entire population of women entrepreneurs in Serbia, and it only applies to the observed sample.

A lack of own capital (−4233) has been identified as a key restriction that impedes women to start their own business. This restriction is stated as one of the most important in all previous studies conducted in Serbia as well. This is logical if one takes into account the fact that in Serbia personal savings are one of the most common sources of initial capital (Erić et al. 2012). Considering the fact that women in Serbia very rarely have any material wealth or savings in their ownership, it is logical that the lack of one's own capital is a key restriction.

The following restrictions on the development of women entrepreneurship that had a statistically significant impact relate to the lack of managerial knowledge and experience (−0.12) and lack of knowledge of the nature of the business (−0.185). Given that women make less than one-fourth of managers in companies in Serbia, it can be expected that they do not have managerial experience. Also, due to the hierarchical relations and subordination that are present in the family, women very often do not have the freedom to make decisions. Lack of experience in decision-making and independent decision-making reduces decisiveness, affects confidence decline, and contributes to an increase in fear of failure (which is also identified as a barrier with a statistically significant impact on women in Serbia) that can lead to the emergence of a barrier to starting one's own business.

Finally, children and responsibilities in the home and family have a somewhat smaller but statistically significant impact on the barriers of women in Serbia to entrepreneurship. This was confirmed by all previous studies (Popović-Pantić 2014; Vrbanac 2018). This points to the fact that in Serbia, the culture of the population, relations in the family, tradition, and the situation in the society to this day have not changed significantly. Lack of state support in the form of a larger number of kindergartens, laws that will equalize the rights of both parents in the field of child care, etc., as well as the retention of traditional family responsibilities leave women in Serbia with too many tasks due to which they often do not decide to accept additional tasks and responsibilities.

6 Discussion and Conclusions

Based on the obtained research results, it can be concluded that the position of women in Serbia on the labor market is very unfavorable, so they represent a traditionally discriminated social group. One way to improve the position of women in society in Serbia is to encourage self-employment and the development of women entrepreneurship. To that end, a large number of measures have been implemented in the form of adopting a large number of strategic documents and legislation aiming to equalize the rights of women with the rights of men. This has led to the development of women entrepreneurship in Serbia, but it is developing very slowly. The development of women entrepreneurship is influenced by a number of factors. Some of them are incentive, while others restrict the development of women entrepreneurship in Serbia.

By empirical research, on a sample of 95 women entrepreneurs, it has been shown that motives that have a statistically significant impact on women in Serbia to start their own business are the need for higher earnings, necessity (unemployment), need for independence in work and autonomy, childcare, and need to provide a better future for the children. Most of these factors were identified by previous studies (Vrbanac 2018; Hugson 2018; Stefanović et al. 2015; Popović-Pantić 2014; Babović 2008, 2012; Gudac-Dodić 2006, 2010; Blagojević 1997), but it has not been proven that they have a statistically significant impact.

One of the novelties of this research is that the opportunities are recognized as a motive for a large number of women, which points to positive trends in the development of women entrepreneurship in Serbia. In Bosnia and Herzegovina, in research conducted by Palalić et al. (2017), empirical results revealed significant differences in entrepreneurial performance between women and men. It was found that gender significantly affects entrepreneurial activities in firms with regard to innovativeness, proactiveness, and risk-taking. Overall, Palalić et al. (2017) reveal that female respondents scored better in entrepreneurial dimensions than did males. Similar results coming from research conducted in Macedonia. Ramadani et al. (2013) revealed that women entrepreneurs are motivated to undertake entrepreneurial career due to the existing possibility to realize substantial profit, desire to work exclusively for themselves, and the desire and need to realize significant achievements throughout the career.

The key restrictions on women entrepreneurship in Serbia identified by this research are lack of one's own capital, lack of managerial knowledge and experience, lack of knowledge of the nature of business, childcare, and responsibilities in the home and the family. The obstacles and difficulties that women encounter are not insurmountable. By implementing certain measures the state and local self-government could intervene through appropriate regulations, in order to encourage women to start their own businesses and facilitate their businesses.

Since the key problem of women in entrepreneurship is the provision of initial capital, it is desirable to provide various forms of financial support in the form of grants, favorable loans, guarantees, etc. However, it is not desirable to emphasize publicly too often that women entrepreneurs should be provided with special incentives and benefits, as it is now, because it appears as favoring one group of people, which is less capable and successful and needs help. Instead, we should work on promoting successful women entrepreneurs while providing various incentives for new ones who will look up to them. Highlighting the model of a successful woman entrepreneur in Serbia as a new model that combines some of the traditional characteristics of women from this region with modern business would thus become a desirable model for the generations of the women to come.

Also, resolving seemingly small problems, such as the organization of work of kindergartens, schools, or hospitals, loan guarantees, or the organization of free specialized courses for women, could greatly alleviate the problems and barriers that many women encounter when making the decision to initiate own business and implementing it. Given the studies conducted so far in Serbia, we think that future studies on the opportunities to and restrictions on the development of women entrepreneurship should be more comprehensive with the need to conduct longitudinal studies and to monitor the work of successful women entrepreneurs longer in order to identify the key factors for the successful operation of enterprises whose owners or managers are women.

References

Aidis R (2002) Why less? The gendered aspects of small- and medium-sized Enterprise (SME) ownership under economic transition. Tinbergen Institute Discussion Paper No. 2002-055/2, 1–31.doi:https://doi.org/10.2139/ssrn.318679

Aritonović I (2009) Društveni položaj žena u Srbiji u doba Kraljevine Jugoslavije. (Social status of women in Serbia in the era of the Kingdom of Yugoslavia). Baština 27:233–257

Babović M (2008) The position of women on the labour market in Serbia. UNDP Serbia and Gender Equality Council, Government of the Republic of Serbia, Belgrade. https://www.undp.org/content/dam/serbia/Publications%20and%20reports/UNDP_SRB_The_Position_of_Women_on_the_Labour_Market_in_Serbia.pdf. Accessed 3 May 2019

Babović M (2012) Ka kvalitetnom praćenju preduzetništva žena u Srbiji: Skraćeni izveštaj na osnovu polazne studije o preduzetništvu žena u Srbiji. Beograd: Program Ujedinjenih nacija za razvoj (Towards quality monitoring of entrepreneurship of women in Serbia: Summary report based on the preliminary study on entrepreneurship of women in Serbia. Belgrade: United Nations Development Program), pp 4–5. http://www.policycafe.rs/financial-research.php#access-to-finance-women. Accessed 8 Oct 2017

Bennett R, Dann S (2000) The changing experience of Australian female entrepreneurs – gender, work & organization. Aust Female Entrep 7(2):75–83. https://doi.org/10.1111/1468-0432.00095

Blagojević M (1997) Roditeljstvo I fertilitet – Srbija devedesetih. (Parenthood and fertility - Serbia in the nineties). Institute for Sociological Research, Faculty of Philosophy, Belgrade

Blagojević M (2006) Seoske ženske organizacije u Vojvodini. (Rural women's organizations in Vojvodina). Pokrajinski zavod za ravnopravnost, Novi Sad

Caliendo M, Fossen F, Kritikos AS (2014) Personality characteristics and the decisions to become and stay self-employed. Small Bus Econ 42(4):787–814. https://doi.org/10.2139/ssrn.1793171

Carter S (2000) Improving the number and performance of women-owned business: some implications for training and advisory services. Educ Train 42(4/5):326–334. https://doi.org/10.1108/00400910010373732

Dawson C, Henley A (2012) "Push" versus "pull" entrepreneurship: an ambiguous distinction? Int J Entrep Behav Res 18(6):697–719. https://doi.org/10.1108/13552551211268139

Erić D, Beraha I, Đuričin S, Kecman N, Jakišić B (2012) Finansiranje malih i srednjih preduzeća u Srbiji (Small and medium size enterprise financing in Serbia). Institut ekonomskih nauka, Čugura print, Beograd (Belgrade)

Fielden SL, Davidson MJ (2005) The way forward for women business owners. In: Fielden SL, Davidson MJ (eds) International handbook of women and small business entrepreneurship. Edward Elgar, Cheltenham, pp 264–272

Gartner WB (1989a) "Who is an entrepreneur?" Is the wrong question. Entrep Theory Pract 3 (1):47–67. https://doi.org/10.1177/104225878801200401

Gartner WB (1989b) Some suggestions for research on entrepreneurial traits and characteristics. Enterp Theory Pract 14(2):27–38. https://doi.org/10.1177/104225878901400103

Global Entrepreneurship Monitoring (2009) Entrepreneurial behaviour and attitudes. https://www.gemconsortium.org/data/key-aps. Accessed 4 May 2019

Gudac-Dodić V (2006) Položaj žene u Srbiji (The status of a woman in Serbia) (1945-2000). In: Perović L (ed) Žene i deca - Srbija u modernizacijskim procesima XIX i XX veka. (Women and Children - Serbia in the modernization processes of the 19th and 20th century). Helsinki Committee for Human Rights in Serbia, Belgrade, vol. 23, pp. 33–130. http://www.helsinki.org.rs/serbian/doc/sveske23.pdf. Accessed 1 May 2019

Gudac-Dodić V (2010) Under the aegis of the family: women in Serbia. J Int Soc Res 3 (13):110–119. http://www.sosyalarastirmalar.com/cilt3/sayi13kadinsayisipdf/gudacdodic_verax.pdf. Accessed 1 May 2019

Heilman ME, Chen JJ (2003) Entrepreneurship as a solution: the allure of self-employment for women and minorities. Hum Resour Manag Rev 13(2):347–364. https://doi.org/10.1016/S1053-4822(03)00021-4

Henning M, Jardim A (1977) The managerial woman. Anchor Press/Doubleday, Garden City. https://doi.org/10.1177/019263657806241527

Holienka M, Jančovičová Z, Kovacicova Z (2016) Women entrepreneurship in Visegrad Region and its drivers. Acta Univ Agric 64(6):1899–1910. https://doi.org/10.11118/actaun201664061899

Hughes KD (2006) Exploring motivation and success among Canadian women entrepreneurs. J Small Bus Entrep 19(2):107–120. https://doi.org/10.1080/08276331.2006.10593362

Hugson M (2018) Men in Serbia: changes, resistances and challenges - results of research on men and gender equality, IMAGES Serbia 2018. Center E8, Belgrade. https://promundoglobal.org/wp-content/uploads/2018/06/IMAGES-Srbija-ENG-print-1.pdf. Accessed 1 May 2019

Ismail K, Ahmad A, Gadar K, Yunus N (2012) Stimulating factors on women entrepreneurial intention. Bus Manag Dyn 2(6):20–28

Ivanović-Đukić M, Radosavljević M (2018) Preduzetnički proces. (Entrepreneurial process). Faculty of Economics, Niš

Ivanović-Đukić M, Lepojević V, Stefanović S, Van Stel A, Petrović J (2018) Contribution of entrepreneurship to economic growth: a comparative analysis of south-east transition and developed European countries. Int Rev Entrep 16(2):257–276
Jianakoplos NA, Bernasek A (2007) Are women more risk averse? Econ Inq 36(4):620–630. https://doi.org/10.1111/j.1465-7295.1998.tb01740.x
Kirkwood J (2009) Motivational factors in a push-pull theory of entrepreneurship. Gen Manag 24 (5):346–354. https://doi.org/10.1108/17542410910968805
Lebakeng MA (2008) An exploration of women entrepreneurship in Lesotho. North-West University, Potchefstroom (Unpublished MBA mini-dissertation)
Leszczyński D (2014) The investigation into motivations, success factors and barriers among women small business owners: an overview of extant literature. Int J Manag Econ 39:108–125. https://doi.org/10.2478/ijme-2014-0024
Lewis P (2013) The search for an authentic entrepreneurial identity: difference and professionalism among women business owners. Gend Work Organ 20(3):252–266. https://doi.org/10.1111/j.1468-0432.2006.00317.x
Lockyer J, George S (2012) What women want: barriers to female entrepreneurship in the west midlands. Int J Gend Entrep 4(2):179–195. https://doi.org/10.1108/17566261211234661
Mallon M, Kohen L (2001) Time for a change? Women's accounts of the move from organizational careers to self-employment. Br J Manag 12(3):217–230. https://doi.org/10.1111/1467-8551.00195
McClelland (1961) The achieving society. Princeton, Van Nostrand Company
Mishra SP (1996) Factors affecting women entrepreneurship in small and cottage industries in India. International Labour Organization, Swedish International Development Cooperation Agency
Nikolić-Ristanović V (2012) Human trafficking between profit and survival. In: Selih A, Zavrsnik A (eds) Crime and transition in Central and Eastern Europe. Springer, New York, pp 205–227
Palalić R, Ramadani V, Dana LP (2017) Entrepreneurship in Bosnia and Herzegovina: focus on gender. Eur Bus Rev 29(4):476–496. https://doi.org/10.1108/EBR-05-2016-0071
Petković S, Ivanović Đukić M (2018) Entrepreneurship in Serbia. In Palalić R, Dana LP, Ramadani V (eds) Entrepreneurship in former Yugoslavia - diversity, institutional constraints and prospects. Springer, Cham, Switzerland, pp 107–130. ISBN 978–3–319-77633-0. ISBN 978-3-319-77634-7 (eBook)
Poggesi S, Mari M, De Vita L (2015) Family and work–life balance mechanisms: what is their impact on the performance of Italian female service firms? Int J Entrep Innov 16(1):43–53. https://doi.org/10.5367/ijei.2015.0173
Popović-Pantić S (2013) Žensko preduzetništvo kroz samozapošljavanje u Srbiji tokom tranzicije: uporedna analiza i empirijsko istraživanje. Neobjavljena doktorska disertacija. (Women entrepreneurship through self-employment in Serbia during transition: comparative analysis and empirical research. Unpublished doctoral dissertation). Faculty of Economics, Belgrade
Popović-Pantić S (2014) Žensko preduzetništvo u Srbiji: Evolucija od socijalne ka ekonomskoj kategoriji. (Women entrepreneurship in Serbia: evolution from social to economic category). Poslovna ekonomija 8(2):143–162. https://doi.org/10.5937/PosEko1402143P
Ramadani V, Gërguri S, Dana LP, Tašaminova T (2013) Women entrepreneurs in the Republic of Macedonia: waiting for directions. Int J Entrep Small Bus 19(1):95–121. https://doi.org/10.1504/IJESB.2013.054330
Rotter JB (1966) Generalized expectancies for internal versus external locus of control of reinforcement. Psychol Monogr Gen Appl 109(80):1–28
Sanchez JC, Licciardello O (2012) Gender differences and attitudes in entrepreneurial intentions: the role of career choice. J Womens Entrep Educ 8(1–2):7–27
Schere J (1982) Tolerance of ambiguity as a discriminating variables between entrepreneurs and managers. Proc Acad Manag 42(4):404–408
Schumpeter JA (1934) The theory of economic development. Harvard University Press, Cambridge
Schumpeter J (1947) The creative response in economic history. J Econ Hist 7(2):149–159

Sloka B, Kantane I, Avotins V, Jermolajeva E (2014) Analysis of entrepreneur's motivation to start business (comparative studies in Latvia in comparison with Canada, USA, Mexico). Eur Integration Stud 8:152–158. https://doi.org/10.5755/j01.eis.0.8.6839
Statistical Office of the Republic of Serbia (2017) Women and men in the Republic of Serbia. http://publikacije.stat.gov.rs/G2017/Pdf/G20176008.pdf. Accessed 3 May 2019
Stefanović S, Ivanović-Đukić M, Janković-Milić V (2013) The analysis of key challenges and constraints to the stability and growth of an entrepreneurial sector in Serbia. J Balkan Near East Stud 15(3):346–365. https://doi.org/10.1080/19448953.2013.789330
Stefanović S, Ivanović-Đukić M, Lepojević V (2015) Analiza preferencija žena u Republici Srbiji, XX Međunarodni naučni skup: Regionalni razvoj i demografski tokovi zemalja Jugoistočne Evrope (Analysis of the preference of women in the republic of Serbia, 20th international scientific conference: regional development and demographic flows of the countries of south-East Europe). Faculty of Economics, Niš, pp 337–351 26. 06. 2015. ISBN 978-86-6139-104-0
Stojanović-Jovanović B, Jovanović S (2015) Sociomedical aspects of women's life in Serbia during XX century. Hist Med 12(1):35–40. https://doi.org/10.5937/pomc12-8613
Tomski P (2014) Entrepreneurship as a career choice. The empirical perspective. Pol J Manag Stud 9:244–253
Verheul I, Stel A, Thurik R (2006) Explaining female and male entrepreneurship at the country level. Entrep Reg Dev 18:151–183. https://doi.org/10.1080/08985620500532053
Verheul I, Carree M, Thurik R (2009) Allocation and productivity of time in new ventures of female and male entrepreneurs. Small Bus Econ 33(3):273–291. https://doi.org/10.1007/s11187-009-9174-x
Vrbanac M (2018) Barijere i pokretači ženskog preduzetništva u Srbiji. Neobjavljena doktorska disretacija. (Barriers and drivers of women entrepreneurship in Serbia. Unpublished doctoral dissertation). Union University, Belgrade
Vučetić R (2007) Žena u gradu. Između rezervata privatnog i osvajanja mesta u javnom životu (A woman in the city. Between a reservation of private and conquering a place in the public life) (1918-1941). In: Ristović M (ed) Privatni život kod Srba u dvadesetom veku (Private life of Serbs in the twentieth century). Clio, Belgrade, pp 131–164
Vukmirović N (2011) Entrepreneurship development and breaking the vicious cycle of poverty. Economic development and entrepreneurship in transition economies: a review of current policy approaches, REDETE 2011. University of Banja Luka, Faculty of Economics, Banja Luka
Yukongdi V (2018) Motivational factors, facilitators, obstacles and gender differences: an exploratory study of Thai entrepreneurs. PEOPLE Int J Soc Sci 4(1):288–297. https://doi.org/10.20319/pijss.2018.41.288297
Zlatkov Cvetković M (2015) Women entrepreneurship in Serbia: a qualitative study of the perceived enabling factors for the female entrepreneurship. Unpublished master thesis. Swedish University of Agricultural Sciences, Department of Economics, Uppsala
Zwan P, Verheul I, Thurik R (2012) The entrepreneurial ladder, gender, and regional development. Small Bus Econ 39(3):627–643. https://doi.org/10.1007/s11187-011-9334-7

Maja Ivanović-Đukić, Ph.D., is a full professor at the University of Niš, Faculty of Economics. She has been an active researcher in entrepreneurship, management of SMEs, and corporate social responsibility. As an author and coauthor she wrote more than 100 scientific publications published in international journals as well as in the leading national journals and international conference proceedings. She took part in two international projects TEMPUS and ERASMUS +, two scientific projects financed by the national ministries, and three projects financed by local community. She was a member of organization and scientific committees of five international conferences.

Saša Petković, Ph.D., is an Associate Professor at the University of Banja Luka, Faculty of Economics. His subjects are entrepreneurship, economics and management of SMEs and management of entrepreneurial projects, theoretical economics, and entrepreneurship scientific areas. He authored or coauthored 33 published research papers in scientific journals and proceedings of the correspondent conferences and nine monographs (five in Springer Publishing). He carried out research and scientific stays in several countries: USA, UK, Brazil, Spain, Germany, Austria, Holland, Bulgaria, Slovenia, Hungary, Croatia, Serbia, Poland, etc. Besides his work at the faculty, he has been engaged in the work of international development organization CARE International Balkans since 1999 as a project manager with Head of Office in Sarajevo and Branch Office in Banja Luka.

Women's Entrepreneurship in Slovenia

Jasna Auer Antoncic, Bostjan Antoncic, and Robert D. Hisrich

Abstract This chapter focuses on women entrepreneurship in Slovenia. The importance of women entrepreneurs is discussed. Their characteristics are described. Results of a survey on characteristics of women and men entrepreneurs are reported. The results give an answer to the research question: what are characteristics of women entrepreneurs in Slovenia? The study focused on some characteristics of women's entrepreneurs, predominantly demographic and sociological. We contributed to knowledge about women entrepreneurship by providing some new insights on the characteristics of women entrepreneurs. Women entrepreneurs tended to be educated with work experience, and they have an important impact on the Slovenian economy.

1 Introduction

Women-owned businesses are growing and making substantial contributions to innovation, employment, and wealth creation in the world economies (Brush et al. 2006, 2009). Slovenia (Slovene: Slovenija), formerly a constituent republic of Yugoslavia, is bounded on the North by Austria, on the North East by Hungary, on the South East and South by Croatia, and on the West by Italy and the Adriatic Sea. Slovenia covers an area of 20,251 square kilometers (land: 20,273 sq. km.; water: 122 sq. km.). Ljubljana is the capital of the Republic of Slovenia. (Funk and

J. A. Antoncic
Faculty of Management, University of Primorska, Koper, Slovenia

B. Antoncic (✉)
School of Economics and Business, University of Ljubljana, Ljubljana, Slovenia
e-mail: bostjan.antoncic@ef.uni-lj.si

R. D. Hisrich
Bridgestone Professor of International Marketing and the Director of the Global Management Center and International Programs, Kent State University, Kent, OH, USA

R. Palalić et al. (eds.), *Women's Entrepreneurship in Former Yugoslavia*, Contributions to Management Science,
https://doi.org/10.1007/978-3-030-45253-7_8

Exhibit 1 Piran. Source: photo by Bostjan Antoncic

Wagnalls New World Encyclopedia 2016, in Panthi et al. 2018, 131). Slovenia in demographic terms (Panthi et al. 2018, 133):

- Population: 2,063,768 (2015)
- Ethnic groups: Slovene 83.1%, Serb 2%, Croat 1.8%, Bosniak 1.1%, other or unspecified 12% (2002 census)
- Languages: Slovenian (official) 91.1%, Serbo-Croatian 4.5%, other or unspecified 4.4%, Italian (official, only in municipalities where Italian national communities reside), Hungarian (official, only in municipalities where Hungarian national communities reside) (2002 census)
- Religions: Catholic 57.8%, Muslim 2.4%, Orthodox 2.3%, other Christian 0.9%, unaffiliated 3.5%, other or unspecified 23%, no religion 10.1% (2002 census)

Slovenia has many tourist attractions such as the Slovenian coastal towns (see Piran in Exhibits 1 and 2).

Slovenia's GDP (current US$) is 43.072 billion and the per capita (current US$) is 20,873 in 2015 (World Bank Data 2016). Although Slovenia only accounted for the 8% of the total area of the former Yugoslavia, their economy was the most developed in terms of industry and other production. Slovenia is a member of the OECD and European Union (Panthi et al. 2018, 134). Slovenia had a relatively high gender equality index, a score of 68.4 out of 100 in 2017, above the EU-28 average, ranking tenth in the European Union (EIGE 2018).

Exhibit 2 Piran. Source: photo by Bostjan Antoncic

This chapter focuses on women entrepreneurship in Slovenia. First, the importance of women entrepreneurs is discussed. Second, their characteristics are described. Third, results of a survey on the characteristic of women and men entrepreneurs are reported. Finally, the results, limitations, future research possibilities, and conclusions are presented.

2 The Importance of Women's Entrepreneurs

Female entrepreneurs are important to the economic development of a country; they contribute to the job creation, to the economic growth, and to the diversity in the economy (Tominc and Rebernik 2006; in Tominc et al. 2019). "On average in the European Union the overall unemployment rates are a bit lower than those of women–the overall unemployment rate in 2017 is 7.8%, but 7.9% for women. . . . The self-employment rate is defined as the number of self-employed people, both own-account self-employed and employers (self-employed people with employees) relative to the number of employed people (OECD 2017), covering a very wide range of activities. On average, women in the EU are only 57% as likely to be self-employed as men (OECD 2017). . . . The women's self-employment rate in Slovenia is just below the EU average (11.4% in 2017)" (Tominc et al. 2019, 43).

Table 1 The involvement in entrepreneurship in Slovenia in 2018

Entrepreneurs	Men	Women
Emerging entrepreneurs (% of population: 2.84; GEM ranking 42/49)($n = 55$)	3.7% in the population 67.6% in the entrepreneurs	1.9% in the population 32.4% in the entrepreneurs
New entrepreneurs (% of population: 3.64; GEM ranking 32/49) ($n = 71$)	5.3% in the population 74.7% in the entrepreneurs	1.9% in the population 25.3% in the entrepreneurs
Total early entrepreneurial activity (% of population: 6.37; GEM ranking 25/49) ($n = 124$)	8.80% in the population (GEM ranking 38/49) 71.1% in the entrepreneurs	3.80% in the population (GEM ranking 46/49) 28.9% in the entrepreneurs
Established entrepreneurs (% of population: 6.84; GEM ranking 40/49) ($n = 139$)	8.87% in the population (GEM ranking 27/49) 66.7% in the entrepreneurs	4.69% in the population (GEM ranking 28/49) 33.3% in the entrepreneurs

Source: Rebernik et al. (2019, 37)

The involvement of men and women in entrepreneurship in Slovenia in 2018 is indicated in Table 1. The overall involvement in entrepreneurship in Slovenia is quite low; according to the GEM ranking Slovenia is in the lower half of GEM countries. Women are less involved in entrepreneurship than men; they represent about 30% of the entrepreneurs. In emerging entrepreneurs, women represent 1.9% of the population and 32.4% of entrepreneurs. In new entrepreneurs, women represent 1.9% of the population and 25.3% of entrepreneurs. In total new entrepreneurial activity, women represent 3.8% of the population and 28.9% of entrepreneurs. In established entrepreneurs, women represent 4.7% of the population and 33.3% of entrepreneurs.

Data on entrepreneurs having sole proprietorships in Slovenia (Bisnode 2017, 7; in Friskovec 2018) indicate that women have a considerably longer business history and fewer fluctuations in the opening and closing of business activities than men (90% of women's entrepreneurs have been in business for at least 5 years or more, only 10% less than 5 years, and no women have been in business for less than 3 years; only 43% of male entrepreneurs work for 5 years or more, 25% for 3–5 years, 15% for 1–3 years, and 17% for less than 1 year). Slovenian women entrepreneurs have had a significant impact in the Slovenian economy according to the Bisnode Indicator of Women Impact (BIWI) (Bisnode 2019): (1) Slovenia ranks second after Poland among 13 analyzed countries (Austria, Belgium, Czech Republic, Denmark, Finland, Germany, Hungary, Norway, Poland, Serbia, Slovakia, Slovenia, and Switzerland) in the total impact. (2) Based on the ratio between the number of employees in enterprises whose owners are women and the proportion of the number of enterprises run by women (the ratio for Slovenia 150), there are four countries with Slovenia being one of them, where companies owned by women employ more people than companies, which have men in leadership positions.

(3) The ratio of income to enterprises owned by women and the share of women-run enterprises (the ratio for Slovenia 97) indicates that there is no higher revenue in any country compared to the average in the economy; in most of the countries in which women are in the leading positions, on average, they are significantly lower than those owned by men, with the smallest difference being recorded in Slovenia. (4) The ratio between the share of net profits in enterprises with women in leading positions and the share in the number of women-run enterprises (the ratio for Slovenia 156) indicates that in all countries, except Slovenia, women entrepreneurs have a lower net profit than their male counterparts; in Slovenia, the profitability of women is on average 56% higher than in the economy.

3 Characteristics of Women Entrepreneurs

Men and women leaders/entrepreneurs have some similarities and differences (Hisrich and Brush 1986; Hughes et al. 1999; Antoncic et al. 2002): (1) Men have a strong opinion, are persuasive, goal oriented, innovative, and idealistic, and possess a high level of self-confidence; they have enthusiasm and high energy level along with a need to be their own boss. (2) Women are flexible and tolerant, goal oriented, creative, and realistic, possess a medium level of self-confidence, have enthusiasm and energy, and are able to cope with the social and business environment.

A comparison between men and women entrepreneurs is indicated in Table 2. Reasons and motives for starting new businesses have been historically similar for female and male entrepreneurs (Glas 1998): (1) Key reasons are not being satisfied with the workplace, the perception and exploitation of a profitable opportunity, and other reasons such as unemployment and family business tradition. (2) Key motives are independence, achievements, money, and career/security. In addition, men and women differ on the Big Five personality factors (Antoncic et al. 2015, 830): "relative to women, men tend to score higher in openness, lower on conscientiousness, lower on extraversion, and lower on agreeableness." The relationship of openness and conscientiousness with new value creation was found more important for female entrepreneurs than for male entrepreneurs (Auer Antoncic et al. 2018). Slovenian women entrepreneurs were found in comparison to their male counterparts (Sirec and Mocnik 2012, 25, 26, 31) to have a higher need for achievement; are willing to tolerate lower risks; have a lower need for autonomy/independence; are somewhat more prepared to respect rules and established working procedures; feel more uncomfortable when they need to shoulder responsibility for deciding how and when to do their work; estimate cognitive social capital in the sense of a positive relationship against entrepreneurship better; assess relational social capital substantially lower than cognitive social capital; and miss out on state and local government support more often.

Tominc and Rebernik (2004) found that when starting new firms, women in Slovenia rarely exploited opportunities in comparison to other GEM countries and

Table 2 A comparison between men and women entrepreneurs

Characteristic	Men entrepreneurs	Women entrepreneurs
Motivation	• Achievements—a tendency for things to happen • Personal independence—Self-image related to corporate status is irrelevant • Satisfaction with work resulting from the desire to control	• Achievements—Achieving the goal • Independence—Do it yourself
Starting point	• Dissatisfaction with the current job • Parallel to the school, the previous part, or the upgrading of the previous work • Completion of military service or loss of service • Opportunity to buy	• Frustration with work • Interest and recognition of opportunities in the known field • Change in personal circumstances
Resources	• Personal assets and savings • Bank financing • Investors • Loans of friends and family	• Personal assets and savings • Personal loans
Previous employment	• Experiences with similar work • A recognized specialist or someone who has had great achievements in this field • Knowledge from a variety of business functions	• Experience in the business field • Experience at the middle management level or at the administrative level in this field • Experience in service areas
Personal characteristics	• Strong opinion and convincing • Targeting • Innovative and idealistic • High level of self-confidence • Enthusiasm and energy • He must be his own gentleman	• Flexible and tolerant • Targeting • Creative and realistic • Average level of self-confidence • Enthusiasm and energy • Ability to face social and business armor
History	• Age of establishment: 25–35 • Father was self-employed • High school-oriented business or technical (usually an engineer) • Firstborn	• Age of foundation: 35–45 • Father was self-employed • High school orientation in social sciences • Firstborn
Support groups	• Friends, professional acquaintances (lawyers, accountants) • Business partners • Spouse	• Close friends • Spouse • Family • Women's professional associations • Branch associations
Types of established businesses	• Industry or construction	• Services—Education, counseling, or public relations

Source: Hisrich and Brush (1986); Antoncic et al. (2002, 97)

that necessity drove women in Slovenia into entrepreneurship more often in comparison to other GEM countries. In addition, women starting a new firm were convinced they possessed necessary education, skills, and experiences to start a new business. Zver (2015, 32) compared three women entrepreneurs in Slovenia and discovered that despite the differences of age, all three female entrepreneurs tended to be similar in a certain way and were different from men in their management style; women entrepreneurs were being promoted recently, but not as much as needed to realize their goals; they were encouraged and supported by their close associates. All three female entrepreneurs advised women to have trust in themselves and in their abilities, to boldly decide on their own independent business, and to not look at the negative environmental influences, as it is worth it to prove themselves in the business world.

Zagernik (2015, 28) on the basis of interviews with four Slovenian women entrepreneurs found: (1) Competences are very important in connection with entrepreneurship. In their work, women are using all types of competences: general, working, organizational, and managerial; in addition to these, important components of competences are also crucial, which help them to be more successful or more effective day to day so they can carry out a new task. (2) For startup entrepreneurship, competences were key for the successful completion of the activity; if an entrepreneur wants and has the will to do so, she can coordinate everything; in the event of a problem or obstacle, she finds a solution and solves the problem. (3) Women entrepreneurs were positively oriented and were striving for and achieving goals. (4) Women entrepreneurs had positive thinking and a vision for the future. Friskovec (2018, 32) compared four women's entrepreneurs in Saleska Valley in Slovenia and found that: (1) Male entrepreneurs are still more developed than female entrepreneurs, but more and more women are involved in entrepreneurship; women prefer not to choose an independent entrepreneurial path. (2) Women have the same opportunities for being entrepreneurs as men, but women must work harder to achieve a certain goal and to prove themselves. (3) Women entrepreneurship is developing more and more, which is supported by an incubator, where more and more women entrepreneurs are involved every year; other organizations offer support in various forms. (4) When deciding about entrepreneurship, women in the current environment have enough incentives and support; they themselves must decide to overcome fears and become successful entrepreneurs.

In light of these research results, some of which reflected the idea that women were inferior to men in business terms (Ahl 2006), this study focused on the research question: what are characteristics of women entrepreneurs in Slovenia?

4 Methodology

Data were collected from a random sample of Slovenian population via e-mail using a developed questionnaire. A total of 801 usable responses were received (about half female and half male), including 140 usable responses from practicing entrepreneurs. The majority of questions in the questionnaire were closed-ended with response categories. Entrepreneurship was assessed through a measure of entrepreneurship activity and intention (Antoncic et al. 2015, 2016), which classifies people into four entrepreneurship-related groups: (1) practicing entrepreneurs (have their own firm), (2) potential entrepreneurs (have the intention to found their own firm in the next 3 years), (3) maybe-entrepreneurs (maybe they will establish their own firm in the future), and (4) non-entrepreneurs (have no intention to establish their own firm). Four demographic variables (age, education, work experience, and marital status) were included in the questionnaire. Four sociological aspects of entrepreneurship (My father is/was an entrepreneur. My mother is/was an entrepreneur. I personally know many entrepreneurs. My friends are entrepreneurs.) were measured on a Likert-type scale ranging from 1—very untrue to 5—very true. The data were analyzed by the percentages of responses of the two groups (men and women) being compared (crosstabulations, comparisons of means, and using Chi-square and t-tests).

5 Findings

The results of the comparison of the type of entrepreneurs of men and women, with significant differences (Chi-Square 15.4, 3 df, sig. 0.001), are presented in Table 3. Practicing entrepreneurs (people that own their own businesses) represent 17.5% of the sample, 22.6% of men, and 12.3% of women. This result is consistent with

Table 3 Entrepreneurship of men and women

			Gender		
			Male	Female	Total
Entrepreneurship	**Non-entrepreneur**	**Count**	**228**	**253**	**481**
		% within entrepreneurship	47.4%	52.6%	100.0%
		% within gender	56.7%	63.4%	60.0%
	Maybe-entrepreneur	**Count**	**73**	**82**	**155**
		% within entrepreneurship	47.1%	52.9%	100.0%
		% within gender	18.2%	20.6%	19.4%
	Potential entrepreneur	**Count**	**10**	**15**	**25**
		% within entrepreneurship	40.0%	60.0%	100.0%
		% within gender	2.5%	3.8%	3.1%
	Practicing entrepreneur	**Count**	**91**	**49**	**140**
		% within entrepreneurship	65.0%	35.0%	100.0%
		% within gender	22.6%	12.3%	17.5%
Total		**Count**	**402**	**399**	**801**
		% within entrepreneurship	50.2%	49.8%	100.0%
		% within gender	100.0%	100.0%	100.0%

Pearson Chi-Square 15.4, 3 df, sig. 0.001

Table 4 Age of entrepreneurs by gender

			Gender		
			Male	Female	Total
Age	**25–34 years**	**Count**	**20**	**13**	**33**
		% within age	60.6%	39.4%	100.0%
		% within gender	22.0%	26.0%	23.4%
	35–44 years	**Count**	**15**	**14**	**29**
		% within age	51.7%	48.3%	100.0%
		% within gender	16.5%	28.0%	20.6%
	45–54 years	**Count**	**27**	**11**	**38**
		% within age	71.1%	28.9%	100.0%
		% within gender	29.7%	22.0%	27.0%
	55–64 years	**Count**	**15**	**10**	**25**
		% within age	60.0%	40.0%	100.0%
		% within gender	16.5%	20.0%	17.7%
	65 years and more	**Count**	**14**	**2**	**16**
		% within age	87.5%	12.5%	100.0%
		% within gender	15.4%	4.0%	11.3%
Total		**Count**	**91**	**50**	**141**
		% within age	64.5%	35.5%	100.0%
		% within gender	100.0%	100.0%	100.0%

Pearson Chi-Square 6.9, 4 df, sig. 0.140

previous research. For example, Rebernik et al. (2019) found men (65%) are more present as practicing entrepreneurship than women (35%). Congruently, women are more present in other groups (potential entrepreneurs, maybe-entrepreneurs, and non-entrepreneurs).

As indicated in Table 4, male entrepreneurs tend to be a little bit older than woman entrepreneurs (especially in the group of over 65 years old), but the difference is not statistically significant (Chi-Square 6.9, 4 df, sig. 0.140).

Also, as indicated in Table 5, the difference in education level is not statistically significant (Chi-Square 2.9, 3 df, sig. 0.405) between the two groups. Nevertheless, women have higher percentages at the level of the graduate degree (10.2% vs. 6.6% of men) and the college/undergraduate degree (57.1% vs. 46.2% of men); women entrepreneurs are somewhat more educated than their male counterparts (Tables 6 and 7).

In terms of years of work experience, a statistically significant difference between men and women was found (Chi-Square 10.3, 4 df, sig. 0.036). The longest work experience classification for women was from 5 to 10 years (30%), whereas for men in the longest work experience classification over 30 years (37.4%). In addition, while some men (6.6%) were in the starting entrepreneurs' group (5 years or less), no women were in this group. In general, women tended to have shorter work experience than men, but were not found among the novice entrepreneurs in this study.

Table 5 Education of entrepreneurs by gender

			Gender		Total
			Male	Female	
Education	**Vocational School**	**Count**	**5**	**2**	**7**
		% within education	71.4%	28.6%	100.0%
		% within gender	5.5%	4.1%	5.0%
	High School	**Count**	**38**	**14**	**52**
		% within education	73.1%	26.9%	100.0%
		% within gender	41.8%	28.6%	37.1%
	College or University Undergraduate Study	**Count**	**42**	**28**	**70**
		% within education	60.0%	40.0%	100.0%
		% within gender	46.2%	57.1%	50.0%
	Graduate Study	**Count**	**6**	**5**	**11**
		% within education	54.5%	45.5%	100.0%
		% within gender	6.6%	10.2%	7.9%
Total		**Count**	**91**	**49**	**140**
		% within education	65.0%	35.0%	100.0%
		% within gender	100.0%	100.0%	100.0%

Pearson Chi-Square 2.9, 3 df, sig. 0.405

In terms of marital status, a statistically significant difference occurred between men and women (Chi-Square 7.8, 2 df, sig. 0.020). While the proportion of married women entrepreneurs was less than half (48.0%), for men this proportion was much higher (70.3%). It appears that women entrepreneurs are totally focused on their company's performance.

Results of the comparison of four sociological aspects of entrepreneurship (My father is/was an entrepreneur. My mother is/was an entrepreneur. I personally know many entrepreneurs. My friends are entrepreneurs.) are presented in Table 8. Statistically significant differences were not found between women entrepreneurs and men entrepreneurs. Some slight differences in mean levels were found higher for women in having father and mother entrepreneurs.

Table 6 Work experience of entrepreneurs by gender

			Gender		
			Male	Female	Total
Work experience (number of years)	**5 years or less**	**Count**	**6**	**0**	**6**
		% within work experience	100.0%	0.0%	100.0%
		% within gender	6.6%	0.0%	4.3%
	5–10 years	**Count**	**11**	**15**	**26**
		% within work experience	42.3%	57.7%	100.0%
		% within gender	12.1%	30.0%	18.4%
	10–20 years	**Count**	**17**	**11**	**28**
		% within work experience	60.7%	39.3%	100.0%
		% within gender	18.7%	22.0%	19.9%
	20–30 years	**Count**	**23**	**10**	**33**
		% within work experience	69.7%	30.3%	100.0%
		% within gender	25.3%	20.0%	23.4%
	more than 30 years	**Count**	**34**	**14**	**48**
		% within work experience	70.8%	29.2%	100.0%
		% within gender	37.4%	28.0%	34.0%
Total		**Count**	**91**	**50**	**141**
		% within work experience	64.5%	35.5%	100.0%
		% within gender	100.0%	100.0%	100.0%

Pearson Chi-Square 10.3, 4 df, sig. 0.036

Table 7 Marital status of entrepreneurs by gender

			Gender		
			Male	Female	Total
Marital status	**Single**	**Count**	**17**	**13**	**30**
		% within marital status	56.7%	43.3%	100.0%
		% within gender	18.7%	26.0%	21.3%
	Married	**Count**	**64**	**24**	**88**
		% within marital status	72.7%	27.3%	100.0%
		% within gender	70.3%	48.0%	62.4%
	Other	**Count**	**10**	**13**	**23**
		% within marital status	43.5%	56.5%	100.0%
		% within gender	11.0%	26.0%	16.3%
Total		**Count**	**91**	**50**	**141**
		% within marital status	64.5%	35.5%	100.0%
		% within gender	100.0%	100.0%	100.0%

Pearson Chi-Square 7.8, 2 df, sig. 0.020

Table 8 Sociological aspects of entrepreneurship by gender

Items	Gender	*n*	Mean	Std. deviation	Std. error mean
My father is/was an entrepreneur	Male	91	2.18	1.724	0.181
	Female	49	2.51	1.870	0.266
My mother is/was an entrepreneur	Male	91	1.58	1.273	0.133
	Female	49	1.94	1.580	0.225
I personally know many entrepreneurs	Male	91	3.86	1.250	0.131
	Female	49	3.71	1.339	0.190
My friends are entrepreneurs	Male	91	3.39	1.260	0.132
	Female	49	3.48	1.360	0.193

* Difference sig. < 0.05 (no significant differences)

6 Discussion

In Slovenia, women entrepreneurs have significant economic importance with their enterprises tending to be much more profitable than the average in the economy. Our research showed that the percentage of women as practicing entrepreneurship was 35% and versus 65% of men which indicates there is some gender gap (women were almost half as likely as men in the EU to be self-employed: 9.9% vs. 17.8%, OECD/EU 2016). The age distribution of entrepreneurs was found to be similar between women and men, with a slight difference (male entrepreneurs tended to be a little older than women entrepreneurs, especially in the group of over 65 years old men are more represented). Women entrepreneurs were found to be somewhat more educated than male entrepreneurs, especially in terms of having a graduate and/or an undergraduate degree. Women entrepreneurs indicated a shorter work experience than men and women were not found among the novice entrepreneurs. A big difference between men and women entrepreneurs was found in the marital status, with more male entrepreneurs being married than female entrepreneurs. Men and women entrepreneurs were found to be similar in sociological aspects, with a slightly larger number of women having father and mother entrepreneurs than men. This result might reflect more women emerging from a family business tradition.

Overall, women entrepreneurship in Slovenia is very important and profitable. The age distribution of women's entrepreneurs was balanced, except the proportion in the over 65 years old group was somewhat lower. Women entrepreneurs tended to be educated with work experience over 5 years or more.

7 Recommendations

The results of this study indicate that economic policy makers should further support the development of women entrepreneurship in Slovenia. In general, policy measures to encourage and support women's entrepreneurship are well described by the OECD and the EU (OECD/EU 2016): (1) Promote a positive attitude through role models and ambassadors. (2) Develop entrepreneurship skills through training courses and mentoring. (3) Facilitate access to finance through financial literacy and a range of financing instruments. (4) Build entrepreneurial networks and ensure linkages to mainstream infrastructures. (5) Promote work–life balance and access to social protection; this is particularly important in Slovenia with the impact of family policies aimed at price reduction in the cost of childcare (OECD/EU 2016, 27): "There is a need to ensure that family polices are supportive of women's labor market participation in general and women entrepreneurship in particular. For example, estimates suggest that a price reduction of 50% in the cost of childcare would lead to an increase in the labor force by 6.5–10% (Gong et al. 2010; Kalb 2009)."

8 Limitations, Future Research, and Conclusions

The study focused only on some characteristics of women's entrepreneurs, predominantly demographic and sociological. Important personality gender differences related to entrepreneurship may also exist (Antoncic et al. 2015). Some cell counts in the crosstabulations in the data analysis were less than five. The study design was more quantitative in nature. Qualitative data would add more information and insights on women entrepreneurship in Slovenia in future research.

This study answered the research question concerning the characteristics of women entrepreneurs in Slovenia by conducting a quantitative study on a random sample from the overall population of Slovenia. We contributed to knowledge about women entrepreneurship by providing some new insights on the characteristics of women entrepreneurs. Women entrepreneurs tended to be educated with work experience, and they have an important impact on the Slovenian economy. Women entrepreneurship in Slovenia remains an important economic force and has a bright future.

Acknowledgments This work was supported by the Slovenian Research Agency [project/grant numbers P5-0117, P5-0049].

References

Ahl H (2006) Why research on women entrepreneurs needs new directions. Entrep Theory Pract 30 (5):595–621

Antoncic B, Hisrich RD, Petrin T, Vahcic A (2002) Podjetnistvo. GV Založba, Ljubljana, Slovenia

Antoncic B, Bratkovic Kregar T, Singh G, DeNoble AF (2015) The big five personality-entrepreneurship relationship: evidence from Slovenia. J Small Bus Manag 53(3):819–841. https://doi.org/10.1111/jsbm.12089

Antoncic B, Auer Antoncic J, Aaltonen HM (2016) Marketing self-efficacy and firm creation. J Small Bus Enterp Dev 23(1):90–104. https://doi.org/10.1108/JSBED-07-2015-0093

Auer Antoncic J, Antoncic B, Kobal Grum D, Ruzzier M (2018) The big five personality of the SME manager and their company's performance. J Dev Entrep 23(4):1–23. https://doi.org/10.1142/S1084946718500218

Bisnode (2017) Bilten: marec 2017. Accessed by Friskovec (2018), 21 July 2018, https://www.bisnode.si/globalassets/slovenia/bilten/bilten-marec-2017-final.pdf

Bisnode (2019) Indeks podjetja Bisnode o vplivu žensk. https://www.bisnode.si/znanja/nase-misli/indeks-podjetja-bisnode-o-vplivu-ensk/. Accessed 9 July 2019

Brush C, Carter N, Gatewood E, Greene P, Hart M (eds) (2006) Growth-oriented women entrepreneurs and their businesses: a global research perspective. Edward Elgar, Cheltenham, UK

Brush CG, De Bruin A, Welter F (2009) A gender-aware framework for women's entrepreneurship. Int J Gend Entrep 1(1):8–24

EIGE (2018) Gender equality index 2017: Slovenia. European Institute for Gender Equality, Vilnius, Lithuania. https://eige.europa.eu/sites/default/files/documents/20181372_mh0218189enn_pdf_si.pdf. Accessed 9 July 2019

Friskovec K (2018) Zensko podjetništvo v Saleski dolini. Univerza v Mariboru, Ekonomsko-poslovna fakulteta, Maribor, Slovenia. https://dk.um.si/IzpisGradiva.php?lang=slv&id=71702. Accessed 9 July 2019

Funk & Wagnalls New World Encyclopedia (2016) Slovenia data. data.worldbank.org. Accessed 10 March 2017

Glas M (1998) Eastern Europe: Slovenia. In: Morrison A (ed) Entrepreneurship: an international perspective. Butterworth-Heinemann, Oxford, UK, pp 108–124

Gong X, Breunig R, King A (2010) How responsive is female labour supply to child care costs? New Australian estimates. IZA Discussion Paper no. 5119

Hisrich RD, Brush CG (1986) The woman entrepreneur: starting, financing, and managing a successful new business. Lexington Books, Lexington, MA

Hughes RL, Ginnett RC, Curphy GJ (1999) Leadership: enhancing the lessons of experience, 3rd edn. Irwin/McGraw-Hill, Boston, MA

Kalb G (2009) Children, labour supply and child care: challenges for empirical analysis. Aust Econ Rev 42(3):276–299

OECD (2017) The missing entrepreneurs: policies for self-employment and entrepreneurship. OECD Publishing, Paris

OECD/EU (2016) Policy brief on Women's entrepreneurship. Publications Office of the European Union, Luxembourg. https://www.oecd.org/cfe/smes/Policy-Brief-on-Women-s-Entrepreneurship.pdf. Accessed 10 July 2019

Panthi L, Antoncic B, Hisrich RD (2018) Entrepreneurship in Slovenia. In: Palalic R, Dana L-P, Ramadani V (eds) Entrepreneurship in former Yugoslavia: diversity, institutional constraints and prospects. Springer, Cham, Switzerland, pp 131–143. https://doi.org/10.1007/978-3-319-77634-7

Rebernik M, Tominc P, Sirec K, Bradac Hojnik B, Rus M, Crnogaj K (2019) Neizkoriscen podjetniski potencial: GEM Slovenija 2018, (Slovenski podjetniški observatorij), 1st edn. Univerzitetna založba Univerze v Mariboru, Maribor. https://doi.org/10.18690/978-961-286-265-7

Sirec K, Mocnik D (2012) Gender specifics in entrepreneurs' personal characteristics. JEEMS 17 (1):11–39

Tominc P, Rebernik M (2004) The scarcity of female entrepreneurship. Drustvena istrazivanja 13 (4–5):779–802

Tominc P, Rebernik M (2006) Female entrepreneurial growth aspirations in Slovenia: an unexploited resource. In: Brush CG, Carter MN, Gatewood JE, Greene GP, Hart MM (eds) Growth-oriented women entrepreneurs and their businesses: a global research perspective. New horizons in entrepreneurship. Edward Elgar, Camberley Surrey, UK, pp 330–348

Tominc P, Rebernik M, Bradac Hojnik B, Sirec K (2019) Danube region entrepreneurship observatory: entrepreneurship ecosystem, women and youth entrepreneurship. Pearson, Harlow,

UK. http://ipmmp.um.si/podonavski-podjetniski-observatorij/ppo-monografije/?r=1073. Accessed 5 July 2019
World Bank Data (2016) Country profile: Slovenia. https://data.worldbank.org/country/slovenia
Zagernik S (2015) Percepcija kompetenc slovenskih podjetnic. Univerza v Mariboru, Fakulteta za organizacijske vede, Kranj. https://dk.um.si/IzpisGradiva.php?lang=slv&id=53867. Accessed 9 July 2019
Zver D (2015) Zensko podjetnistvo v Sloveniji. Univerza v Mariboru, Ekonomsko-poslovna fakulteta, Maribor. https://dk.um.si/IzpisGradiva.php?lang=slv&id=54624. Accessed 5 July 2019

Jasna Auer Antoncic, Ph.D., is an Associate Professor of Entrepreneurship at the Faculty of Management, University of Primorska, where she teaches and conducts business research work. Her main research interests include employee satisfaction, psychology of entrepreneurship, intrapreneurship, and business growth. She has written three books in the area of entrepreneurship, as well as several business research articles. The titles of the books were *Employee Satisfaction, Intrapreneurship and Growth* (2009), *Entrepreneurship Cases—Founding and Management of Firms* (2013), and *Family Business Characteristics in Slovenia* (2015). Her articles have been published in scientific and academic journals such as *Industrial Management & Data Systems*, *Journal of Small Business and Enterprise Development*, *Journal of Developmental Entrepreneurship*, *Journal of Enterprising Culture*, and *Management*. She received the Best Paper Award at the 2010 IBER (Business) and ITLC (Education) conferences, Las Vegas.

Bostjan Antoncic, Ph.D., is a Professor of Entrepreneurship at the School of Economics and Business, University of Ljubljana. His areas of expertise include corporate entrepreneurship, entrepreneurial networks, entrepreneurial personality, and international entrepreneurship. He has written several books—more than ten in the area of entrepreneurship alone, as well as several business research articles. The titles of the books were, for example, *Entrepreneurship* (2002, 2008), *Entrepreneurship Cases—Growth and Development* (2002), *Entrepreneurship Cases—Start-Up, Momentum and Growth* (2005), *The Personal Resource-Acquisition Network of the Entrepreneur and Small Firm Growth* (2007), *Business Plan Preparation Guidebook* (2008), and *Entrepreneurship Cases—Founding and Management of Firms* (2013). His papers have been published in academic journals such as the *Journal of Business Venturing*, *Entrepreneurship and Regional Development*, *Industrial Management & Data Systems*, *Technovation*, *Transformations in Business & Economics*, *Journal of Business Economics and Management*, and *Journal of Small Business Management*.

Robert D. Hisrich is the Bridgestone Chair of International Marketing and Associate Dean of Graduate and International Programs at the College of Business Administration at Kent State University. He holds a B.A. from DePauw University and an M.B.A. and a doctorate from the University of Cincinnati. Professor Hisrich's research pursuits are focused on entrepreneurship and venture creation: entrepreneurial ethics, corporate entrepreneurship, women and minority entrepreneurs, venture financing, and global venture creation. He teaches courses and seminars in these areas, as well as in marketing management, and product planning and development. His interest in global management and entrepreneurship resulted in two Fulbright Fellowships in Budapest, Hungary; honorary degrees from Chuvash State University (Russia) and University of Miskolc (Hungary); and being a visiting faculty member in universities in Austria, Australia, Ireland, and Slovenia. Professor Hisrich serves on the editorial boards of several prominent journals in entrepreneurial scholarship, is on several boards of directors, and is author or coauthor of over 300 research articles appearing in journals such as *Journal of Marketing, Journal of Marketing Research, Journal of Business Venturing, Journal of Developmental Entrepreneurship, and Entrepreneurship Theory and Practice*. Professor Hisrich has authored, coauthored, or edited 46 books or their editions, including *Marketing* (2000, 2nd ed.), *How to Fix and Prevent the 13 Biggest Problems That Derail Business* (2004), *Technology Entrepreneurship* (2015, 2nd ed.), *Entrepreneurial Finance* (2015), *International Entrepreneurship* (2016, 3rd ed.), *Advanced Introduction to Corporate Venturing* (2016), *Effective Entrepreneurial Management* (2017), and *Entrepreneurship* (2017, 10th ed.).

Women's Entrepreneurship in the Former Yugoslavia: Toward the Future

Ramo Palalić, Léo-Paul Dana, and Emil Knezović

Abstract This chapter comprehends briefly women's entrepreneurship, and it gives a concise and understandable review of each chapter's material. In this chapter, all ex-Yugoslavian countries are revised separately in terms of women's entrepreneurship, its status, and its future perspectives. Additionally, authors provided the final words on this topic with an extension of possible steps recommended as the future research.

1 Toward the Future

Women entrepreneurship in recent times has been advancing a lot. Industrialized countries had started this phenomenon even in the nineteenth century. Although it is traced in the Europe in the nineteenth century, as well as in the Balkans, as Vuković (2015) argued, real development was barely seen in the region of ex-Yugoslavia, however. It was due to the state systems that the whole Balkan countries had. Another reason was that women's primary role was to nurture their children (Gross and Szabo 1992; Palalić et al. 2018a) and had no time for extracurricular activities like entrepreneurial ones.

The former Yugoslavia was under the emancipation process of females in society after WWII (Simić 2011), and more precisely it dated from 1945 till now. Although this process was seen in this region as progressive, but women roles were not seen on the surface, rather hidden and limited, and yet they were involved in specific activities such as clerical and manufacturing (Mežnarić 1985) and agricultural. No

R. Palalić · E. Knezović (✉)
Faculty of Business and Administration, International University of Sarajevo, Ilidža, Bosnia and Herzegovina
e-mail: rpalalic@ius.edu.ba; eknezovic@ius.edu.ba

L.-P. Dana
Dalhousie University, Halifax, NS, Canada
e-mail: lp.dana@Montpellier-BS.com

R. Palalić et al. (eds.), *Women's Entrepreneurship in Former Yugoslavia*, Contributions to Management Science,
https://doi.org/10.1007/978-3-030-45253-7_9

exposure of women as entrepreneurial leaders was traced in the region that will represent an exemplary leadership of this category. All former republics of ex-Yugoslavia (Alpeza et al. 2018; Mustafa and Krasniqi 2018; Palalić et al. 2018c; Palalić and Bičo 2018; Petković and Ivanović Đukić 2018; Ramadani et al. 2018), except Slovenia (Palalić et al. 2018b), did not meaningfully support entrepreneurship development regardless of gender, yet it was considered as a destructive phenomenon to society (Dana et al. 2018; Palalić et al. 2018b).

After the resolution of Yugoslavia, in the early 1990s, a transition wave from the West gripped the region, and the economic and political transition (Ramadani and Schneider 2013) of the region started. However, this transition has taken a few decades, and still, many obstacles for entrepreneurship development (Palalic 2017) are opposing the true entrepreneurship advancements. Entrepreneurship of females was not delved deeply. Being gender-sensitive issue in this region, after the crash of the "Yugopluralist model" (Dana 2010), women entrepreneurship development is yet to start.

The *Slovenian* case, regarding women entrepreneurship, is having a good standing. Although more men are involved in businesses than women, still women's entrepreneurship plays a significant role in Slovenian economic development. The age of female and male entrepreneurs is more or less the same, while education level of female entrepreneurs is higher than the male ones. In conclusion, Slovenian business landscape created a kind of balanced gender entrepreneurs, which contributes to its society development.

Croatia sees female entrepreneurship as one of the vital parts of its national economy. Being a woman entrepreneur in Croatia is very challenging and sometimes depriving due to many obstacles and factors that negatively influence women entrepreneurship. One of the instruments that the Croatian government uses for development of female entrepreneurship is the *Croatia Women in Business Program*, which was established in 2011. The program helps women oriented toward entrepreneurship to establish their entrepreneurial career through a variety of training, seminars, workshops, and consultancies (EBRD 2019). Over 50 projects have been implemented through this program across Croatia. It should be noted that other nonprofit organizations, like CESI (CESI 2019), contribute to women entrepreneurship since 2015, as well as many others.[1] This entrepreneurship aspect in Croatia has potential, and it is fully supported by the government, which dedicated the state's 6-year strategy to its development (*Strategy of Development of Women Entrepreneur, 2014–2020*).

Women entrepreneurship in *Bosnia* is undeveloped. The State Ministry for Entrepreneurship does not exist. Due to complex state system structure, each entity has its own Ministry for Entrepreneurship. In awaiting for the state strategy for entrepreneurship in general, and yet to be thought for women entrepreneurship strategy, women entrepreneurs started to launch their own platforms to promote female entrepreneurial activities via several platforms, and among them are

[1]For more information, please see chapter "Women's Entrepreneurship in Croatia".

"Poduzetnice" and "Udruženje poslovnih žena (2020)". One of them designed a women entrepreneurship 2-year action plan from 2018 to 2020 (Poduzetnice 2018).

Bosnian government is not doing enough regarding women entrepreneurship. There are no reliable data available for this aspect since the state structure is decentralized, and thus the data are not uniformed. Data uniformity is important because a good strategy must be based on valid data for the whole country. However, women entrepreneurship has potential, but it is far behind developed and supported by its government compared to Slovenia and Croatia.

Serbian women in the labor market are still discriminated, which resulted in their aspirations to be self-employed. There are some means to support women entrepreneurship, but these are limited and dependent on many internal and external factors. Women entrepreneurs are highly motivated, but obstacles like capital, managerial experience, familiarity to a business, and house obligations are defocusing women's potentials in their entrepreneurial activities.

Kosovo, as a newly emergent economy in the Balkans, provides a wonderful place for new businesses whose taxation policy is truly favorable. Its economy is based on SMEs (99%) with unnoticed presence of large corporations. From the total number of companies, over 10% are owned by female entrepreneurs. A decade ago, the number of registered female entrepreneurs was higher compared to males (Hoxha and Krasniqi 2008), and one of the reasons was that an international community and other organizations had enormously supported this trend (Ramadani et al. 2015). This trend has its growth, but still, it is at the inception stage, due to different cultural and political factors (Ramadani and Dana 2013; Welsh et al. 2017), as well as gender issues, which are specifically related to this region (Palalic 2017).

North Macedonia has a very favorable entrepreneurial environment for new business comers. Among former Yugoslavian republics, which were not accepted by the EU, this country is the best regarding the establishing of new businesses. Women entrepreneurship in this country has challenges, and the foremost one is nonexisting database for women entrepreneurs, which could be a good basis for strategy design by the government. Secondly, females are faced with time limit for their personal and professional development regarding entrepreneurial aspirations. Additionally, work–life balance is critical, which does not provide more time for further education in entrepreneurship field. However, all these observed limitations that businesswomen (current and prospective ones) face with could be turned into opportunities if appropriate actions are undertaken by important figures (governmental, nongovernmental, and others) to support women entrepreneurship in this country.

Women in *Montenegro* face difficulties regarding their entrepreneurship perspective. Mostly, the cultural values, based on patriarchy, restrict women to develop their entrepreneurial mindset fully. Also, a low number of women in political and any other decision-making, as well as in leadership positions, show this stumbling block that does not allow this phenomenon to advance and further develop. Factors like finance access, appropriate knowledge in business field, family obligations, as well as gray economy deeply hamper women entrepreneurship development in Montenegro.

Finally, former Yugoslavian republics, even to some extent those who are already EU members, shall adopt the policy proscribed by the OECD/EU (2019) suggesting to reduce the gender gap in entrepreneurship. In overall, the tendency of reducing this gap is positive, but it is mostly due to low motivation of men to be self-employed (OECD 2019). While the situation in the EU could be exemplary to the Balkan countries, in reality, there is a much bigger gap between male and female entrepreneurs when it comes to non-EU countries. Male entrepreneurs are 50% more successful in business growth than female ones (OECD 2019). Anecdotally speaking, a huge gap exists in former Yugoslavian republics. Partially, it is due to the transition from one economic system to another that takes a lot of time (except Slovenia and Croatia), with fewer improvements in entrepreneurship development in general. Another issue, which should be researched diligently, is the regional culture that is impregnated in people's mindset, which is reflected furtherly in a low entrepreneurship development.

Taking into consideration that the EU provides many decent funds for gender entrepreneurship, governments of ex-Yugoslavian republics should work jointly on reduction of gender entrepreneurship gap and advance female entrepreneurship through certain development programs provided by the EU.

References

Alpeza M, Oberman Peterka S, Has M (2018) Entrepreneurship in Croatia. In: Palalić R, Dana L-P, Ramadani V (eds) Entrepreneurship in former Yugoslavia: diversity, institutional constraints and prospects. Springer, Heidelberg. https://doi.org/10.1007/978-3-319-77634-7_6

Center for Education, Counselling and Research-CESI (2019). http://www.cesi.hr/en/project-free-rural-women-and-entrepreneurship/. Accessed 15 Jan 2020

Dana LP (2010) When economies change hands: A survey of entrepreneurship in emerging markets of Europe from the Balkans to the Baltic States. Routledge, Heidelberg

Dana L-P, Palalić R, Ramadani V (2018) Entrepreneurship in former Yugoslavia: an introduction. In: Palalić R, Dana L-P, Ramadani V (eds) Entrepreneurship in former Yugoslavia: diversity, institutional constraints and prospects. Springer, Heidelberg. https://doi.org/10.1007/978-3-319-77634-7_1

EBRD-European Bank for Reconstruction and Development (2019). https://www.ebrd.com/croatia.html. Accessed 15 Jan 2020

Gross M, Szabo A (1992) Prema hrvatskome građanskom društvu: društveni razvoj u civilnoj Hrvatskoj i Slavoniji šezdesetih i sedamdesetih godina 19. stoljeća. Globus, Zagreb

Hoxha D, Krasniqi B (2008) Female entrepreneurship in Kosovo: does gender difference hypothesis hold? Int J Bus Manag Sci 1(1):49–61

Mežnarić S (1985) Theory and reality: the status of employed women in Yugoslavia. In: Wolchik SL, Meyer AG (eds) Women, state and party in Eastern Europe. Duke University, Durham, NC, pp 214–220

Mustafa M, Krasniqi BA (2018) Entrepreneurship in Kosovo. In: Palalić R, Dana L-P, Ramadani V (eds) Entrepreneurship in former Yugoslavia: diversity, institutional constraints and prospects. Springer, Heidelberg. https://doi.org/10.1007/978-3-319-77634-7_6

OECD/European Union (2019) The missing entrepreneurs 2019: policies for inclusive entrepreneurship. OECD, Paris. https://doi.org/10.1787/3ed84801-en

Palalic R (2017) The phenomenon of entrepreneurial leadership in gazelles and mice: a qualitative study from Bosnia and Herzegovina. World Rev Entrep Manag Sustain Dev 13(2/3):211–236
Palalić R, Bičo A (2018) Entrepreneurship in Bosnia and Herzegovina. In: Palalić R, Dana L-P, Ramadani V (eds) Entrepreneurship in former Yugoslavia: diversity, institutional constraints and prospects. Springer, Heidelberg. https://doi.org/10.1007/978-3-319-77634-7_2
Palalić R, Ramadani V, Dana L-P, Ratten V (2018a) Gender entrepreneurial leadership in family businesses: a case study from Bosnia & Herzegovina. In: Ratten V, Dana L-P, Ramadani V (eds) Women entrepreneurship in family business. Routledge, London
Palalić R, Dana L-P, Ramadani V (eds) (2018b) Entrepreneurship in former Yugoslavia: diversity, institutional constraints and prospects. Springer, Heidelberg
Palalić R, Bičo A, Ramadani V, Dana L-P (2018c) Entrepreneurship in Montenegro. In: Palalić R, Dana L-P, Ramadani V (eds) Entrepreneurship in former Yugoslavia: diversity, institutional constraints and prospects. Springer, Heidelberg. https://doi.org/10.1007/978-3-319-77634-7_6
Petković S, Ivanović Đukić M (2018) Entrepreneurship in Serbia. In: Palalić R, Dana L-P, Ramadani V (eds) Entrepreneurship in former Yugoslavia: diversity, institutional constraints and prospects. Springer, Heidelberg. https://doi.org/10.1007/978-3-319-77634-7_6
Poduzetnice (2018) https://poduzetnice.ba/akcioni-plan-za-razvoj-poduzetnistva-zena-u-federaciji-bosne-i-hercegovine-2018-2020-radna-verzija/. Accessed 17 Jan 2020
Ramadani V, Dana L-P (2013) The state of entrepreneurship in the Balkans: evidence from selected countries. In: Ramadani V, Schneider CR (eds) Entrepreneurship in the Balkans: diversity, support and prospects. Springer, Heidelberg, pp 217–250
Ramadani V, Schneider RC (2013) Introduction. In: Ramadani V, Schneider RC (eds) Entrepreneurship in the Balkans: diversity, support, and prospects. Springer, Cham, pp 1–14
Ramadani V, Hisrich RD, Gërguri-Rashiti S (2015) Female entrepreneurs in transition economies: insights from Albania, Macedonia and Kosovo. World Rev Entrep Manag Sustain Dev 11 (4):391–413
Ramadani V, Rexhepi G, Dana L-P, Gerguri-Rashiti S, Ratten V (2018) Entrepreneurship in Macedonia. In: Palalić R, Dana L-P, Ramadani V (eds) Entrepreneurship in former Yugoslavia: diversity, institutional constraints and prospects. Springer, Heidelberg. https://doi.org/10.1007/978-3-319-77634-7_6
Simić I (2011) Socijalizam i položaj žena u nauci, Kontinuirana edukacija - Položaj žena u nauci
Udruženje poslovnih žena (2020) https://upzbih.ba. Accessed 17 Jan 2020
Vuković K (2015) Počeci poduzetništva žena u znanstvenim i književnim djelima hrvatskih autora. Društvena istraživanja: časopis za opća društvena pitanja 24(1):133–151
Welsh DHB, Kaciak E, Trimi S, Mainardes EW (2017) Women entrepreneurs and family firm heterogeneity: evidence from an emerging economy. Group Decis Negot 27(3):445–465

Ramo Palalić is the Coordinator of Leadership and Entrepreneurship Centre at the IUS. Dr. Palalić's research interests are entrepreneurship, leadership, marketing, and small and family business management. As an Assistant Professor, Dr. Palalić teaches at all three study cycles in the above areas. Apart from this, he is actively involved in business projects in the areas of entrepreneurial leadership and marketing management, in private and public organizations. He has authored and coauthored many articles in reputable international journals, several books, and many book chapters. Additionally, he is serving a few journals as reviewer/editorial board member.

Léo-Paul Dana is Professor at Dalhousie University in Canada. A graduate of McGill University and HEC-Montreal, he has served as Professor and President of the Scientific Council at Montpellier Business School and was formerly Marie Curie Fellow at Princeton University and Visiting Professor at INSEAD. He has published extensively in a variety of journals including *Entrepreneurship & Regional Development, Entrepreneurship: Theory & Practice, International Business Review, International Small Business Journal, Journal of Business Research, Journal of Small Business Management, Journal of World Business, Small Business Economics,* and *Technological Forecasting & Social Change.*

Emil Knezović is the Head of Department of Economics and Management at the International University of Sarajevo. His research and teaching expertise include human resource management, entrepreneurship, small business management, and marketing. So far, he has published several articles in refereed international and national journals. He has been engaged as a researcher in several projects, among which is Horizon2020 Systemic Action for Gender Equality. Before joining academia, he worked in the real estate and transport industry where occasionally he still serves as a consultant.

The manufacturer's authorised representative in the EU is Springer Nature Customer Service Centre GmbH, Europaplatz 3, 69115 Heidelberg, Germany. If you have any concerns regarding our products, please contact ProductSafety@springernature.com

Printed and bound by CPI Group (UK) Ltd, Croydon, CR0 4YY
30/09/2026
02225697-0002